Contents

Preface

This Special Edition of *Conformity and Conflict: Readings in Cultural Anthropology* offers a carefully selected series of sixteen articles that perfectly complement the chapters in my textbook, *Cultural Anthropology*, Fourth Edition. Each essay provides rich material for discussion about particular topics in greater depth than the textbook can provide. The arrangement of the articles follows the table of contents of the textbook, with each textbook chapter paired with an article that addresses a related topic.

Questions included at the end of each article ask students to make connections between the *Conformity and Conflict* article and the content of the Miller chapter. They also provide excellent critical thinking opportunities.

The collection includes classic and memorable pieces, such as "Eating Christmas in the Kalahari" and "Life without Chiefs," as well as newer essays that relate to contemporary issues such as "Medical Anthropology: Improving Nutrition in Malawi" and "The Road to Refugee Resettlement." Many of the topics addressed, as in "Baseball Magic," and "Japanese Hip-Hop and the Globalization of Popular Culture," for example, will be directly engaging to students' interests and experience. The first essay in the collection, "Anthro Shock," establishes the relevance of cultural anthropology from the start.

Students will find the material in the essays interesting and important. They will also appreciate the fact that this streamlined version of the longer version of *Conformity and Conflict* is a more cost-effective and environmentally responsible option than a reader that contains far more articles than can be assigned in one semester.

I am pleased that Allyn & Bacon decided to publish this reader as a companion to *Cultural Anthropology*, and I hope that you are, too.

Barbara D. Miller
Professor of Anthropology & International Affairs
George Washington University
Washington, DC

WORLD MAP AND GEOGRAPHICAL PLACEMENT OF READINGS

The numbers on this map correspond to the reading numbers. Screened maps also accompany the readings, and boxed areas on those maps highlight the subject locations. Readings labeled as "cross-cultural" on this global map do not include boxed areas.

14

8

Special Edition

Conformity and Conflict

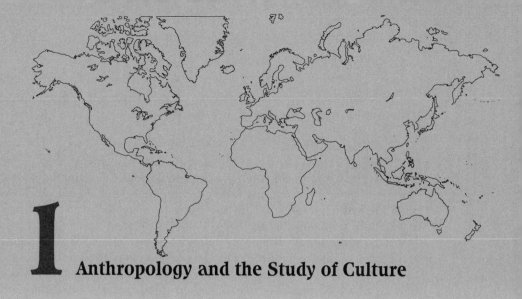

I Anthropology and the Study of Culture

Career Advice for Anthropology Undergraduates

John T. Omohundro

Although anthropologists regularly use their skills in the world of work, and employers are beginning to recognize the value of employees who are trained in anthropology, many Americans still do not fully understand what anthropology is and have little idea what students who major in anthropology can do for them. Worse, students themselves may not consciously recognize the work skills that anthropology has taught them or how to translate these skills into a language prospective employers can understand. John Omohundro tackles this problem of recognition and translation in this selection. Using a concept he calls "transcultural presentation," he lists some of the skills that anthropology teaches students and shows how these skills can be translated by graduating students into résumé language for employers.

John T. Omohundro, Career Advice for Anthropology Undergraduates from *Careers in Anthropology* © 2007. Reprinted with permission from The McGraw-Hill Companies .

The following scene happens at least once a semester. A distraught student pokes her (or his) head through my office door.

"Scuse me. . . . Are you busy? I need to ask you something."

"No, Grebbleberry, come in, sit down. What's bothering you?"

"Well, I really like anthropology. In fact, I want to drop my major in [deleted] and declare anthropology. But I told my parents and they were freaked out. My mother cried and my father threatened to cut me off. And my friends think I've lost it completely. Now they have me scared. I'm afraid I won't be able to get a job. What am I going to do?"

This student has all the symptoms of anthro shock. I'm tempted to smile in recognition of the syndrome but to Grebbleberry there is nothing amusing here. I have two answers: the difficult answer and the easy answer. The difficult answer, which I would like to give, is a problem because students are not prepared to believe me. The difficult answer is:

"For most careers, it doesn't matter much what you major in, as long as you like the subject and are good at it. The point of a major in a liberal arts education is to give practice at studying something in depth. One's major is not the same thing as job training. The careers that follow from most undergraduate majors are not and cannot be specified, even if the world doesn't change—but it does, frequently. There is no direct, obvious, and inevitable connection between college disciplines and the occupational titles people carry."

Although many years of teaching and advising convince me that the difficult answer I've just described is true, I don't respond with that answer anymore. First, I have to treat the "anthro shock"—the fear gripping the student that, ". . . mocked and alone, I'm going to starve." So, instead I reply with the easy answer:

"Take courage. There are many things you can do for a living that use your anthropological knowledge and skills. I can help you discover them and prepare for them."

Only then does the student's color begin to return; the anthro shock is in remission. Later, perhaps, after we've begun a career development program, I might introduce the difficult answer. But Grebbleberry still won't believe me, because my answer goes against most of what pundits, peers, parents, and even some professors have told her. This article presents some of the evidence that I have gathered for the claims made in the "easy" answer, to assist advisors to respond quickly and effectively to anthro shock.

Becoming a Career Advisor

Good advice is sorely needed and in short supply. Too many of the students I have supervised appeared flustered and ill-prepared when people ask them naive but usually sincere questions about what anthropology is, what it is good for, and what the student is going to "do with it." My advisees usually answered these questions apologetically or parried them with self-deprecating humor. Bill

Gates can get away with being apologetic and self-deprecating; my students need to present themselves more positively. Furthermore, many students and parents acquire their understanding of anthropology through students rather than professors, so it behooves us to raise the quality of the understanding that our major students impart. In turn, by improving their self-presentation our students will become more confident, more ambitious, and ultimately more successful in finding good work.

My career advising grew out of efforts to be a good teacher of the liberal arts, one who helps students move on to self-actualization in the world after college. The advising also grew out of my research in adaptive problem-solving by residents of small coastal communities in Newfoundland. Using the adaptive problem-solving approach, I ask, how do students find out about the world of work and how do they find their place in it? Twenty years ago, I began to develop career workshops within my department, then expanded them into workshops at anthropology conferences, and lately assembled those materials into a workbook, *Careers in Anthropology* (1998).[1] I use the book as a supplementary text in courses, as a workbook in careers workshops, and as an advising guide to students who declare anthropology as a major. This article is drawn from that book.

Because my experience with careers has been limited to academic ones, I collaborate with my college's career planning counselor. Lacking important parts of the whole picture, we are insufficient individually to advise anthropology majors. I have learned about résumés, interviews, and employer expectations, while my career planning colleagues have learned about the usefulness of anthropological perspectives and methods. Even if students consult both of us separately, they tend to perceive us as talking past one another, so they sometimes become frustrated and drop out of the process. But when the career planner and I work together, we see the value in each other's knowledge and how to blend it with concepts from our own fields. The career planners, for example, are delighted to learn that anthropology includes training in participant observation, object reconstruction and cataloging, and cognitive mapping, among other activities. They in turn have taught me what employers call those activities and how to highlight them on student résumés to increase what linguistic anthropologists call "indexicality," or talking on the same wavelength.

While working with the career planners, and counseling and tracking my advisees, I discovered that undergraduate anthropology alumni not only find meaningful work in which they use their anthropology, but they can use their anthropology to get hired to do that work. To demonstrate this idea I drafted and field tested exercises in which anthropological research techniques, such as ethnosemantics, life history, demography, participant observation, social network analysis, key informant interviews, and survey data analysis, are applied to the tasks of selecting and pursuing interesting work. I also realized that when they are advising for careers, professors can use anthropological perspectives

---

[1]John T. Omohundro, *Careers in Anthropology* (Mountain View, CA: Mayfield Publishing Company, 1998).

and data-collection techniques to better understand what students and employers know and need. Let us look briefly at what that might be.

Career Planning in Cross-Cultural Perspective

Except for a handful of publications distributed by the American Anthropological Association, few anthropologists have addressed the subject of career planning for undergraduate majors. One exception, James Spradley's "Career Education from a Cultural Perspective,"[2] shaped my conception of the problem. Spradley observes that in most cultures, such as the Amish in northern New York, the Inuit in central Canada, or the Masai in Kenya, children live close to the world of adult work. As they approach their own adulthood, youths understand clearly what adult work is and what they must do to take it up. There aren't many choices, but there isn't much anxiety either. The transition is smooth and supported by ritual, such as coming-of-age ceremonies.

The modern West, Spradley continues, is quite different. Career options are unclear to the beginner. A gulf yawns between their lives and what adults do. What kinds of careers are there over that gulf? What do people do in those positions? How do I decide which position is for me? How do I cross this gulf and get into the picture? The small-scale, nonindustrial cultures allowed twenty years of enculturation to adult careers. By comparison, Spradley observes, the postindustrial world expects youths to make a more complex transition from sixteen years of schooling to adult work in a matter of months or as little as a single weekend. And our culture has no ritual to ease the change.

It takes each student a while to assemble some kind of bridge across that gulf between college life and adult life. The average length of time in the U.S. between graduating with a B.A. and getting hired is six months to one year. That delay isn't usually because there aren't any jobs for liberal arts students. The delay is largely a cultural problem: new graduates simply don't know what to do next. A career counselor at Dartmouth College puts the problem like this: "Although liberal arts majors are qualified for dozens of jobs, they have no idea how to market themselves successfully."[3] They eventually figure it out and get back in the picture. Two years after graduation, two-thirds are employed full time (many of the others are in further study). Three-quarters of the employed are in positions related to their field of study.

My counseling efforts have aimed to enculturate students to the career life while they are still in college, thus abbreviating that liminal state after the baccalaureate degree. Of course, that's a tactical calculation. Looking back on sixteen years of formal education and looking ahead to a worklife of forty or more

[2]James P. Spradley, "Career Education from a Cultural Perspective," in Larry McClure and Carolyn Buan (eds.), *Essays in Career Education* (Portland, OR: Northwest Regional Educational Laboratory, 1973), pp. 3–16.

[3]Burton Nadler, *Liberal Arts Power: What It Is and How to Sell It on Your Resume,* 2nd ed. (Princeton, NJ: Peterson's, 1989).

years, many of my advisees want to enter a liminal state for awhile. Neverthe-less, other students are eager to move on. Those who made the effort during their college years to select a starting career, identify some employers, and pre-pare themselves for that career were rewarded by finding interesting work more quickly than those who waited until after they graduated. Students will have to make some time for this work in a busy college life. As my career planning col-league says, "Looking for a job is itself a job."

If students take up this job of career planning, their anthropology teach-ers can be valuable motivators and informants. However, not all professors say much about careers to their advisees or their classes. I know this is so because for years I have advised students from other colleges who sought me out at con-ferences, or when they were home visiting their parents, because they were suf-fering from anthro shock untreated by their own professors.

Why are some professors avoiding giving career advice? Some feel that after years in the ivory tower they don't understand the work world that their students want to enter. Times have changed, they say, since they were looking for a posi-tion. It is widely repeated in the college community that after graduation many students will enter careers that don't exist yet. Also, it is widely repeated that most people change careers (not just employers, but lines of work) several times in their working life. My career planning colleagues have amassed evidence to sup-port these popular conceptions. So, "how can we know what to advise students today?" some of my colleagues wonder. Other professors define career advice, just as they do elementary writing instruction, as a task someone else should do.

A third reason that some professors avoid counseling for careers is that they don't approve of the idea of college as a place to credential people for jobs. In their view, student "vocationalism," or seeing college as a route to a good ca-reer, shifts the professor's role from liberator of young minds to gatekeeper of yuppiedom. Professors who teach critical approaches to culture want to in-culcate resistance and a desire to change, not a desire to join, the system.

Anthropologist Michael Moffatt, in an insightful ethnography of residence halls and student culture, caused me to re-think student concern about jobs.[4] Moffatt suggests that professors who disdain student "vocationalism" are being hypocritical. After all, professors got their job by going to college, so why shouldn't the students want the same? Students expect that what they call their "job" will place them in the American middle classes, where their occupation will be a key element in their identity. They expect that job to offer them chal-lenge, growth, rewards, security, and a chance to make the world a better place—all of which are goals deserving support from anthropology professors.

Translating the Skills

What does the student need to find that job and thus meet those goals? Career advice is partly a matter of teaching students to imagine themselves in a new

[4]Michael Moffat, *Coming of Age in New Jersey* (Brunswick, NJ: Rutgers University Press, 1986).

way (the ethnographic "other's" way) and to construct a few basic models of what it's like in the working world.

Imagining themselves in a new way involves learning what employers (one of those ethnographic "others") really want (or think they want) and then reviewing one's education and experience for evidence of having acquired those desirable qualities. Seen in an anthropological light, this process may be called "trans-cultural self-presentation" and is similar to what the ethnographer initiates when entering the field and attempting to build rapport. Here are some data to assist that process.

Anthro shock contains the fear that one will acquire no marketable skills. "Marketable skills" implies there are other kinds as well. In fact, there are few skills that a liberal arts student acquires that aren't marketable. But there are temporary enthusiasms influencing which skills are considered desirable this year and what vocabulary is used to describe those skills. Anthropology students are well equipped to examine language, identify trends, and adapt to them by translating their own skills and knowledge into language appropriate for the setting.

Table 1 describes some skills that anthropology majors have an opportunity to develop at my college and, I am sure, at many other undergraduate institutions supporting a major. These are phrased in language immediately recognizable by the anthropology student and teacher.

Table 2 identifies twelve abilities often acquired through the undergraduate anthropology major. Fewer students and teachers will recognize their major as rephrased in this table, but employers will take notice. I advise my students to select anthropology and other courses intentionally to increase their competence in the abilities listed in Table 1 and then, when presenting themselves to potential graduate schools or employers, to highlight those abilities in the terms used in Table 2. Summer jobs, internships, volunteer work, as well as college classes may provide practice in the desirable activities (read "marketable skills").

Advanced majors in our senior seminar practice this transcultural self-presentation with exercises in composing résumé language. I begin by examining a résumé as a cultural text, an element in the process of seeking and offering jobs. We consider when and how their intended readers approach résumés. I argue that the résumé, in little more than a page, is intended to provoke interest in the writer as a person who can do (or learn to do) what the reader wants. In one column students list in their own language the experiences, both in their major and in their lives, that they think might have value. In a second column they conduct the "first-order" extraction of what skills and abilities were expected or practiced in those activities. In the third column they rephrase these skills and abilities in résumé language. Usually an anxiety-generating activity, composing résumés this way seems to generate more self-confidence.

What Careers Do Anthropology B.A.'s Pursue?

Students can be brought out of anthro shock by infusions of empirical data. Surveys have been conducted to assess what work anthropology students are

TABLE 1   Some Transferable Skills in the Anthropology Major

—Interacting with people of diverse cultures, making allowance for difference in customs and beliefs

—Providing insight into social problems by supplying information about how problems—such as aging, conflict, or bereavement—are dealt with in other cultures

—Interviewing people to obtain information about their attitudes, knowledge, and behavior

—Using statistics and computers to analyze data

—Adapting approaches used in public relations, marketing, or politics to different population groups

—Appraising; classifying; and cataloging rare, old, or valuable objects

—Repairing, reconstructing, and preserving cultural artifacts by selecting chemical treatment, temperature, humidity, and storage methods

—Drawing maps and constructing scale models

—Photographing sites, objects, people, and events

—Interpreting or translating

—Using scientific equipment and measuring devices

—Analyzing craft techniques

—Cooperating in an ethnographic or archaeological research team

—Making policy based on social science research data, problem-solving methods, and professional ethical standards

—Designing research projects and applying for grants

—Producing a research paper in appropriate format and style

—Orally presenting research results

—Applying a variety of ethnographic data collection techniques: ethnosemantics, proxemics, life histories, ethnohistory, folklore, event analysis, genealogies, etc.

—Producing and editing a scholarly journal

—Leading a pre-professional organization such as a student anthropology society or honors society

—Developing public relations for a museum, field project, or conference

—Designing, building, installing, and acting as docent for museum exhibits

—Coaching, instructing, tutoring, and team-teaching with peers

—Studying a second language

Source: Adapted from John T. Omohundro, *Careers in Anthropology* (Mountain View, CA: Mayfield, 1998).

prepared for and what fields alumni actually entered. In *Anthropology and Jobs,* H. Russell Bernard and Willis Sibley identified thirteen fields that the anthropology B.A. could enter with no additional training.[5] These included journalism, police work, and the travel or tour industry. They also identified twenty-eight fields the anthropology B.A. could enter if additional training, up to the M.A. or M.S. level in the appropriate discipline, was acquired. These

[5]H. Russell Bernard and Willis E. Sibley, *Anthropology and Jobs: A Guide for Undergraduates,* American Anthropological Association special publication (Washington, DC: American Anthropological Association, 1975).

TABLE 2   Résumé Language for Anthropological Abilities

Social agility—In an unfamiliar social or career-related setting, you learn to size up quickly the "rules of the game." You can become accepted more quickly than you could without anthropology.

Observation—As you must often learn about a culture from within it, you learn how to interview and observe as a participant.

Planning—You learn how to find patterns in the behavior of a cultural group. This allows you to generalize about their behavior and predict what they might do in a given situation.

Social sensitivity—While other people's ways of doing things may be different from your own, you learn the importance of events and conditions that have contributed to this difference. You also recognize that other cultures view your ways as strange. You learn the value of behaving toward others with appropriate preparation, care, and understanding.

Accuracy in interpreting behavior—You become familiar with the range of behavior in different cultures. You learn how to look at cultural causes of behavior before assigning causes yourself.

Challenging conclusions—You learn that analyses of human behavior are open to challenge. You learn how to use new knowledge to test past conclusions.

Interpreting information—You learn how to use data collected by others, reorganizing or interpreting it to reach original conclusions.

Simplifying information—As anthropology is conducted among publics as well as about them, you learn how to simplify technical information for communication to non-technical people.

Contextualizing—Attention to details is a trait of anthropology. However, you learn that any detail might not be as important as its context, and can even be misleading when context is ignored.

Problem-solving—Often functioning within a cultural group, or acting upon culturally sensitive issues, you learn to approach problems with care. Before acting, you learn how to identify the problem, set your goals, decide upon the actions you will take, and calculate possible effects on other people.

Persuasive writing—Anthropology strives to represent the behavior of one group to another group, and is in continual need of interpretation. You learn the value of bringing someone else to your view through written argument.

Social perspective—You learn how to perceive the acts of individuals and local groups as cause and effect of larger sociocultural systems. This enables you to "act locally and think globally."

Source: John T. Omohundro, *Careers in Anthropology* (Mountain View, CA: Mayfield, 1998).

fields included dietetics, market research, city planning, museums, personnel, and community development, to name a few.

Ten years later, two of my students conducted a survey of anthropology alumni from 32 liberal arts colleges in the northeast U.S.[6] Of the 616 respondents, 62% worked in the profit sector, 9% in the non-profit sector, and 6% in government. 16% were still in a graduate or professional school.

[6]Lawrence W. Kratts and Clarissa Hunter, "Undergraduate Alumni Survey Results," *Anthropology Newsletter* (November 1986).

The respondents' occupations were sorted into seventeen categories. Academics accounted for 10%, some of whom were in disciplines other than anthropology, but managers ("director," "administrator," etc.) dominated at 19%. It appears that a large number of anthropology majors become actors in a bureaucracy, supervising others. Medicine, communications, and business together accounted for another 16% of respondents' current positions.

Does this range of work positions outside of anthropology, as usually conceived, signal a failure on our part to place our advisees in positions that will utilize their major? I don't think so, and neither do the alumni. 71% of the northeast alumni agreed with the statement, "my anthropology education helps me in my current work." An owner of a small business wrote, "All aspects of the [antique] business are satisfying: attending antique shows, unearthing an early item, researching its age and provenance, restoring or repairing it, and educating a potential customer about it. . . ."

Most (81%) of the alumni returning the survey claimed they were satisfied and challenged by their current work, and 74% felt their decision to major in anthropology was a good one. Some alumni waxed enthusiastic about anthropology as the foundation for a liberal arts education. A banker urged current majors, "Go for it: no one in business will ever hold a liberal arts education against you. . . . In the long run this will mark you as superior to a crowd of business students. . . ." Alumni highlighted the value in their current work of cultural relativism, examining human behavior holistically, and using qualitative research methods, all acquired in the major. A social services administrator reported, "I work as a management analyst in a county social services agency. While it is difficult to get an anthro degree recognized as relevant, the anthropological approach is, I feel, one of the best for this sort of job. I'm always translating. . . ."

More recent surveys of alumni, such as the six colleges in the North Carolina system in 1988[7] and a SUNY Plattsburgh survey in 1993,[8] produced similar results. The majority of anthropology majors are 1) glad they majored in anthropology, 2) using some or all of the skills and perspectives they acquired in the major, and 3) enjoying their work, even if few of them are hanging out shingles bearing the title "anthropologist."

Along with their satisfaction, the alumni have some complaints and some advice for current students and their teachers. Overall, alumni were disappointed with the quality and quantity of career advice they received while undergraduates. They also see now that they would have benefitted from more careful choices of electives and course work outside of anthropology.

The northeast alumni urged current students to take courses in math, statistics, communications, economics, science, and computing. This advice matches that offered by alumni from most majors, who recommend courses in

[7]Stanton Tefft, with Cathy Harris and Glen Godwin, "North Carolina Undergraduate Alumni Survey," *Anthropology Newsletter* (January 1988).

[8]James Armstrong, personal communication, 1993.

administration, writing, interpersonal relations, economics, accounting, and math. In our northeast survey, anthropology alumni also strongly urged students to gain as much practical experience as possible through field schools, lab and methods courses, senior theses, independent research projects, overseas study, and collaboration with professors' research.

Conclusion

The purpose of this essay has been to help anthropology teachers deal with anthro shock among their students. I advocate swift first aid with the easy answer, but it is essential to have the evidence to back up that answer. I also advocate cooperation with careers planning professionals. Anthropology offers many marketable skills, or good training for a variety of fields of work, but students, working within the world view of college life and transcript semantics, often don't know how to translate their abilities into ones the rest of the world wants.

Surveys of alumni show that they pursue many lines of work, enjoy their work, are using their anthropological perspective and skills, and are glad they majored in anthropology. Their self-descriptions in surveys suggest that they majored in anthropology because its fundamental concepts and methods for understanding human behavior matched their long-established dispositions. After college, they found satisfying employment in positions where those same dispositions—now more developed through the major—were welcome and useful. This led me to a self-discovery theory of liberal arts education. That is, college is not a place where the student, as a blank slate ready to become a cog, learns "what I need to know to get a job." Instead, college is a place where the student discovers "what I like to do" and then refines his or her ability to do it. I've discovered that many career planning professionals knew this all along.

In sum, the evidence is that anthropology students not only find meaningful work, but they can use their anthropology to get that work, and we teachers can use our anthropology to improve our career advising. Not every anthropologist feels comfortable giving career advice, for several reasons, some of which I sympathize with and some I don't. Not every student needs to rush from college to a career, either, but I have discussed here some ways to help them if they want to move along.

Postscript: Grebbleberry recovered and is now doing fine as a technical illustrator in Oregon, coupling her artistic ability to her love of archaeology.

Connection Questions

1. Give three examples of how people mentioned in the Miller chapter are putting their anthropology training and education to work.

2. How would an anthropology degree or coursework benefit you in the career field you plan to enter or your life goals more generally?

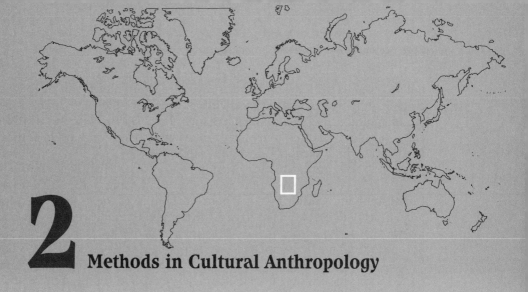

2 Methods in Cultural Anthropology

Eating Christmas in the Kalahari

Richard Borshay Lee

What happens when an anthropologist living among the !Kung of Africa decides to be generous and to share a large animal with everyone at Christmastime? This compelling account of the misunderstanding and confusion that resulted takes the reader deeper into the nature of culture. Richard Lee carefully traces how the !Kung perceived his generosity and taught the anthropologist something about his own culture.

The !Kung Bushmen's knowledge of Christmas is thirdhand. The London Missionary Society brought the holiday to the southern Tswana tribes in the early nineteenth century. Later, native catechists spread the idea far and wide among the Bantu-speaking pastoralists, even in the remotest corners of the Kalahari Desert. The Bushmen's idea of the Christmas story, stripped to its essentials, is "praise the birth of white man's god-chief"; what keeps their interest in the

Reprinted from *Natural History*, December 1969; copyright © Natural History Magazine, Inc., 1969.

holiday high is the Tswana-Herero custom of slaughtering an ox for his Bushmen neighbors as an annual goodwill gesture. Since the 1930s, part of the Bushmen's annual round of activities has included a December congregation at the cattle posts for trading, marriage brokering, and several days of trance dance feasting at which the local Tswana headman is host.

As a social anthropologist working with !Kung Bushmen, I found that the Christmas ox custom suited my purposes. I had come to the Kalahari to study the hunting and gathering subsistence economy of the !Kung, and to accomplish this it was essential not to provide them with food, share my own food, or interfere in any way with their food-gathering activities. While liberal handouts of tobacco and medical supplies were appreciated, they were scarcely adequate to erase the glaring disparity in wealth between the anthropologist, who maintained a two-month inventory of canned goods, and the Bushmen, who rarely had a day's supply of food on hand. My approach, while paying off in terms of data, left me open to frequent accusations of stinginess and hardheartedness. By their lights, I was a miser.

The Christmas ox was to be my way of saying thank you for the cooperation of the past year; and since it was to be our last Christmas in the field, I was determined to slaughter the largest, meatiest ox that money could buy, insuring that the feast and trance dance would be a success.

Through December I kept my eyes open at the wells as the cattle were brought down for watering. Several animals were offered, but none had quite the grossness that I had in mind. Then, ten days before the holiday, a Herero friend led an ox of astonishing size and mass up to our camp. It was solid black, stood five feet high at the shoulder, had a five-foot span of horns, and must have weighed 1,200 pounds on the hoof. Food consumption calculations are my specialty, and I quickly figured that bones and viscera aside, there was enough meat—at least four pounds—for every man, woman, and child of the 150 Bushmen in the vicinity of /ai/ai who were expected at the feast.

Having found the right animal at last, I paid the Herero £20 ($56) and asked him to keep the beast with his herd until Christmas day. The next morning word spread among the people that the big solid black one was the ox chosen by /ontah (my Bushman name; it means, roughly, "whitey") for the Christmas feast. That afternoon I received the first delegation. Ben!a, an outspoken sixty-year-old mother of five, came to the point slowly.

"Where were you planning to eat Christmas?"

"Right here at /ai/ai," I replied.

"Alone or with others?"

"I expect to invite all the people to eat Christmas with me."

"Eat what?"

"I have purchased Yehave's black ox, and I am going to slaughter and cook it."

"That's what we were told at the well but refused to believe it until we heard it from yourself."

"Well, it's the black one," I replied expansively, although wondering what she was driving at.

"Oh, no!" Ben!a groaned, turning to her group. "They were right." Turning back to me she asked, "Do you expect us to eat that bag of bones?"

"Bag of bones! It's the biggest ox at /ai/ai."

"Big, yes, but old. And thin. Everybody knows there's no meat on that old ox. What did you expect us to eat off it, the horns?"

Everybody chuckled at Ben!a's one-liner as they walked away, but all I could manage was a weak grin.

That evening it was the turn of the young men. They came to sit at our evening fire. /gaugo, about my age, spoke to me man-to-man.

"/ontah, you have always been square with us," he lied. "What has happened to change your heart? That sack of guts and bones of Yehave's will hardly feed one camp, let alone all the Bushmen around /ai/ai." And he proceeded to enumerate the seven camps in the /ai/ai vicinity, family by family. "Perhaps you have forgotten that we are not few, but many. Or are you too blind to tell the difference between a proper cow and an old wreck? That ox is thin to the point of death."

"Look, you guys," I retorted, "that is a beautiful animal, and I'm sure you will eat it with pleasure at Christmas."

"Of course we will eat it; it's food. But it won't fill us up to the point where we will have enough strength to dance. We will eat and go home to bed with stomachs rumbling."

That night as we turned in, I asked my wife, Nancy, "What did you think of the black ox?"

"It looked enormous to me. Why?"

"Well, about eight different people have told me I got gypped; that the ox is nothing but bones."

"What's the angle?" Nancy asked. "Did they have a better one to sell?"

"No, they just said that it was going to be a grim Christmas because there won't be enough meat to go around. Maybe I'll get an independent judge to look at the beast in the morning."

Bright and early, Halingisi, a Tswana cattle owner, appeared at our camp. But before I could ask him to give me his opinion on Yehave's black ox, he gave me the eye signal that indicated a confidential chat. We left the camp and sat down.

"/ontah, I'm surprised at you; you've lived here for three years and still haven't learned anything about cattle."

"But what else can a person do but choose the biggest, strongest animal one can find?" I retorted.

"Look, just because an animal is big doesn't mean that it has plenty of meat on it. The black one was a beauty when it was younger, but now it is thin to the point of death."

"Well, I've already bought it. What can I do at this stage?"

"Bought it already? I thought you were just considering it. Well, you'll have to kill it and serve it, I suppose. But don't expect much of a dance to follow."

My spirits dropped rapidly. I could believe that Ben!a and /gaugo just might be putting me on about the black ox, but Halingisi seemed to be an impartial critic. I went around that day feeling as though I had bought a lemon of a used car.

In the afternoon it was Tomazo's turn. Tomazo is a fine hunter, a top trance performer . . . and one of my most reliable informants. He approached the subject of the Christmas cow as part of my continuing Bushman education.

"My friend, the way it is with us Bushmen," he began, "is that we love meat. And even more than that, we love fat. When we hunt we always search for the fat ones, the ones dripping with layers of white fat: fat that turns into a clear, thick oil in the cooking pot, fat that slides down your gullet, fills your stomach and gives you a roaring diarrhea," he rhapsodized.

"So, feeling as we do," he continued, "it gives us pain to be served such a scrawny thing as Yehave's black ox. It is big, yes, and no doubt its giant bones are good for soup, but fat is what we really crave, and so we will eat Christmas this year with a heavy heart."

The prospect of a gloomy Christmas now had me worried, so I asked Tomazo what I could do about it.

"Look for a fat one, a young one . . . smaller, but fat. Fat enough to make us //gom (evacuate the bowels), then we will be happy."

My suspicions were aroused when Tomazo said that he happened to know a young, fat, barren cow that the owner was willing to part with. Was Tomazo working on commission, I wondered? But I dispelled this unworthy thought when we approached the Herero owner of the cow in question and found that he had decided not to sell.

The scrawny wreck of a Christmas ox now became the talk of the /ai/ai water hole and was the first news told to the outlying groups as they began to come in from the bush for the feast. What finally convinced me that real trouble might be brewing was the visit from u!au, an old conservative with a reputation for fierceness. His nickname meant spear and referred to an incident thirty years ago in which he had speared a man to death. He had an intense manner; fixing me with his eyes, he said in clipped tones:

"I have only just heard about the black ox today, or else I would have come here earlier. /ontah, do you honestly think you can serve meat like that to people and avoid a fight?" He paused, letting the implications sink in. "I don't mean fight you, /ontah; you are a white man. I mean a fight between Bushmen. There are many fierce ones here, and with such a small quantity of meat to distribute, how can you give everybody a fair share? Someone is sure to accuse another of taking too much or hogging all the choice pieces. Then you will see what happens when some go hungry while others eat."

The possibility of at least a serious argument struck me as all too real. I had witnessed the tension that surrounds the distribution of meat from a kudu or gemsbok kill, and had documented many arguments that sprang up from a real or imagined slight in meat distribution. The owners of a kill may spend up to two hours arranging and rearranging the piles of meat under the gaze of a circle of recipients before handing them out. And I knew that the Christmas feast at /ai/ai would be bringing together groups that had feuded in the past.

Convinced now of the gravity of the situation, I went in earnest to search for a second cow; but all my inquiries failed to turn one up.

The Christmas feast was evidently going to be a disaster, and the incessant complaints about the meagerness of the ox had already taken the fun out of it for me. Moreover, I was getting bored with the wisecracks, and after losing my temper a few times, I resolved to serve the beast anyway. If the meat fell short, the hell with it. In the Bushmen idiom, I announced to all who would listen:

"I am a poor man and blind. If I have chosen one that is too old and too thin, we will eat it anyway and see if there is enough meat there to quiet the rumbling of our stomachs."

On hearing this speech, Ben!a offered me a rare word of comfort. "It's thin," she said philosophically, "but the bones will make a good soup."

At dawn Christmas morning, instinct told me to turn over the butchering and cooking to a friend and take off with Nancy to spend Christmas alone in the bush. But curiosity kept me from retreating. I wanted to see what such a scrawny ox looked like on butchering, and if there *was* going to be a fight, I wanted to catch every word of it. Anthropologists are incurable that way.

The great beast was driven up to our dancing ground, and a shot in the forehead dropped it in its tracks. Then, freshly cut branches were heaped around the fallen carcass to receive the meat. Ten men volunteered to help with the cutting. I asked /gaugo to make the breast bone cut. This cut, which begins the butchering process for most large game, offers easy access for removal of the viscera. But it also allows the hunter to spot-check the amount of fat on an animal. A fat game animal carries a white layer up to an inch thick on the chest, while in a thin one, the knife will quickly cut to bone. All eyes fixed on his hand as /gaugo, dwarfed by the great carcass, knelt to the breast. The first cut opened a pool of solid white in the black skin. The second and third cut widened and deepened the creamy white. Still no bone. It was pure fat; it must have been two inches thick.

"Hey /gau," I burst out, "that ox is loaded with fat. What's this about the ox being too thin to bother eating? Are you out of your mind?"

"Fat?" /gau shot back. "You call that fat? This wreck is thin, sick, dead!" And he broke out laughing. So did everyone else. They rolled on the ground, paralyzed with laughter. Everybody laughed except me; I was thinking.

I ran back to the tent and burst in just as Nancy was getting up. "Hey, the black ox. It's fat as hell! They were kidding about it being too thin to eat. It was a joke or something. A put-on. Everyone is really delighted with it."

"Some joke," my wife replied. "It was so funny that you were ready to pack up and leave /ai/ai."

If it had indeed been a joke, it had been an extraordinarily convincing one, and tinged, I thought, with more than a touch of malice, as many jokes are.

Nevertheless, that it was a joke lifted my spirits considerably, and I returned to the butchering site where the shape of the ox was rapidly disappearing under the axes and knives of the butchers. The atmosphere had become festive. Grinning broadly, their arms covered with blood well past the elbow, men packed chunks of meat into the big cast-iron cooking pots, fifty pounds to the load, and muttered and chuckled all the while about the thinness and worthlessness of the animal and /ontah's poor judgment.

We danced and ate that ox two days and two nights; we cooked and distributed fourteen potfuls of meat and no one went home hungry and no fights broke out.

But the "joke" stayed in my mind. I had a growing feeling that something important had happened in my relationship with the Bushmen and that the clue lay in the meaning of the joke. Several days later, when most of the people had dispersed back to the bush camps, I raised the question with Hakekgose, a Tswana man who had grown up among the !Kung, married a !Kung girl, and who probably knew their culture better than any other non-Bushman.

"With us whites," I began, "Christmas is supposed to be the day of friendship and brotherly love. What I can't figure out is why the Bushmen went to such lengths to criticize and belittle the ox I had bought for the feast. The animal was perfectly good and their jokes and wisecracks practically ruined the holiday for me."

"So it really did bother you," said Hakekgose. "Well, that's the way they always talk. When I take my rifle and go hunting with them, if I miss, they laugh at me for the rest of the day. But even if I hit and bring one down, it's no better. To them, the kill is always too small or too old or too thin; and as we sit down on the kill site to cook and eat the liver, they keep grumbling, even with their mouths full of meat. They say things like, 'Oh, this is awful! What a worthless animal! Whatever made me think that this Tswana rascal could hunt!' "

"Is this the way outsiders are treated?" I asked.

"No, it is their custom; they talk that way to each other, too. Go and ask them."

/gaugo had been one of the most enthusiastic in making me feel bad about the merit of the Christmas ox. I sought him out first.

"Why did you tell me the black ox was worthless, when you could see that it was loaded with fat and meat?"

"It is our way," he said, smiling. "We always like to fool people about that. Say there is a Bushman who has been hunting. He must not come home and announce like a braggart, 'I have killed a big one in the bush!' He must first sit down in silence until I or someone else comes up to his fire and asks, 'What did you see today?' He replies quietly, 'Ah, I'm no good for hunting. I saw nothing at all [pause] just a little tiny one.' Then I smile to myself," /gaugo continued, "because I know he has killed something big.

"In the morning we make up a party of four or five people to cut up and carry the meat back to the camp. When we arrive at the kill we examine it and cry out, 'You mean to say you have dragged us all the way out here in order to make us cart home your pile of bones? Oh, if I had known it was this thin I wouldn't have come.' Another one pipes up, 'People, to think I gave up a nice day in the shade for this. At home we may be hungry, but at least we have nice cool water to drink.' If the horns are big, someone says, 'Did you think that somehow you were going to boil down the horns for soup?'

"To all this you must respond in kind. 'I agree,' you say, 'this one is not worth the effort; let's just cook the liver for strength and leave the rest for the hyenas. It is not too late to hunt today and even a duiker or a steenbok would be better than this mess.'

"Then you set to work nevertheless; butcher the animal, carry the meat back to the camp and everyone eats," /gaugo concluded.

Things were beginning to make sense. Next, I went to Tomazo. He corroborated /gaugo's story of the obligatory insults over a kill and added a few details of his own.

"But," I asked, "why insult a man after he has gone to all that trouble to track and kill an animal and when he is going to share the meat with you so that your children will have something to eat?"

"Arrogance," was his cryptic answer.

"Arrogance?"

"Yes, when a young man kills much meat he comes to think of himself as a chief or a big man, and he thinks of the rest of us as his servants or inferiors. We can't accept this. We refuse one who boasts, for someday his pride will make him kill somebody. So we always speak of his meat as worthless. This way we cool his heart and make him gentle."

"But why didn't you tell me this before?" I asked Tomazo with some heat.

"Because you never asked me," said Tomazo, echoing the refrain that has come to haunt every field ethnographer.

The pieces now fell into place. I had known for a long time that in situations of social conflict with Bushmen I held all the cards. I was the only source of tobacco in a thousand square miles, and I was not incapable of cutting an individual off for noncooperation. Though my boycott never lasted longer than a few days, it was an indication of my strength. People resented my presence at the water hole, yet simultaneously dreaded my leaving. In short I was a perfect target for the charge of arrogance and for the Bushman tactic of enforcing humility.

I had been taught an object lesson by the Bushmen; it had come from an unexpected corner and had hurt me in a vulnerable area. For the big black ox was to be the one totally generous, unstinting act of my year at /ai/ai and I was quite unprepared for the reaction I received.

As I read it, their message was this: There are no totally generous acts. All "acts" have an element of calculation. One black ox slaughtered at Christmas does not wipe out a year of careful manipulation of gifts given to serve your own ends. After all, to kill an animal and share the meat with people is really no more than the Bushmen do for each other every day and with far less fanfare.

In the end, I had to admire how the Bushmen had played out the farce—collectively straight-faced to the end. Curiously, the episode reminded me of the

Good Soldier Schweik and his marvelous encounters with authority. Like Schweik, the Bushmen had retained a thoroughgoing skepticism of good intentions. Was it this independence of spirit, I wondered, that had kept them culturally viable in the face of generations of contact with more powerful societies, both black and white? The thought that the Bushmen were alive and well in the Kalahari was strangely comforting. Perhaps, armed with that independence and with their superb knowledge of their environment, they might yet survive the future.

Connection Questions

1. Describe the research methods presented in Miller's text that Richard Lee discusses in his account, "Eating Christmas in the Kalahari."

2. What evidence does Richard Lee provide about the rapport he established with the !Kung Bushmen?

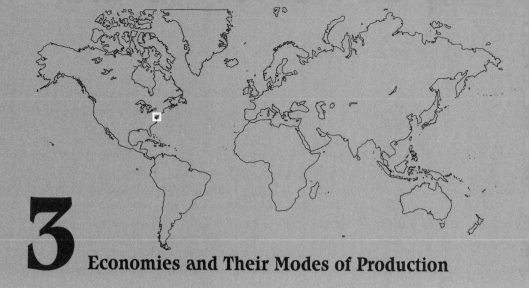

3 Economies and Their Modes of Production

Office Work and the Crack Alternative

Philippe Bourgois

Market economies are standard features of most countries in today's world. Almost everywhere, there is a formal market economy identified by visible, legal, organized economic structures and activities, which economists attempt to measure and governments can tax and regulate. Banks, factories, corporations, retail outlets—these and other publicly organized economic units are usually part of the formal economy.

But underneath the formal economy lies an informal system often called the shadow *or* underground *economy. The shadow economy is usually small-scale, personal, and at times illegal. Governments find it difficult to tax and regulate the shadow economy. Yet it is the shadow economy that provides a living for hundreds of millions of largely poor men and women around the world today.*

In this article, Philippe Bourgois focuses on part of the shadow economy in the United States, the illegal sale of crack by Puerto Rican immigrants in New York City. He argues that the loss of manufacturing jobs in

*New York is a key to understanding the rise of drug dealing in Spanish
Harlem. Manufacturing jobs once provided dignified and stable employment for poorly educated, unskilled Puerto Rican men and women. As factories closed during the 1960s, '70s, and '80s, the unemployed could find
work only in service industries such as security corporations, law firms,
and insurance companies. Because they were uneducated and culturally different, they could hold only minimum wage jobs in such worlds, as they are
usually controlled by educated, largely Anglo people who openly look down
on them. In the end, they could achieve higher status and often higher income in their own ethnic community by dealing drugs. The result has been
a destructive spiral into addiction, murder, and prison. Bourgois concludes
the article with an addendum noting that high employment in the late 1990s
provided more work opportunities for Puerto Ricans in the formal economy
and that crack dealing has largely given way to the less visible sale of marijuana and heroin.*

For a total of approximately three and a half years during the late 1980s and
early 1990s, I lived with my wife and young son in an irregularly heated, rat-
filled tenement in East Harlem, New York. This two-hundred-square-block
neighborhood—better known locally as *El Barrio* or Spanish Harlem—is visibly impoverished yet it is located in the heart of New York, the richest city in
the Western Hemisphere. It is literally a stone's throw from multimillion-dollar
condominiums. Although one in three families survived on some form of public assistance in 1990, the majority of El Barrio's 110,600 Puerto Rican and
African-American residents fall into the ranks of the working poor.[1] They eke
out an uneasy subsistence in entry-level service and manufacturing jobs in one
of the most expensive cities in the world.

   The public sector (e.g., the police, social welfare agencies, the Sanitation
Department) has broken down in El Barrio and does not function effectively.
This has caused the legally employed residents of the neighborhood to lose control of their streets and public spaces to the drug economy. My tenement's block
was not atypical and within a few hundred yards' radius I could obtain heroin,
crack, powder cocaine, hypodermic needles, methadone, Valium, angel dust,
marijuana, mescaline, bootleg alcohol, and tobacco. Within two hundred feet
of my stoop there were three competing crack houses selling vials at two, three,
and five dollars. Several doctors operated "pill mills" on the blocks around me,

---

[1]According to the 1990 Census, in East Harlem 48.3 percent of males and 35.2 percent of females
over sixteen were officially reported as employed—compared to a citywide average of 64.3 percent
for men and 49 percent for women. Another 10.4 percent of the men and 5.7 percent of the women
in East Harlem were actively looking for legal work. . . . In El Barrio as a whole, 60 percent of all
households reported legally earned incomes. Twenty-six percent received Public Assistance, 6.3 percent received Supplemental Security Income, and 5 percent received Medicaid benefits.

writing prescriptions for opiates and barbiturates upon demand. In the projects within view of my living-room window, the Housing Authority police arrested a fifty-five-year-old mother and her twenty-two-year-old daughter while they were "bagging" twenty-two pounds of cocaine into ten-dollar quarter-gram "Jumbo" vials of adulterated product worth over a million dollars on the streets. The police found twenty-five thousand dollars in cash in small-denomination bills in this same apartment.[2] In other words, there are millions of dollars' worth of business going on directly in front of the youths growing up in East Harlem tenements and housing projects. Why should these young men and women take the subway downtown to work minimum-wage jobs—or even double minimum-wage jobs—in downtown offices when they can usually earn more, at least in the short run, by selling drugs on the street corner in front of their apartment or schoolyard?

This dynamic underground economy is predicated on violence and substance abuse. It has spawned what I call a "street culture" of resistance and self-destruction. The central concern of my study is the relationship of street culture to the worlds of work accessible to street dealers—that is, the legal and illegal labor markets that employ them and give meaning to their lives. I hope to show the local-level implications of the global-level restructuring of the U.S. economy away from factory production and toward services. In the process, I have recorded the words and experiences of some unrepentant victims who are part of a network of some twenty-five street-level crack dealers operating on and around my block. To summarize, I am arguing that the transformation from manufacturing to service employment—especially in the professional office work setting—is much more culturally disruptive than the already revealing statistics on reductions in income, employment, unionization, and worker's benefits would indicate. Low-level service sector employment engenders a humiliating ideological—or cultural—confrontation between a powerful corps of white office executives and their assistants versus a younger generation of poorly educated, alienated, "colored" workers. It also often takes the form of a sharply polarized confrontation over gender roles.

Shattered Working-Class Dreams

All the crack dealers and addicts whom I have interviewed had worked at one or more legal jobs in their early youth. In fact, most entered the labor market at a younger age than the typical American. Before they were twelve years old they were bagging groceries at the supermarket for tips, stocking beers off-the-books in local *bodegas*, or shining shoes. For example, Primo, the night manager at a video game arcade that sells five-dollar vials of crack on the block where I lived, pursued a traditional working-class dream in his early

---

[2]Both of these police actions were reported in the local print and television media, but I am withholding the cities to protect the anonymity of my street address.

adolescence. With the support of his extended kin who were all immersed in a working-class "common sense," he dropped out of junior high school to work in a local garment factory:

> I was like fourteen or fifteen playing hooky and pressing dresses and whatever they were making on the steamer. They was cheap, cheap clothes.
>
> My mother's sister was working there first and then her son, my cousin Willie—the one who's in jail now—was the one they hired first, because his mother agreed: "If you don't want to go to school, you gotta work."
>
> So I started hanging out with him. I wasn't planning on working in the factory. I was supposed to be in school; but it just sort of happened.

Ironically, young Primo actually became the agent who physically moved the factory out of the inner city. In the process, he became merely one more of the 445,900 manufacturing workers in New York City who lost their jobs as factory employment dropped 50 percent from 1963 to 1983 . . .

Almost all the crack dealers had similar tales of former factory jobs. For poor adolescents, the decision to drop out of school and become a marginal factory worker is attractive. It provides the employed youth with access to the childhood "necessities"—sneakers, basketballs, store-bought snacks— that sixteen-year-olds who stay in school cannot afford. In the descriptions of their first forays into legal factory-based employment, one hears clearly the extent to which they, and their families, subscribed to mainstream working-class ideologies about the dignity of engaging in "hard work" rather than education.

Had these enterprising, early-adolescent workers from El Barrio not been confined to the weakest sector of manufacturing in a period of rapid job loss, their teenage working-class dreams might have stabilized. Instead, upon reaching their mid-twenties, they discovered themselves to be unemployable high school dropouts. This painful realization of social marginalization expresses itself across a generational divide. The parents and grandparents of the dealers continue to maintain working-class values of honesty and hard work which conflict violently with the reality of their children's immersion in street culture. They are constantly accused of slothfulness by their mothers and even by friends who have managed to maintain legal jobs. They do not have a regional perspective on the dearth of adequate entry-level jobs available to "functional illiterates" in New York, and they begin to suspect that they might indeed be "*vago bons*" [lazy bums] who do not *want* to work hard and cannot help themselves. Confused, they take refuge in an alternative search for career, meaning, and ecstasy in substance abuse.

Formerly, when most entry-level jobs were found in factories, the contradiction between an oppositional street culture and traditional working-class, masculine, shop-floor culture was less pronounced—especially when the work site was protected by a union. Factories are inevitably rife with confrontational hierarchies. Nevertheless, on the shop-floor, surrounded by older union workers, high school dropouts who are well versed in the latest and toughest street culture styles function effectively. In the factory, being tough and violently macho has high cultural value; a certain degree of opposition to the foreman and the "bossman" is expected and is considered appropriate.

In contrast, this same oppositional street-identity is nonfunctional in the professional office worker service sector that has burgeoned in New York's high-finance-driven economy. It does not allow for the humble, obedient, social interaction—often across gender lines—that professional office workers routinely impose on their subordinates. A qualitative change has occurred, therefore, in the tenor of social interaction in office-based employment. Workers in a mail room or behind a photocopy machine cannot publicly maintain their cultural autonomy. Most concretely, they have no union; more subtly, there are few fellow workers surrounding them to insulate them and to provide them with a culturally based sense of class solidarity.[3] Instead they are besieged by supervisors and bosses from an alien, hostile, and obviously dominant culture who ridicule street culture. Workers like Primo appear inarticulate to their professional supervisors when they try to imitate the language of power in the workplace and instead stumble pathetically over the enunciation of unfamiliar words. They cannot decipher the hastily scribbled instructions—rife with mysterious abbreviations—that are left for them by harried office managers. The "common sense" of white-collar work is foreign to them; they do not, for example, understand the logic for filing triplicate copies of memos or for postdating invoices. When they attempt to improvise or show initiative they fail miserably and instead appear inefficient, or even hostile, for failing to follow "clearly specified" instructions.

Their "social skills" are even more inadequate than their limited professional capacities. They do not know how to look at their fellow co-service workers, let alone their supervisors, without intimidating them. They cannot walk down the hallway to the water fountain without unconsciously swaying their shoulders aggressively as if patrolling their home turf. Gender barriers are an even more culturally charged realm. They are repeatedly reprimanded for harassing female coworkers.

The cultural clash between white "yuppie" power and inner-city "scrambling jive" in the service sector is much more than a superficial question of style. It is about access to power. Service workers who are incapable of obeying the rules of interpersonal interaction dictated by professional office culture will never be upwardly mobile. Their supervisors will think they are dumb or have a "bad attitude." Once again, a gender dynamic exacerbates the confusion and sense of insult experienced by young, male inner-city employees because most supervisors in the lowest reaches of the service sector are women. Street culture does not allow males to be subordinate across gender lines.

---

[3]Significantly, there are subsectors of the service industry that are relatively unionized—such as hospital and custodial work—where there is a limited autonomous space for street culture and working-class resistance.

"Gettin' Dissed"

On the street, the trauma of experiencing a threat to one's personal dignity has been frozen linguistically in the commonly used phrase "to diss," which is short for "to disrespect." Significantly, one generation ago ethnographers working in rural Puerto Rico specifically noted the importance of the traditional Puerto Rican concept of *respeto* in mediating labor relations:

> The good owner "respects" (*respeta*) the laborer. . . . It is probably to the interest of the landowner to make concessions to his best workers, to deal with them on a respect basis, and to enmesh them in a network of mutual obligations.[4]

Puerto Rican street-dealers do not find respect in the entry-level service sector jobs that have increased two-fold in New York's economy since the 1950s. On the contrary, they "get dissed" in the new jobs that are available to them. Primo, for example, remembers the humiliation of his former work experiences as an "office boy," and he speaks of them in a race- and gender-charged idiom:

> I had a prejudiced boss. She was a fucking "ho'," Gloria. She was white. Her name was Christian. No, not Christian, Kirschman. I don't know if she was Jewish or not. When she was talking to people she would say, "He's illiterate."
>
> So what I did one day was, I just looked up the word, "illiterate," in the dictionary and I saw that she's saying to her associates that I'm stupid or something!
>
> Well, I am illiterate anyway.

The most profound dimension of Primo's humiliation was being obliged to look up in the dictionary the word used to insult him. In contrast, in the underground economy, he is sheltered from this kind of threat:

> Rocky [the crack house franchise owner] he would never disrespect me that way. He wouldn't tell me that because he's illiterate too. Plus I've got more education than him. I got a GED. . . .

Primo excels in the street's underground economy. His very persona inspires fear and respect. In contrast, in order to succeed in his former office job, Primo would have had to self-consciously alter his street identity and mimic the professional cultural style that office managers require of their subordinates and colleagues. Primo refused to accept his boss's insults and he was unable to imitate her interactional styles. He was doomed, consequently, to a marginal position behind a photocopy machine or at the mail meter. Behavior considered appropriate in street culture is considered dysfunctional in office settings.

---

[4]Eric Wolf, "San Jose: Subcultures of a 'Traditional' Coffee Municipality," in Julian Stewart (ed.), *The People of Puerto Rico* (Chicago: University of Chicago Press, 1956), p. 235.

In other words, job requirements in the service sector are largely cultural style and this conjugates powerfully with racism.

> I wouldn't have mind that she said I was illiterate. What bothered me was that when she called on the telephone, she wouldn't want me to answer even if my supervisor who was the receptionist was not there. [Note how Primo is so low in the office hierarchy that his immediate supervisor is a receptionist.]
>
> When she hears my voice it sounds like she's going to get a heart attack. She'd go, "Why are you answering the phones?"
>
> That bitch just didn't like my Puerto Rican accent.

Primo's manner of resisting this insult to his cultural dignity exacerbated his marginal position in the labor hierarchy:

> And then, when I did pick up the phone, I used to just sound *Porta'rrrican* on purpose.

In contrast to the old factory sweatshop positions, these just-above-minimum-wage office jobs require intense interpersonal contact with the middle and upper-middle classes. Close contact across class lines and the absence of a working-class autonomous space for eight hours a day in the office can be a claustrophobic experience for an otherwise ambitious, energetic, young, inner-city worker.

Caesar, who worked for Primo as lookout and bodyguard at the crack house, interpreted this requirement to obey white, middle-class norms as an affront to his dignity that specifically challenged his definition of masculinity:

> I had a few jobs like that [referring to Primo's "telephone diss"] where you gotta take a lot of shit from bitches and be a wimp.
>
> I didn't like it but I kept on working, because "Fuck it!" you don't want to fuck up the relationship. So you just be a punk [shrugging his shoulders dejectedly].

One alternative for surviving at a workplace that does not tolerate a street-based cultural identity is to become bicultural: to play politely by "the white woman's" rules downtown only to come home and revert to street culture within the safety of one's tenement or housing project at night. Tens of thousands of East Harlem residents manage this tightrope, but it often engenders accusations of betrayal and internalized racism on the part of neighbors and childhood friends who do not have—or do not want—these bicultural skills.

This is the case, for example, of Ray, a rival crack dealer whose tough street demeanor conflates with his black skin to "disqualify" him from legal office work. He quit a "nickel-and-dime messenger job downtown" in order to sell crack full time in his project stairway shortly after a white woman fled from him shrieking down the hallway of a high-rise office building. Ray and the terrified woman had ridden the elevator together, and, coincidentally, Ray had stepped off on the same floor as her to make a delivery. Worse yet, Ray had been trying to act like a "debonair male" and suspected the contradiction between his inadequate appearance and his chivalric intentions was responsible for the woman's terror:

> You know how you let a woman go off the elevator first? Well that's what I did to her but I may have looked a little shabby on the ends. Sometime my hair not combed. You know. So I could look a little sloppy to her maybe when I let her off first.

What Ray did not quite admit until I probed further is that he too had been intimidated by the lone white woman. He had been so disoriented by her taboo, unsupervised proximity that he had forgotten to press the elevator button when he originally stepped on after her:

> She went in the elevator first but then she just waits there to see what floor I press. She's playing like she don't know what floor she wants to go to because she wants to wait for me to press my floor. And I'm standing there and I forgot to press the button. I'm thinking about something else—I don't know what was the matter with me. And she's thinking like, "He's not pressing the button; I guess he's following me!"

As a crack dealer, Ray no longer has to confront this kind of confusing humiliation. Instead, he can righteously condemn his "successful" neighbors who work downtown for being ashamed of who they were born to be:

> When you see someone go downtown and get a good job, if they be Puerto Rican, you see them fix up their hair and put some contact lens in their eyes. Then they fit in. And they do it! I seen it.
>
> They turn-overs. They people who want to be white. Man, if you call them in Spanish, it wind up a problem.
>
> When they get nice jobs like that, all of a sudden, you know, they start talking proper.

Self-Destructive Resistance

During the 1980s, the real value of the minimum wage for legally employed workers declined by one-third. At the same time, social services were cut. The federal government, for example, decreased the proportion of its contribution to New York City's budget by over 50 percent . . . The breakdown of the inner city's public sector is no longer an economic threat to the expansion of New York's economy because the native-born labor force it shelters is increasingly irrelevant.

New immigrants arrive every day, and they are fully prepared to work hard for low wages under unsavory conditions. Like the parents and grandparents of Primo and Caesar, many of New York's newest immigrants are from isolated rural communities or squalid shanty towns where meat is eaten only once a week and there is no running water or electricity. Half a century ago Primo's mother fled precisely the same living conditions these new immigrants are only just struggling to escape. Her reminiscences about childhood in her natal village reveal the time warp of improved material conditions, cultural dislocation, and crushed working-class dreams that is propelling her second-generation son into a destructive street culture:

> I loved that life in Puerto Rico, because it was a healthy, healthy, healthy life.
>
> We always ate because my father always had work, and in those days the custom was to have a garden in your patio to grow food and everything that you ate.
>
> We only ate meat on Sundays because everything was cultivated on the same little parcel of land. We didn't have a refrigerator, so we ate *bacalao* [salted codfish], which can stay outside and a meat that they call *carne de vieja* [shredded beef], and sardines from a can. But thanks to God, we never felt hunger. My mother made a lot of cornflour.
>
> Some people have done better by coming here, but many people haven't. Even people from my barrio, who came trying to find a better life [*buen ambiente*] just found disaster. Married couples right from my neighborhood came only to have the husband run off with another woman.
>
> In those days in Puerto Rico, when we were in poverty, life was better. Everyone will tell you life was healthier and you could trust people. Now you can't trust anybody.
>
> What I like best was that we kept all our traditions . . . our feasts. In my village, everyone was either an Uncle or an Aunt. And when you walked by someone older, you had to ask for their blessing. It was respect. There was a lot of respect in those days [original quote in Spanish].

The Jewish and Italian-American white workers that Primo's mother replaced a generation ago when she came to New York City in hope of building a better future for her children were largely absorbed into an expanding economy that allowed them to be upwardly mobile. New York's economy always suffered periodic fluctuations, such as during the Great Depression, but those difficult periods were always temporary. The overall trend was one of economic growth. Primo's generation has not been so lucky. The contemporary economy does not particularly need them, and ethnic discrimination and cultural barriers overwhelm them whenever they attempt to work legally and seek service-sector jobs. Worse yet, an extraordinarily dynamic underground drug economy beckons them.

Rather than bemoaning the structural adjustment which is destroying their capacity to survive on legal wages, streetbound Puerto Rican youths celebrate their "decision" to bank on the underground economy and to cultivate their street identities. Caesar and Primo repeatedly assert their pride in their street careers. For example, one Saturday night after they finished their midnight shift at the crack house, I accompanied them on their way to purchase "*El

Sapo Verde" [The Green Toad], a twenty-dollar bag of powder cocaine sold by a new company three blocks away. While waiting for Primo and Caesar to be "served" by the coke seller a few yards away, I engaged three undocumented Mexican men drinking beer on a neighboring stoop in a conversation about finding work in New York. One of the new immigrants was already earning five hundred dollars a week fixing deep-fat-fry machines. He had a straightforward racist explanation for why Caesar—who was standing next to me—was "unemployed":

> OK, OK, I'll explain it to you in one word: Because the Puerto Ricans are brutes! [Pointing at Caesar] Brutes! Do you understand?
>
> Puerto Ricans like to make easy money. They like to leech off of other people. But not us Mexicans! No way! We like to work for our money. We don't steal. We came here to work and that's all [original quote in Spanish].

Instead of physically assaulting the employed immigrant for insulting him, Caesar embraced the racist tirade, ironically turning it into the basis for a new, generational-based, "American-born," urban cultural pride. In fact, in his response, he ridicules what he interprets to be the hillbilly naiveté of the Mexicans who still believe in the "American Dream." He spoke slowly in street-English as if to mark sarcastically the contrast between his "savvy" Nuyorican (New York-born Puerto Rican) identity versus the limited English proficiency of his detractor:

> That's right, m'a man! We is real vermin lunatics that sell drugs. We don't want no part of society. "Fight the Power!"[5]
>
> What do we wanna be working for? We rather live off the system. Gain weight, lay women.
>
> When we was younger, we used to break our asses too [gesturing towards the Mexican men who were straining to understand his English]. I had all kinds of stupid jobs too . . . advertising agencies . . . computers.
>
> But not no more! Now we're in a rebellious stage. We rather evade taxes, make quick money, and just survive. But we're not satisfied with that either. Ha!

Conclusion: Ethnography and Oppression

The underground economy and the social relations thriving off of it are best understood as modes of resistance to subordination in the service sector of the new U.S. economy. This resistance, however, results in individual self destruction and wider community devastation through substance abuse and violence. This complex and contradictory dynamic whereby resistance leads to self-destruction in the inner city is difficult to convey to readers in a clear and re-

---

[5]"Fight the Power" is a rap song composed in 1990 by the African-American group, Public Enemy.

sponsible manner. Mainstream society's "common sense" understanding of social stratification around ethnicity and class assumes the existence of racial hierarchies and blames individual victims for their failures. This makes it difficult to present ethnographic data from inner-city streets without falling prey to a "pornography of violence" or a racist voyeurism.

The public is not persuaded by a structural economic understanding of Caesar and Primo's "self-destruction." Even the victims themselves psychologize their unsatisfactory lives. Similarly, politicians and, more broadly, public policy ignore the fundamental structural economic facts of marginalization in America. Instead the first priority of federal and local social "welfare" agencies is to change the psychological—or at best the "cultural"—orientations of misguided individuals . . . U.S. politicians furiously debate family values while multinational corporations establish global free-trade zones and unionized factory employment in the U.S. continues to disappear as overseas sweatshops multiply. Social science researchers, meanwhile, have remained silent for the most part. They politely ignore the urgent social problems engulfing the urban United States. The few marginal academic publications that do address issues of poverty and racism are easily ignored by the media and mainstream society. . . .

Epilogue

In the six years since this article was first published, four major dynamics have altered the tenor of daily life on the streets of East Harlem and have deeply affected the lives of the crack dealers and their families depicted in these pages: (1) the U.S. economy entered the most prolonged period of sustained growth in its recorded history, (2) the size of the Mexican immigrant population in New York City and especially in East Harlem increased dramatically, (3) the War on Drugs escalated into a quasi-official public policy of criminalizing and incarcerating the poor and the socially marginal, and (4) drug fashion trends among inner-city youth rendered marijuana even more popular and crack and heroin even less popular among Latinos and African Americans.

Crack, cocaine, and heroin are still all sold on the block where I lived, but they are sold less visibly by a smaller number of people. It is still easy to purchase narcotics throughout East Harlem, but much of the drug dealing has moved indoors, out of sight, dealers no longer shouting out the brand names of their drugs. Most importantly, heroin and crack continue to be spurned by Latino and African-American youth who have seen the ravages those drugs committed on the older generations in their community. Nevertheless, in the U.S. inner city there remains an aging hardcore cohort of addicts. In most large cities crack is most visibly ensconced in predominantly African-American neighborhoods on the poorest blocks, often surrounding large public housing projects. In New York City, Puerto Rican households also continue to be at the epicenter of this ongoing, but now more self-contained, stationary cyclone of crack consumption.

In contrast to crack, heroin consumption has increased. Throughout most of the United States, heroin is cheaper and purer than in the early 1990s, belying any claims that the War on Drugs is winnable. Heroin's new appeal, however, is primarily among younger whites outside the ghetto for whom crack was never a drug of choice. It is not a drug of choice among Latino and African-American youth.

To summarize, both heroin and crack continue to be part of a multi-billion-dollar business that ravages inner-city families with special virulence. The younger generations of East Harlem residents, however, are more involved as sellers rather than consumers. Those Latino and African-American youth who do use crack or heroin generally try to hide the fact from their friends.

More important than changing drug-consumption fashions or the posturing of politicians over drug war campaigns has been the dramatic long-term improvement in the U.S. economy resulting in record low rates of unemployment. Somewhat to my surprise, some of the crack dealers and their families have benefited from this sustained economic growth. Slightly less than half have been allowed to enter the lower echelons of the legal labor market. For example, during the summer of 2000: one dealer was a unionized doorman, another was a home health care attendant, another was a plumber's assistant, three others were construction workers for small-time unlicensed contractors, and one was a cashier in a discount tourist souvenir store. Three or four of the dealers were still selling drugs, but most of them tended to be selling marijuana instead of crack or heroin. Three other dealers were in prison with long-term sentences and ironically were probably employed at well below minimum wage in the United States' burgeoning prison-based manufacturing sector. In short, the dramatic improvement in the U.S. economy has forced employers and unions to integrate more formally marginalized Puerto Ricans and African Americans into the labor market than was the case in the late 1980s and early 1990s when the research for this [article] was conducted. Nevertheless, even at the height of the growth in the U.S. economy in the year 2000, a large sector of street youth found themselves excluded. These marginals have become almost completely superfluous to the legal economy; they remain enmeshed in a still-lucrative drug economy, a burgeoning prison system, and a quagmire of chronic substance abuse. From a long-term political and economic perspective, the future does not bode well for inner-city poor of New York. In the year 2000, the United States had the largest disparity between rich and poor of any industrialized nation in the world—and this gap was not decreasing.

Connection Questions

1. Describe the reasons why many Puerto Rican immigrants shifted from working in the formal sector to the informal sector.

2. Generate some comparisons between drug dealing in Spanish Harlem and commercial sex work in Thailand, as described in the Miller text.

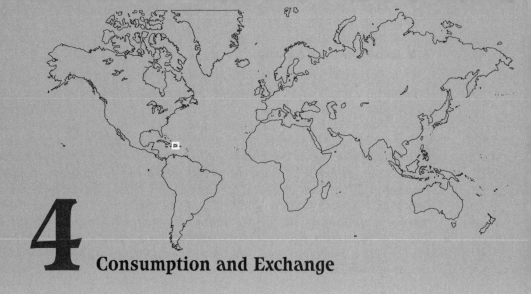

4

Consumption and Exchange

Men's Pleasure, Women's Labor: Tourism for Sex

Denise Brennan

Tourism is a major component of globalization and an increasingly important source of income for many countries. Tourists travel for many reasons: There are sights to see and tastes to appreciate in European winemaking centers and art museums, physical challenges to conquer on treks to Nepal's Himalayas and rides down wild New Zealand rivers, and comfortable luxury to be experienced in countless tropical beach and golfing resorts. However, one attraction for travel that is rarely mentioned, but which is important in several parts of the world, is the lure of sexual gratification. Such is the case in the Dominican Republic town of Sosúa, the subject of this article by Denise Brennan. Sosúa is a travel destination for male European tourists looking for inexpensive sex with island women. It is also the destination for

Reprinted by permission of Waveland Press, Inc. from Denise Brennan, "Globalization, Women's Labor, and Men's Pleasure: Sex Tourism in Sosúa, the Dominican Republic," in *Urban Life*. (Long Grove, IL: Waveland Press, Inc., 2002). All rights reserved.

Dominican women who are attracted to the possibilities—more money including money wires, sponsorship for emigration to Europe, a European visa—of sex work with the European tourists. Tourists easily discover what Sosúa has to offer by surfing the Internet, finding chat lines and advertisements touting sex with "dirt cheap colored girls," and "something for everyone's taste." Brennan's focus, however, is on the Dominican women themselves. They flock to Sosúa for the possible release from poverty and hardship, but rarely achieve these goals. Even when they attain more permanent relationships with clients, the associations rarely last. Describing the lives of three women, Brennan concludes that the unequal association with foreign men usually fails, and that the women do better if they rely on relationships with Dominican men.

Introduction

There is a new sex-tourist destination on the global sexual landscape: Sosúa, the Dominican Republic. A beach town on the north coast, Sosúa has emerged as a place of fantasy for white, European, male sex tourists desiring sex for money with Afro-Caribbean women. But European men are not the only ones who seek to fulfill fantasies in Sosúa. Dominican sex workers also arrive in Sosúa with fantasies: fantasies of economic mobility, visas to Europe, and maybe even romance. For them, Sosúa and its tourists represent an escape. These women migrate from throughout the Dominican Republic with dreams of European men "rescuing" them from a lifetime of foreclosed opportunities and poverty. They hope to meet and marry European men who will sponsor their (and their children's) migration to Europe. Yet, even though more and more women and girls migrate to Sosúa every day, most leave Sosúa's sex trade with little more than they had when they first arrived.

This article explores this paradoxical feature of sex tourism in Sosúa, and examines why women continue to flock to Sosúa and how they make the most of their time while there. Through the sex trade in this one tourist town, we see how globalization affects sex workers and sex tourists differently. In this economy of desire, some dreams are realized, while others prove hollow. White, middle-class and lower-middle class European visitors and residents are much better positioned to secure what they want in Sosúa than poor, black Dominican sex workers and other Dominican migrants who are likely to be disillusioned by Sosúa, tourism, and tourists. Globalization and accompanying transnational processes that unfold—such as tourism and sex tourism—not only open up opportunities but also reproduce unequal, dependent relations along lines of gender, race, class, and nationality.

Dominican women who migrate to Sosúa and its sex trade are motivated by the opportunity to meet, and possibly marry, a foreign tourist. Even if sex workers do not marry clients, Sosúa holds out the promise of establishing a transnational relationship with the aid of new transnational technologies such as fax machines and international money wires. Without these transnational connections, Sosúa's sex trade would be no different than sex work in any other Dominican town. By migrating to Sosúa, these women are engaged in an economic strategy that is both very familiar and something altogether new. I argue that they try to use the sex trade as an *advancement* strategy, not just a *survival* strategy. In short, these marginalized single mothers try to take advantage of the global linkages that exploit them.

Though only a handful of women regularly receive money wires from ex-clients in Europe, and a rarer few actually move to Europe to live with their European sweethearts, success stories of women who are living out this fantasy circulate among the sex workers like Dominicanized versions of the movie *Pretty Woman.* Thus, Sosúa's myth of opportunity goes unchallenged and women, recruited through female social networks of family and close friends who have already migrated to Sosúa, keep on arriving, ready to find their Richard Gere. Yet what the women find there is a far cry from their fantasy images of fancy dinners, nightclubs, easy money, and visas off the island. One sex worker, Carmen,[1] insightfully sums up just how important fantasy is to constructing the image of Sosúa as a place of opportunity. For Carmen, Sosúa is not a place of endless opportunity, but a place of disappointment and unrealized dreams:

> Women come to Sosúa because of a *gran mentira* (big lie). They hear they can make money, and meet a gringo, and they come. . . . They come with their dreams, but then they find out it is all a lie.

Tourism and Sex Tourism in the Global Economy

Work choices available to poor women are determined not only by local factors, but by the Dominican Republic's place in the global economy. Dominican women's internal migration for sex work is a consequence of local economic and social transformations as well as larger, external forces, such as foreign investment in export-processing zones (factories) and tourism. Just as international investors see the Dominican Republic as a site of cheap labor, international tourists know it as a place to buy cheap sex.

The Internet

In sex tourism, first-world travelers/consumers seek exoticized, racialized "native" bodies in the developing world for cut-rate prices. These two components—race and its associated stereotypes and expectations, and the economic

---

[1]I have changed all the names of sex workers and the bars in which they work, as well as bar and restaurant owners.

disparities between the developed and developing worlds—characterize sex-tourist destinations throughout the world. So what are white men "desiring" when they decide to book a flight from Frankfurt, for example, to Puerto Plata (the nearest airport to Sosúa)? I turned to the Internet for answers. Any exploration of the relationship between globalization, women's work choices in the global economy, and women's migration for work must now investigate the role the Internet has in producing and disseminating racialized and sexualized stereotypes in the developing world. In particular, the Internet is quickly and radically transforming the sex trade in the developing world, since on-line travel services make it increasingly easy for potential sex tourists to research sex-tourist destinations and to plan trips. I looked at web sites which post writings from alleged sex tourists who share information about their sex trips. In the process, these web sites advertise not only their services, but also Dominican women as sexual commodities. One such web-site subscriber was impressed by the availability of "dirt cheap colored girls," while another boasted, "When you enter the discos, you will feel like you're in heaven! A tremendous number of cute girls and something for everyone's taste (if you like colored girls like me)!" There is little doubt that race is central to what these sex tourists desire in their travels.

International Tourism: Who Benefits?

International tourism, however, has not benefited local Dominicans—poor Dominicans—as much as many had hoped. Although development and foreign investment have brought first-world hotels and services to Sosúa, the local population still lives in third-world conditions. The most successful resorts in Sosúa are foreign owned, and even though they create employment opportunities for the local population, most of the new jobs are low-paying service jobs with little chance for mobility. Moreover, the multinational resorts that have moved into Sosúa have pushed small hotel and restaurant owners out of business. One restaurant owner, Luis, comments on the effects these large, all-inclusive hotels (tourists pay airfare, lodging, food, and even drinks ahead of time in their home countries) have on the Sosúa economy:

> These tourists hardly change even U.S. $100 to spend outside the hotel. Before the all-inclusive hotels, people would change between U.S. $1000–2000 and it would get distributed throughout the town: some for lodging, for food and entertainment. Now, not only do any of the local merchants [not] get any of the money, but it never even leaves the tourists' home countries—like Germany or Austria—where they pay for their vacation in advance.

Foreign ownership, repatriation of profits, and the monopolistic nature of these all-inclusive resorts make it difficult for the local population in tourist economies, such as in Sosúa, to profit significantly. With tourism as the largest industry in the global economy, it is not unusual for foreign firms to handle all four components of a tourist's stay: airlines, hotels, services, and tour operators. I interviewed the general manager (an Italian citizen) of a German hotel in Sosúa, for example, whose parent company is a German airline company. Eighty percent of the hotel's guests are German, all of whom paid for their travel "package" in Germany. Furthermore, this German company imported most of its management staff from Europe, as well as the furniture, fabrics, and other goods necessary to run the hotel. So much for opportunities for local Dominicans.

Migration Off the Island

Marginalized individuals in the global economy not only turn to tourism as an exit from poverty, but also to migration. Before examining Dominican women's use of the sex trade in Sosúa as a way to migrate overseas, we first must consider the history of migration between the Dominican Republic and New York in the past few decades. This migration circuit and the transnational cultural, political, and economic flows between these two spaces have led many Dominicans to look *fuera* (outside) for solutions to their economic problems rather than within Dominican borders.

Migration to Sosúa

This preoccupation with goods, capital, and opportunities that are "outside" helps explain why sex workers and other Dominican migrants imagine Sosúa as a place of opportunity. These women would go to New York if they could, but they do not have the social networks—immediate family members in New York—to sponsor them for visas. They therefore often view migrating internally to Sosúa as the closest they will ever get to the "outside." Both migration to New York and transnational relationships with foreign tourists are ways to access a middle-class lifestyle and its accompanying commodities. Without migration circuits to New York, these women have a greater chance to get overseas by marrying a tourist (no matter how slight a chance) than they do of obtaining a visa—legally—to the United States. In some ways, hanging out in the tourist bars in Sosúa is a better use of their time than waiting in line for a visa at the U.S. embassy in Santo Domingo.

Strategies for migration, including sex workers' attempts to build transnational ties, are a "response and resistance" to the Dominican Republic's integration into the global economy. This response is informed by ideologies that view New York, Germany, and other outside places as those where individuals are more likely to make economic gains than within the Dominican Republic. Sosúa, with its access to tourists and their vacation money, is the next best alternative to getting off the island. Carla, a first-time sex worker, explains why Sosúa draws women from throughout the country: "We come here because we dream of ticket" (airline ticket). But without a visa—which they can obtain through marriage—Dominican sex workers cannot use the airline ticket Carla describes. These single mothers must depend on their European clients-turned-boyfriends/husbands to sponsor them for visas off the island. These women are at once independent and dependent, strategic and exploited.

Choosing Sex Work in Sosúa over Other Labor Options

A question I routinely posed to sex workers—and which others have asked me, as a fieldworker/anthropologist working with women who sell sex—is why do these Dominican women decide to enter sex work? The majority of these women are mothers and first-time sex workers. With little formal education, few marketable skills, limited social networks, and minimal support from the fathers of their children, poor Dominican women have few opportunities to escape from poverty and periodic crises. Within this context, sex work appears as a potentially profitable alternative, especially in light of the low wages women earn within the insecure and low-paying informal sector. Working as a domestic, a hair stylist in a salon, or a waitress in a restaurant are typical ways sex workers participated in the paid labor market prior to migrating to Sosúa. Each job generally yields under 1000 pesos a month (U.S. $83), whereas sex workers charge 500 pesos for a sexual encounter with a foreign client. Felicia and Margarita, two friends who had migrated from the same town, found these kinds of jobs did not sufficiently provide for their families. They summed up the dilemma for women like themselves who leave school in their early teens, receive no other formal job training, and thus have few well-paying job options open to them:

> If you have a husband who pays for food and the house then you can work in jobs like hair styling. Otherwise it's not possible to work in jobs like this.

Maintaining the view that women's earnings are secondary or supplementary, these women nevertheless became the primary breadwinners once they separated from their husbands.

Since these women could have chosen to enter the sex trade in other Dominican towns, by choosing Sosúa sex workers actively choose to work with foreign rather than Dominican men. The selection of sex work over other work options, and the selection of Sosúa with its tourist clientele, demonstrate that sex work for these women is not just a survival strategy, but rather a strategy of advancement. This "choice" of the sex trade *in Sosúa* presents an important counter example to depictions of *all* sex workers (who are not coerced or forced into prostitution) in *all contexts* as powerless victims of male violence and exploitation.

Yet, without protection under the law, sex workers are vulnerable to clients' actions once they are out of public spaces and in private hotel rooms. These women risk battery, rape, and forced unprotected sex. Sex workers in

Sosúa often discount the risks of violence and AIDS when faced with the potential payoffs of financial stability or a marriage proposal. And most recently, since so many women migrate to Sosúa from throughout the Dominican Republic, sex workers outnumber clients in the bars. Thus, in order to understand why women place themselves in a context of violence and uncertainty, we need to explore fully Sosúa's opportunity myth. How reliable are the payoffs and how high are the risks? Why might women achieve "success" through sex work in Sosúa? Can these poor, single mothers benefit from globalization and the transnational connections it engenders?

Sex Work: Short- and Long-Term Strategies

The payoff from working with foreign tourists can represent considerable long-term financial gains for the sex worker and her extended family—far more than from factory work, for example. Yet, not all women who arrive in Sosúa to pursue sex work desire to establish transnational ties. Some have long-term strategies, such as saving enough money to start a *colmado* (small grocery store) in their yard in their home communities. Others use sex work as a way to make ends meet in the immediate future, such as paying for children's school supplies or medical expenses. However, financial security, no matter how hard fought, often proves fleeting for the poorest segments of Dominican society. An exit from poverty might not be as permanent as the sex workers hope, even if they establish a relationship with a foreign tourist. Relationships go sour, and the extended family's only lifeline from poverty subsequently disintegrates. For every promise a tourist keeps, there are many more stories of disappointment. Even the success stories eventually cannot live up to the myths.

Sex work yields varying levels of rewards. For example, some women have savings accounts or build houses with their earnings, while others do not have enough money to pay the motorcycle taxi fare from their boarding houses to the tourist bars. How are some sex workers able to save, despite the obstacles, while most continue to live day to day? Success at sex work in Sosúa depends on both a planned-out strategy and a commitment to saving money, as well as luck. I cannot emphasize enough the role *chance* plays in sex workers' long-term ties with foreign clients. Whether clients stay in touch with the women is out of the women's control. One sex worker, Carmen, was thus skeptical that the Belgian client with whom she spent time during his three-week vacation in Sosúa actually would follow through on his promises to marry her and move her to Europe:

> I don't absolutely believe that he is going to marry me. You know, sure, when he was here he seemed to love me. But you know people leave and they forget.

In fact, months later, she still had not heard from him. I even helped Carmen write him a letter, which I mailed when I got back to the United States. It was returned to my address, unopened. Had she gotten the address wrong or did he give her a false address along with false proclamations of love and commitment?

Adding to the uncertainty and fragility of transnational relationships are other logistical obstacles to "success." Women must find ways to save money despite the drain on their resources from paying police bribes and living in an expensive tourist town where prices for food and rent are among the highest in the country. All of this combined with competition among sex workers for clients increase the likelihood of leaving Sosúa with little or no money saved. Furthermore, the majority of women arrive in Sosúa without knowing what they are getting into. They have heard of police roundups and know that they must vie with countless other women just like themselves to catch the attention of potential clients, but like most migrants, they are full of hope and dreams and believe that "it will be different for them." In gold-rush fashion, they arrive in Sosúa because they have heard of Sosúa's tourists and money, and they plan, without a specific strategy in mind, to cash in on the tourist boom. It only takes a few days in Sosúa to realize that the only way to quickly make big money is by establishing transnational relationships. New arrivals see veteran sex workers drop by the Codetel office (telephone and fax company) every day, hoping for faxes from clients in Europe or Canada. For those newcomers who want to receive money wires or marriage proposals from tourists overseas, they learn that they must establish similar ongoing transnational relationships.

Sex Workers' Stories

In order to explore how sex workers' time in Sosúa measures up to their fantasy images, I turn to the divergent experiences of three sex workers. Their stories underscore the difficulties of establishing a transnational relationship, as well as its fragility. Through sex workers' accounts of their relationships with foreign men, we get a sense of just how wildly unpredictable the course of these relationships can be.

Elena and Jürgen: Building and Breaking Transnational Ties

This story begins with Elena's release from jail. After being held for two days, twenty-two-year-old Elena went to the beach. When I saw her, back at her one-room wooden house, she was ecstatic. At the beach she had run into Jürgen, a German client who had just returned to Sosúa to see her. They had been sending faxes to one another since he left Sosúa after his last vacation, and he had mentioned in one of his faxes that he would be returning. He did not know where she lived, but figured he would find her that evening at the Anchor, Sosúa's largest tourist bar and a place where tourists go to drink, dance, and pick up sex workers. He brought her presents from Germany, including perfume and a matching gold necklace and bracelet. Elena was grinning ear to ear as she showed off her gifts, talking about Jürgen like a smitten schoolgirl:

I am cancelling everything for the weekend and am going to spend the entire time with him. We will go the beach and he will take me to nightclubs and to restaurants.

Elena began preparing for the weekend. Her two sisters who lived with her, ages fourteen and sixteen, would look after her six-year-old daughter, since Elena would stay with Jürgen in his tourist hotel. She chose the evening's outfit carefully, with plenty of help from her sisters, daughter, and a friend (a young sex worker) who lives with them since she has very little money. Elena provides for these four girls with her earnings from sex work. They all rotate between sharing the double bed and sleeping on the floor. Spending time with a tourist on his vacation means Elena would receive more gifts, maybe even some for her family, and would make good money. So they helped primp Elena, selecting billowy rayon pants that moved as she did, and a black lycra stretch shirt with long sheer sleeves that was cropped to reveal her slim stomach. She was meeting Jürgen at the Anchor, where I saw her later on, and she stood out in the crowd.

As soon as Jürgen's vacation ended, he went back to Germany with plans to return in a couple of months. Since he was self-employed in construction in Germany, he wanted to live part of the year in the Dominican Republic. Elena was very upset that Jürgen had left. She was incredibly shaken up and could not stop crying. I had heard sex workers often distinguish between relationships with tourists *por amor* (love) or *por residence* (residence/visas), but Elena's tears broke down that distinction. I realized then that Elena might be in love with Jürgen.

Unlike Carmen's relationship with her Belgian client, which ended with broken promises, Jürgen kept his word and wired money and kept in touch through faxes. Even more surprisingly, Jürgen returned to Sosúa only two months later. Within days of his arrival, he rented a two-bedroom apartment that had running water and an electrical generator (for daily blackouts). He also bought beds, living room furniture, and a large color TV. Elena was living out the fantasy of many sex workers in Sosúa: She was sharing a household with a European man who supported her and her dependents. Jürgen paid for food that Elena and her sisters prepared, and had cable TV installed. He also paid for Elena's daughter to attend a private school, and came home one day with school supplies for her. Occasionally, Jürgen took Elena, her daughter, and her sisters out to eat at one of the tourist restaurants that line the beach.

Elena had moved up in the world: Eating in tourist restaurants, sending a daughter to private school, and living in a middle-class apartment were all symbols of her increased social and economic mobility. As a female head of household who had been taking care of her daughter and sisters with her earnings from sex work, Elena quit sex work soon after meeting Jürgen and lived off of the money he gave her. Sex work, and the transnational relationship it had built, altered Elena's life as well as the lives of those who depended on her. But for how long?

As it turned out, Jürgen was not Elena's or the family's salvation. Soon after Elena and Jürgen moved in together, Elena found out she was pregnant.

Both she and Jürgen were very happy about having a baby. He had a teenage son living with his ex-wife in Germany and relished the idea of having another child. At first, he was helpful around the house and doted on Elena. But the novelty soon wore off and he returned to his routine of spending most days in the German-owned bar beneath their apartment. He also went out drinking at night, with German friends, hopping from bar to bar. He was drunk, or nearly so, day and night. Elena saw him less and less frequently and they fought often, usually over money.

Eventually he started staying out all night. On one occasion, a friend of Elena's (a sex worker) saw Jürgen at the Anchor talking with and later leaving with a Haitian sex worker. Elena knew he was cheating on her. But she did not want to raise this with Jürgen, explaining that men "do these things" and instead, she focused her anger on the fact that he was not giving her enough money to take care of the household. Ironically, Elena had more disposable income before she began to live with Jürgen. Back then, she would go out dancing and drinking with her friends—not looking for clients—but just to have fun. Now, without an income of her own, she was dependent upon Jürgen not only for household expenses but for her entertainment as well.

On more than one occasion I served as interpreter between the two during their attempts at "peace negotiations" after they had not spoken to one another for days. Since Elena does not speak any German or English, she asked me to help her understand why Jürgen was mad at her as well as to communicate her viewpoint to him. In preparation for one of these "negotiations," Elena briefed me on what she wanted me to explain to Jürgen:

> I want to know why he is not talking to me? And why is he not giving me any money? He is my *esposo* [husband in consensual union] and is supposed to give me money. I need to know if he is with me or with someone else. He pays for this house and paid for everything here. I need to know what is going on. You know I was fine living alone before, I'm able to do that. I took care of everything before, this is not a problem. But I need to know what is going to happen.

Since they were living together, and Jürgen was paying the bills, Elena considered them to be married. To Elena and her friends, Jürgen, as an *esposo*, was financially responsible for the household. But Jürgen saw things differently. He felt Elena thought he was "made of money" and was always asking him for more. He asked me to translate to her:

> I'm not a millionaire. I told Elena last week that I don't like her always asking for money. She did not listen. She asks me for money all day long. I don't want to be taken advantage of.

One day, without warning, Jürgen packed his bags and left for Germany for business. Elena knew this day would come, that Jürgen had to go to Germany to work. But she did not expect their relationship would be in such disarray, and that he would depart without leaving her money (although he did leave some food money with her younger sisters who turned it over to Elena). In Jürgen's absence, Elena took her daughter out of the private school, since the tuition soon became overdue, and she started working part-time at a small Dominican-owned restaurant. Once Jürgen returned to Sosúa from Germany a couple of months later, they split up for good. Elena moved out of their apartment back to the labyrinth of shanties on dirt paths off the main road. Her economic and social mobility was short-lived. She had not accumulated any savings or items she could pawn during her time with Jürgen. Jürgen never gave her enough money so that she could set some aside for savings. And all the things he bought for the apartment were his, not hers. When they vacated the apartment he took all of the furniture and the TV.

Her relationship with Jürgen dramatically changed Elena's life; she was, after all, having his child. But her social and economic status remained as marginal as ever. Even though she was living out many sex workers' fantasies of "marrying" a foreign tourist, she still lived like many poor Dominicans, struggling day to day without access to resources to build long-term economic security. When she and Jürgen fought, and he withheld money from her, she was less economically independent than she was as a sex worker, when she was certain to earn around 500 pesos a client. Although sex workers take on great risks—AIDS, abuse, and arrest—and occupy a marginal and stigmatized status in Dominican society, Elena's status as the "housewife" of a German resident was fragile and constantly threatened.

Jürgen now lives, Elena has heard, somewhere in Asia. Elena is back living in the same conditions as before she met Jürgen, except with one more child. She has not returned to sex work and makes significantly less money working in a restaurant. Her older married sisters (who also live in Sosúa) now help take care of their younger sisters, and Elena sends what money she can, though less than in her sex work days, to help out her parents.

Luisa's Money Wires

Luisa is an example of a sex worker whose transnational connections were those other sex workers envied, but her "success," like Elena's, ended without warning. She, quite remarkably, received U.S. $500 every two weeks from a client in Germany, who wanted her to leave sex work and start her own clothing store. She told him she had stopped working the tourist bars, and that she used the money to buy clothes for the store. Yet, when he found out that she was still working in the sex trade, had not opened a store, and was living with a Dominican boyfriend, he stopped wiring money.

At this juncture, Luisa was in over her head. She had not put any of the money in the bank in anticipation of the day when the money wires might dry up. She was renting a two-bedroom house that was twice the size and rent of friends' apartments. And, she sent money home to her mother in Santo Domingo, who was taking care of her twelve-year-old son. She also supported her Dominican boyfriend, who did not have a steady job. Other sex workers called him a *chulo* (pimp) since he lived off Luisa's earnings and money wires. They saw Luisa as foolish for bankrolling her boyfriend, especially since he was not the father of her son. She began hocking her chains and rings in one of Sosúa's half-dozen pawn shops. She eventually moved out of the house into a smaller apartment with her Dominican boyfriend, and returned to sex work.

As lucky as Luisa was to meet this German client at the Anchor, most of the women working the Anchor night after night never receive a single money wire transfer. Those who do generally receive smaller sums than Luisa did, on a much more infrequent and unpredictable basis. As Luisa's story demonstrates, a sex worker's luck can change overnight. There is no guarantee that money wires will continue once they begin. Luisa had no way of knowing that she would lose her "meal ticket," nor can she be certain that she will ever find another tourist to replace him. Furthermore, women cannot count on earning money in sex work indefinitely. Luisa is in her early thirties and knows that over the next few years it will be increasingly difficult to compete with the young women in the bars (some are as young as sixteen and seventeen, most are between nineteen and twenty-five). Yet, once sex workers make the decision to leave Sosúa and the sex trade, they face the same limited opportunities they confronted before they moved to Sosúa. They are still hampered by limited education, lack of marketable job skills, and not "knowing the right people." In fact, obstacles to economic and social mobility might have increased, especially if they are rumored to have AIDS. They might have to battle gossip in their home community and the stigma associated with sex work. After years of working in bars they might have a substance-abuse problem. And, they return to children who have grown up in their absence.

Carmen's Diversification Strategy

Carmen's story, compared to Elena's and Luisa's, is one of relative success, in which her relationships with Dominican clients figure prominently. In fact, supplementing uncertain income from foreign tourists by working with Dominican clients, as well as establishing long-term relationships with Dominican *amigos/clientes fijos* (friends/regular clients), supplies Carmen with a steady flow of income. Another sex worker, Ani, explains the function of *amigos*:

> You don't always have a client. You need *amigos* and *clientes fijos*. If you have a problem, like something breaks in your house, or your child is sick and you need money for the doctor or medicine, they can help.

For Carmen, working with Dominicans has proven much more reliable than establishing ties with foreign men. Carmen has saved enough money from four years in sex work to build a small house in Santo Domingo (the capital city five hours away where she will retire to take care of her mother and children). She has managed to save more money than most sex workers. I asked her why she thinks she was able to save money, while many of her friends do not have an extra centavo, and she answered:

> Because they give it to their men. Their husbands wait at home and drink while their women work. Not me. If I'm in the street with all the risks of disease and the police, I'm keeping the money or giving it to my kids. I'm not giving it to a man, no way. If women don't give the money to their men, they (the men) beat them.

She is careful not to let the men in her life know how much money she has saved in the bank (unlike Luisa), or the sources of the money. She has a steady relationship in particular with Jorge, who is her economic safety net, especially in times of crises. She describes their relationship:

> He is very young [she scrunched her nose up in disapproval of this point]. He lives with his mother in Santiago and works in a *zona franca* [factory in an export-processing zone]. He gives me money, even though he does not make a lot. He bought me furniture for the new house.

At times, the money Jorge gives Carmen is the only money she has. By establishing a relationship with a Dominican man, she has been able to supplement her unpredictable income from sex work. Though the money he gives her is in smaller sums than transnational money wires other sex workers receive, it is money she can count on, on a regular basis.

Carmen has not only diversified her clientele and focused on achieving one specific goal (building a house) but also has set up clear personal limitations working in a dangerous trade. Since she has a serious fear of the police, she refuses to work when they are making arrests outside of the tourist bars where many of the sex workers congregate to talk, smoke, or greet customers. At one point when the police seemed to be making more arrests than usual, Carmen quit going to the tourist bars altogether. Instead, she took a bus to a small Dominican town about thirty miles away to work in a bar that caters to Dominican clients. Thus, she developed an alternate plan to working in Sosúa when necessary.

By pursuing local Dominican clients as well as trying to establish transnational connections, sex work is paying off for Carmen in the long term. Carmen refused to be seduced by the promise of a tourist enclave and the sweet talk of foreign tourists. Instead, she treated Sosúa as any other Dominican town with "brothels" and set up a roster of local regular clients. Carmen's gains have been slow and modest. Nevertheless, she saved enough money to begin constructing a small house. Thus far it has taken her four years, and she still needs enough money for windows. But she will leave Sosúa with her future, and her family's, more secure than when she first arrived. Stories about modest successes like Carmen's are not as glamorous as those with transnational dimensions. Rather, stories of transnational relationships and quick, big money circulate among the sex workers, like those of Elena and Luisa. Their more immediate and visible ascension from poverty is regaled and fuels the illusion of Sosúa as a place to get rich quick.

Conclusion

Foreign sex tourists clearly benefit from their geographic position in the global economy, as they travel with ease (no visa is needed to enter the Dominican Republic), and buy sex for cheaper prices than in their home countries. Dominican sex workers, in contrast, face innumerable constraints due to their country's marginal position in the global economy. Sosúa's sex trade is but one more site where, broadly, we can observe globalization exacerbating inequality and, more specifically, we can situate tourism and sex tourism as both relying on and reproducing inequalities in the global economy.

Like most prospectors in search of quick money, few sex workers find what they were hoping for. It is not surprising, however, that such women, despite the obstacles to fulfilling their "fantasies," continue to arrive every day. Women from the poorest classes have no other work options that pay as well as the sex trade with tourists. Nor do most other work options offer the opportunity to establish long-term relationships with foreign men. Although most transnational relationships are unlikely to alter sex workers' long-term economic and social status, these women make far more financial gains than do sex workers without such a relationship, and earn more than they would from other accessible labor options (such as domestic service or factory work).

Sex workers also can make gains without transnational connections. Though difficult to achieve, these gains might prove more durable than those relying on a transnational relationship. Carmen's transnational ties never paid off, and consequently she did not come into a lot of money all at once. But she still managed to save what she could over time. Her house represents security, but it does not catapult her out of *los pobres* (the poor). Her "success" is not on the same level as women with ongoing relationships with European men. But while these ties could dissolve at any time, Carmen's house will still be there. She looks forward to the day she completes her house and leaves Sosúa and its sex trade:

> When I leave here I want to sit on the front porch of my new house with my mother and my children and drink a cold glass of juice. I want a peaceful life. No Sosúa, no men giving you problems.

Connection Questions

1. Is sex tourism a form of consumerism as Miller defines it?

2. How has globalization affected the economy in Sosúa?

3. Do you think that the sex trade in Sosúa is a form of exploitation, as that term is defined in the Miller text?

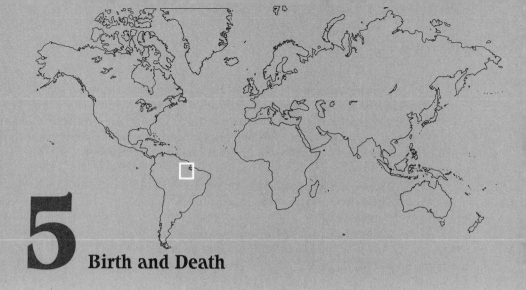

5 Birth and Death

Mother's Love: Death without Weeping

Nancy Scheper-Hughes

Kinship systems are based on marriage and birth. Both, anthropologists assume, create ties that can link kin into close, cooperative, enduring structures. What happens to such ties, however, in the face of severe hardship imposed by grinding poverty and urban migration? Can we continue to assume, for example, that there will be a close bond between mother and child? This is the question pursued by Nancy Scheper-Hughes in the following article about the mother–infant relationship among poor women in a Brazilian shantytown. The author became interested in the question following a "baby die-off" in the town of Bom Jesus in 1965. She noticed that mothers seemed to take these events casually. After twenty-five years of research in the Alto do Cruzeiro shantytown there, she has come to see such indifference as a cultural response to high rates of infant death due to poverty and malnutrition. Mothers, and surrounding social institutions such as the Catholic church, expect babies to die easily. Mothers concentrate their support on babies who are "fighters" and let themselves grow attached to their children only

Reprinted from *Natural History*, October 1989; copyright © Natural History Magazine, Inc., 1989.

45

when they are reasonably sure that the offspring will survive. The article also provides an excellent illustration of what happens to kinship systems in the face of poverty and social dislocation. Such conditions may easily result in the formation of woman-headed families and in a lack of the extended kinship networks so often found in more stable, rural societies.

> I have seen death without weeping
> The destiny of the Northeast is death
> Cattle they kill
> To the people they do something worse
> —Anonymous Brazilian singer (1965)

"Why do the church bells ring so often?" I asked Nailza de Arruda soon after I moved into a corner of her tiny mud-walled hut near the top of the shantytown called the Alto do Cruzeiro (Crucifix Hill). I was then a Peace Corps volunteer and a community development/health worker. It was the dry and blazing hot summer of 1965, the months following the military coup in Brazil, and save for the rusty, clanging bells of N.S. das Dores Church, an eerie quiet had settled over the market town that I call Bom Jesus da Mata. Beneath the quiet, however, there was chaos and panic. "It's nothing," replied Nailza, "just another little angel gone to heaven."

Nailza had sent more than her share of little angels to heaven, and sometimes at night I could hear her engaged in a muffled but passionate discourse with one of them, two-year-old Joana. Joana's photograph, taken as she lay propped up in her tiny cardboard coffin, her eyes open, hung on a wall next to one of Nailza and Ze Antonio taken on the day they eloped.

Nailza could barely remember the other infants and babies who came and went in close succession. Most had died unnamed and were hastily baptized in their coffins. Few lived more than a month or two. Only Joana, properly baptized in church at the close of her first year and placed under the protection of a powerful saint, Joan of Arc, had been expected to live. And Nailza had dangerously allowed herself to love the little girl.

In addressing the dead child, Nailza's voice would range from tearful imploring to angry recrimination: "Why did you leave me? Was your patron saint so greedy that she could not allow me one child on this earth?" Ze Antonio advised me to ignore Nailza's odd behavior, which he understood as a kind of madness that, like the birth and death of children, came and went. Indeed, the premature birth of a stillborn son some months later "cured" Nailza of her "inappropriate" grief, and the day came when she removed Joana's photo and carefully packed it away.

More than fifteen years elapsed before I returned to the Alto do Cruzeiro, and it was anthropology that provided the vehicle of my return. Since 1982 I have returned several times in order to pursue a problem that first attracted my attention in the 1960s. My involvement with the people of the Alto do Cruzeiro now spans a quarter of a century and three generations of parenting in a community where mothers and daughters are often simultaneously pregnant.

The Alto do Cruzeiro is one of three shantytowns surrounding the large market town of Bom Jesus in the sugar plantation zone of Pernambuco in Northeast Brazil, one of the many zones of neglect that have emerged in the shadow of the now tarnished economic miracle of Brazil. For the women and children of the Alto do Cruzeiro the only miracle is that some of them have managed to stay alive at all.

The Northeast is a region of vast proportions (approximately twice the size of Texas) and of equally vast social and developmental problems. The nine states that make up the region are the poorest in the country and are representative of the Third World within a dynamic and rapidly industrializing nation. Despite waves of migrations from the interior to the teeming shantytowns of coastal cities, the majority still live in rural areas on farms and ranches, sugar plantations and mills.

Life expectancy in the Northeast is only forty years, largely because of the appallingly high rate of infant and child mortality. Approximately one million children in Brazil under the age of five die each year. The children of the Northeast, especially those born in shantytowns on the periphery of urban life, are at a very high risk of death. In these areas, children are born without the traditional protection of breast-feeding, subsistence gardens, stable marriages, and multiple adult caretakers that exists in the interior. In the hillside shantytowns that spring up around cities or, in this case, interior market towns, marriages are brittle, single parenting is the norm, and women are frequently forced into the shadow economy of domestic work in the homes of the rich or into unprotected and oftentimes "scab" wage labor on the surrounding sugar plantations, where they clear land for planting and weed for a pittance, sometimes less than a dollar a day. The women of the Alto may not bring their babies with them into the homes of the wealthy, where the often-sick infants are considered sources of contamination, and they cannot carry the little ones to the riverbanks where they wash clothes because the river is heavily infested with schistosomes and other deadly parasites. Nor can they carry their young children to the plantations, which are often several miles away. At wages of a dollar a day, the women of the Alto cannot hire baby sitters. Older children who are not in school will sometimes serve as somewhat indifferent caretakers. But any child not in school is also expected to find wage work. In most cases, babies are simply left at home alone, the door securely fastened. And so many also die alone and unattended.

Bom Jesus da Mata, centrally located in the plantation zone of Pernambuco, is within commuting distance of several sugar plantations and mills. Consequently, Bom Jesus has been a magnet for rural workers forced off their small subsistence plots by large landowners wanting to use every available piece of land for sugar cultivation. Initially, the rural migrants to Bom Jesus were squatters who were given tacit approval by the mayor to put up temporary straw huts on each of the three hills overlooking the town. The Alto do Cruzeiro is the oldest, the largest, and the poorest of the shantytowns. Over the past three decades many of the original migrants have become permanent residents, and the primitive and temporary straw huts have been replaced by small homes (usually of two rooms) made of wattle and daub, sometimes covered with plaster. The more affluent residents use bricks and tiles. In most Alto homes, dangerous kerosene lamps have been replaced by light bulbs. The once tattered rural garb, often fashioned from used sugar sacking, has likewise been replaced by store-bought clothes, often castoffs from a wealthy *patrão* (boss). The trappings are modern, but the hunger, sickness, and death that they conceal are traditional, deeply rooted in a history of feudalism, exploitation, and institutionalized dependency.

My research agenda never wavered. The questions I addressed first crystallized during a veritable "die-off" of Alto babies during a severe drought in 1965. The food and water shortages and the political and economic chaos occasioned by the military coup were reflected in the handwritten entries of births and deaths in the dusty, yellowed pages of the ledger books kept at the public registry office in Bom Jesus. More than 350 babies died in the Alto during 1965 alone—this from a shantytown population of little more than 5,000. But that wasn't what surprised me. There were reasons enough for the deaths in the miserable conditions of shantytown life. What puzzled me was the seeming indifference of Alto women to the death of their infants, and their willingness to attribute to their own tiny offspring an aversion to life that made their death seem wholly natural, indeed all but anticipated.

Although I found that it was possible, and hardly difficult, to rescue infants and toddlers from death by diarrhea and dehydration with a simple sugar, salt, and water solution (even bottled Coca-Cola worked fine), it was more difficult to enlist a mother herself in the rescue of a child she perceived as ill-fated for life or better off dead, or to convince her to take back into her threatened and besieged home a baby she had already come to think of as an angel rather than as a son or daughter.

I learned that the high expectancy of death, and the ability to face child death with stoicism and equanimity, produced patterns of nurturing that differentiated between those infants thought of as thrivers and survivors and those thought of as born already "wanting to die." The survivors were nurtured, while stigmatized, doomed infants were left to die, as mothers say, *a mingua*, "of neglect." Mothers stepped back and allowed nature to take its course. This pattern, which I call mortal selective neglect, is called passive infanticide by anthropologist Marvin Harris. The Alto situation, although culturally specific in the form that it takes, is not unique to Third World shantytown communities and may have its correlates in our own impoverished urban communities in some cases of "failure to thrive" infants.

I use as an example the story of Zezinho, the thirteen-month-old toddler of one of my neighbors, Lourdes. I became involved with Zezinho when I was called in to help Lourdes in the delivery of another child, this one a fair and robust little tyke with a lusty cry. I noted that while Lourdes showed great inter-

est in the newborn, she totally ignored Zezinho who, wasted and severely malnourished, was curled up in a fetal position on a piece of urine- and feces-
soaked cardboard placed under his mother's hammock. Eyes open and vacant,
mouth slack, the little boy seemed doomed.

When I carried Zezinho up to the community day-care center at the top of
the hill, the Alto women who took turns caring for one another's children (in
order to free themselves for part-time work in the cane fields or washing clothes)
laughed at my efforts to save Ze, agreeing with Lourdes that here was a baby
without a ghost of a chance. Leave him alone, they cautioned. It makes no sense
to fight with death. But I did do battle with Ze, and after several weeks of force-
feeding (malnourished babies lose their interest in food), Ze began to succumb
to my ministrations. He acquired some flesh across his taut chest bones, learned
to sit up, and even tried to smile. When he seemed well enough, I returned him
to Lourdes in her miserable scrap-material lean-to, but not without guilt about
what I had done. I wondered whether returning Ze was at all fair to Lourdes and
to his little brother. But I was busy and washed my hands of the matter. And
Lourdes did seem more interested in Ze now that he was looking more human.

When I returned in 1982, there was Lourdes among the women who
formed my sample of Alto mothers—still struggling to put together some sem-
blance of life for a now grown Ze and her five other surviving children. Much
was made of my reunion with Ze in 1982, and everyone enjoyed retelling the
story of Ze's rescue and of how his mother had given him up for dead. Ze would
laugh the loudest when told how I had had to force-feed him like a fiesta turkey.
There was no hint of guilt on the part of Lourdes and no resentment on the part
of Ze. In fact, when questioned in private as to who was the best friend he ever
had in life, Ze took a long drag on his cigarette and answered without a trace of
irony, "Why my mother, of course!" "But of course," I replied.

Part of learning how to mother in the Alto do Cruzeiro is learning when to
let go of a child who shows that it "wants" to die or that it has no "knack" or no
"taste" for life. Another part is learning when it is safe to let oneself love a child.
Frequent child death remains a powerful shaper of maternal thinking and practice. In the absence of firm expectation that a child will survive, mother love as
we conceptualize it (whether in popular terms or in the psychobiological notion of maternal bonding) is attenuated and delayed with consequences for infant survival. In an environment already precarious to young life, the emotional
detachment of mothers toward some of their babies contributes even further to
the spiral of high mortality–high fertility in a kind of macabre lock-step dance
of death.

The average woman of the Alto experiences 9.5 pregnancies, 3.5 child
deaths, and 1.5 stillbirths. Seventy percent of all child deaths in the Alto occur
in the first six months of life, and 82 percent by the end of the first year. Of all
deaths in the community each year, about 45 percent are of children under the
age of five.

Women of the Alto distinguish between child deaths understood as natural (caused by diarrhea and communicable diseases) and those resulting from

sorcery, the evil eye, or other magical or supernatural afflictions. They also recognize a large category of infant deaths seen as fated and inevitable. These hopeless cases are classified by mothers under the folk terminology "child sickness" or "child attack." Women say that there are at least fourteen different types of hopeless child sickness, but most can be subsumed under two categories—chronic and acute. The chronic cases refer to infants who are born small and wasted. They are deathly pale, mothers say, as well as weak and passive. They demonstrate no vital force, no liveliness. They do not suck vigorously; they hardly cry. Such babies can be this way at birth or they can be born sound but soon show no resistance, no "fight" against the common crises of infancy: diarrhea, respiratory infections, tropical fevers.

The acute cases are those doomed infants who die suddenly and violently. They are taken by stealth overnight, often following convulsions that bring on head banging, shaking, grimacing, and shrieking. Women say it is horrible to look at such a baby. If the infant begins to foam at the mouth or gnash its teeth or go rigid with its eyes turned back inside its head, there is absolutely no hope. The infant is "put aside"—left alone—often on the floor in a back room, and allowed to die. These symptoms (which accompany high fevers, dehydration, third-stage malnutrition, and encephalitis) are equated by Alto women with madness, epilepsy, and worst of all, rabies, which is greatly feared and highly stigmatized.

Most of the infants presented to me as suffering from chronic child sickness were tiny, wasted famine victims, while those labeled as victims of acute child attack seemed to be infants suffering from the deliriums of high fever or the convulsions that can accompany electrolyte imbalance in dehydrated babies.

Local midwives and traditional healers, praying women, as they are called, advise Alto women on when to allow a baby to die. One midwife explained: "If I can see that a baby was born unfortuitously, I tell the mother that she need not wash the infant or give it a cleansing tea. I tell her just to dust the infant with baby powder and wait for it to die." Allowing nature to take its course is not seen as sinful by these often very devout Catholic women. Rather, it is understood as cooperating with God's plan.

Often I have been asked how consciously women of the Alto behave in this regard. I would have to say that consciousness is always shifting between allowed and disallowed levels of awareness. For example, I was awakened early one morning in 1987 by two neighborhood children who had been sent to fetch me to a hastily organized wake for a two-month-old infant whose mother I had unsuccessfully urged to breast-feed. The infant was being sustained on sugar water, which the mother referred to as *soro* (serum), using a medical term for the infant's starvation regime in light of his chronic diarrhea. I had cautioned the mother that an infant could not live on *soro* forever.

The two girls urged me to console the young mother by telling her that it was "too bad" that her infant was so weak that Jesus had to take him. They were coaching me in proper Alto etiquette. I agreed, of course, but asked, "And what do *you* think?" Xoxa, the eleven-year-old, looked down at her dusty flip-flops and blurted out, "Oh, Dona Nanci, that baby never got enough to eat, but you must never say that!" And so the death of hungry babies remains one of the best kept secrets of life in Bom Jesus da Mata.

Most victims are waked quickly and with a minimum of ceremony. No tears are shed, and the neighborhood children form a tiny procession, carrying the baby to the town graveyard where it will join a multitude of others. Although a few fresh flowers may be scattered over the tiny grave, no stone or wooden cross will mark the place, and the same spot will be reused within a few months' time. The mother will never visit the grave, which soon becomes an anonymous one.

What, then, can be said of these women? What emotions, what sentiments motivate them? How are they able to do what, in fact, must be done? What does mother love mean in this inhospitable context? Are grief, mourning, and melancholia present, although deeply repressed? If so, where shall we look for them? And if not, how are we to understand the moral visions and moral sensibilities that guide their actions?

I have been criticized more than once for presenting an unflattering portrait of poor Brazilian women, women who are, after all, themselves the victims of severe social and institutional neglect. I have described these women as allowing some of their children to die, as if this were an unnatural and inhuman act rather than, as I would assert, the way any one of us might act, reasonably and rationally, under similarly desperate conditions. Perhaps I have not emphasized enough the real pathogens in this environment of high risk: poverty, deprivation, sexism, chronic hunger, and economic exploitation. If mother love is, as many psychologists and some feminists believe, a seemingly natural and universal maternal script, what does it mean to women for whom scarcity, loss, sickness, and deprivation have made that love frantic and robbed them of their grief, seeming to turn their hearts to stone?

Throughout much of human history—as in a great deal of the impoverished Third World today—women have had to give birth and to nurture children under ecological conditions and social arrangements hostile to child survival, as well as to their own well-being. Under circumstances of high childhood mortality, patterns of selective neglect and passive infanticide may be seen as active survival strategies.

They also seem to be fairly common practices historically and across cultures. In societies characterized by high childhood mortality and by a correspondingly high (replacement) fertility, cultural practices of infant and child care tend to be organized primarily around survival goals. But what this means is a pragmatic recognition that not all of one's children can be expected to live. The nervousness about child survival in areas of northeast Brazil, northern India, or Bangladesh, where a 30 percent or 40 percent mortality rate in the first years of life is common, can lead to forms of delayed attachment and a casual or benign neglect that serves to weed out the worst bets so as to enhance the life chances of healthier siblings, including those yet to be born. Practices similar to those that I am describing have been recorded for parts of Africa, India, and Central America.

Life in the Alto do Cruzeiro resembles nothing so much as a battlefield or an emergency room in an overcrowded inner-city public hospital. Consequently, morality is guided by a kind of "lifeboat ethics," the morality of triage. The seemingly studied indifference toward the suffering of some of their infants, conveyed in such sayings as "little critters have no feelings," is understandable in light of these women's obligation to carry on with their reproductive and nurturing lives.

In their slowness to anthropomorphize and personalize their infants, everything is mobilized so as to prevent maternal overattachment and, therefore, grief at death. The bereaved mother is told not to cry, that her tears will dampen the wings of her little angel so that she cannot fly up to her heavenly home. Grief at the death of an angel is not only inappropriate, it is a symptom of madness and of a profound lack of faith.

Infant death becomes routine in an environment in which death is anticipated and bets are hedged. While the routinization of death in the context of shantytown life is not hard to understand, and quite possible to empathize with, its routinization in the formal institutions of public life in Bom Jesus is not as easy to accept uncritically. Here the social production of indifference takes on a different, even a malevolent, cast.

In a society where triplicates of every form are required for the most banal events (registering a car, for example), the registration of infant and child death is informal, incomplete, and rapid. It requires no documentation, takes less than five minutes, and demands no witnesses other than office clerks. No questions are asked concerning the circumstances of the death, and the cause of death is left blank, unquestioned and unexamined. A neighbor, grandmother, older sibling, or common-law husband may register the death. Since most infants die at home, there is no question of a medical record.

From the registry office, the parent proceeds to the town hall, where the mayor will give him or her a voucher for a free baby coffin. The full-time municipal coffinmaker cannot tell you exactly how many baby coffins are dispatched each week. It varies, he says, with the seasons. There are more needed during the drought months and during the big festivals of Carnaval and Christmas and São Joao's Day because people are too busy, he supposes, to take their babies to the clinic. Record keeping is sloppy.

Similarly, there is a failure on the part of city-employed doctors working at two free clinics to recognize the malnutrition of babies who are weighed, measured, and immunized without comment and as if they were not, in fact, anemic, stunted, fussy, and irritated starvation babies. At best the mothers are told to pick up free vitamins or a health "tonic" at the municipal chambers. At worst, clinic personnel will give tranquilizers and sleeping pills to quiet the hungry cries of "sick-to-death" Alto babies.

The church, too, contributes to the routinization of, and indifference toward, child death. Traditionally, the local Catholic church taught patience and resignation to domestic tragedies that were said to reveal the imponderable workings of God's will. If an infant died suddenly, it was because a particular saint had claimed the child. The infant would be an angel in the service of his or her heavenly patron. It would be wrong, a sign of a lack of faith, to weep for a child with such good fortune. The infant funeral was, in the past, an event celebrated with joy. Today, however, under the new regime of "liberation theology," the bells of N.S. das Dores parish church no longer peal for the death of Alto babies, and no priest accompanies the procession of angels to the cemetery where their bodies are disposed of casually and without ceremony. Children bury children in Bom Jesus da Mata. In this most Catholic of communities, the coffin is handed to the disabled and irritable municipal gravedigger, who often chides the children for one reason or another. It may be that the coffin is larger than expected and the gravedigger can find no appropriate space. The children do not wait for the gravedigger to complete his task. No prayers are recited and no sign of the cross made as the tiny coffin goes into its shallow grave.

When I asked the local priest, Padre Marcos, about the lack of church ceremony surrounding infant and childhood death today in Bom Jesus, he replied: "In the old days, child death was richly celebrated. But those were the baroque customs of a conservative church that wallowed in death and misery. The new church is a church of hope and joy. We no longer celebrate the death of child angels. We try to tell mothers that Jesus doesn't want all the dead babies they send him." Similarly, the new church has changed its baptismal customs, now often refusing to baptize dying babies brought to the back door of a church or rectory. The mothers are scolded by the church attendants and told to go home and take care of their sick babies. Baptism, they are told, is for the living; it is not to be confused with the sacrament of extreme unction, which is the anointing of the dying. And so it appears to the women of the Alto that even the church has turned away from them, denying the traditional comfort of folk Catholicism.

The contemporary Catholic church is caught in the clutches of a double bind. The new theology of liberation imagines a kingdom of God on earth based on justice and equality, a world without hunger, sickness, or childhood mortality. At the same time, the church has not changed its official position on sexuality and reproduction, including its sanctions against birth control, abortion, and sterilization. The padre of Bom Jesus da Mata recognizes this contradiction intuitively, although he shies away from discussions on the topic, saying that he prefers to leave questions of family planning to the discretion and the "good consciences" of his impoverished parishioners. But this, of course, sidesteps the extent to which those good consciences have been shaped by traditional church teachings in Bom Jesus, especially by his recent predecessors. Hence, we can begin to see that the seeming indifference of Alto mothers toward the death of some of their infants is but a pale reflection of the official indifference of church and state to the plight of poor women and children.

Nonetheless, the women of Bom Jesus are survivors. One woman, Biu, told me her life history, returning again and again to the themes of child death, her first husband's suicide, abandonment by her father and later by her second husband, and all the other losses and disappointments she had suffered in her long forty-five years. She concluded with great force, reflecting on the days of Carnaval '88 that were fast approaching:

> No, Dona Nanci, I won't cry, and I won't waste my life thinking about it from morning to night. . . . Can I argue with God for the state that I'm in? No! And so I'll dance and I'll jump and I'll play Carnaval! And yes, I'll laugh and people will wonder at a *pobre* like me who can have such a good time.

And no one did blame Biu for dancing in the streets during the four days of Carnaval—not even on Ash Wednesday, the day following Carnaval '88 when we all assembled hurriedly to assist in the burial of Mercea, Biu's beloved *casula,* her last-born daughter who had died at home of pneumonia during the festivities. The rest of the family barely had time to change out of their costumes. Severino, the child's uncle and godfather, sprinkled holy water over the little angel while he prayed: "Mercea, I don't know whether you were called, taken, or thrown out of this world. But look down at us from your heavenly home with tenderness, with pity, and with mercy." So be it.

Connection Questions

1. Discuss whether low life expectancy in Bom Jesus is a result of indirect infanticide.

2. What are the major proximate, intermediate, and ultimate causes of death of the infants in Bom Jesus?

3. In Chapter 7, Miller discusses the concept of bonding. What is your perspective on this concept and how does it affect your reaction to the lack of bonding exhibited by mothers in Bom Jesus?

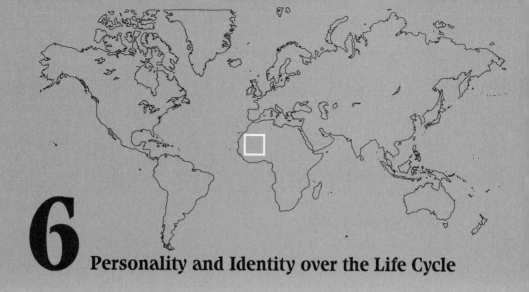

6
Personality and Identity over the Life Cycle

A Woman's Curse?

Meredith F. Small

Many societies around the world treat menstruating women as taboo. Seen as unclean, such women may be evicted from the kitchen, admonished not to touch men's belongings, excluded from sacred places, and even required to sleep in a separate menstrual hut. It is this last requirement that attracted Beverly Strassmann to study the West African Dogon. Among the Dogon, menstruating women crowd each night into a small, cramped menstrual hut built outside village walls. Although they dislike doing so, they believe, as do Dogon men, that their condition is a danger to the gods. Disaster may befall their village if they fail to conform.

Strassmann looked for another explanation, however. Based on years of observation in several Dogon villages, she concluded that the custom serves as an overt sign of a woman's condition that can be used by men to infer the paternity of children. If a woman goes to the menstrual hut, she is clearly not pregnant or lactating. If she is absent and not lactating, chances are she is pregnant. The hut signals information about a woman that would otherwise be hidden.

In this article, Meredith Small describes Strassmann's study and shows that Strassmann has also collected data that says something about the impact

Reprinted by permission of the New York Academy of Sciences from *The Sciences*, January/February 1999.

of menstruation for women in this country. Dogon women menstruate about 110 times during their fertile lives; Western women do so approximately 350 times. Dogon women menstruate less because they are pregnant more often and because they nurse their babies for at least 20 months. Menstruation rarely, if ever, occurs under these conditions. Western women do neither and use birth control pills to bring on menstruation month after month. The high menstruation rate, Small concludes, may be the cause of higher cancer rates. She concludes with the admonition that in the West, we should work with the body, not against it.

The passage from girlhood to womanhood is marked by a flow of blood from the uterus. Without elaborate ceremony, often without discussion, girls know that when they begin to menstruate, their world is changed forever. For the next thirty years or so, they will spend much energy having babies, or trying not to, reminded at each menstruation that either way, the biology of reproduction has a major impact on their lives.

Anthropologists have underscored the universal importance of menstruation by documenting how the event is interwoven into the ideology as well as the daily activities of cultures around the world. The customs attached to menstruation take peculiarly negative forms: the so-called menstrual taboos. Those taboos may prohibit a woman from having sex with her husband or from cooking for him. They may bar her from visiting sacred places or taking part in sacred activities. They may forbid her to touch certain items used by men, such as hunting gear or weapons, or to eat certain foods or to wash at certain times. They may also require that a woman paint her face red or wear a red hip cord, or that she segregate herself in a special hut while she is menstruating. In short, the taboos set menstruating women apart from the rest of their society, marking them as impure and polluting.

Anthropologists have studied menstrual taboos for decades, focusing on the negative symbolism of the rituals as a cultural phenomenon. Perhaps, suggested one investigator, taking a Freudian perspective, such taboos reflect the anxiety that men feel about castration, an anxiety that would be prompted by women's genital bleeding. Others have suggested that the taboos serve to prevent menstrual odor from interfering with hunting, or that they protect men from microorganisms that might otherwise be transferred during sexual intercourse with a menstruating woman. Until recently, few investigators had considered the possibility that the taboos—and the very fact of menstruation—might instead exist because they conferred an evolutionary advantage.

In the mid-1980s the anthropologist Beverly I. Strassmann of the University of Michigan in Ann Arbor began to study the ways men and women have evolved to accomplish (and regulate) reproduction. Unlike traditional anthropologists, who focus on how culture affects human behavior, Strassmann was convinced that the important role played by biology was being neglected.

Menstruation, she suspected, would be a key for observing and understanding the interplay of biology and culture in human reproductive behavior.

To address the issue, Strassmann decided to seek a culture in which making babies was an ongoing part of adult life. For that she had to get away from industrialized countries, with their bias toward contraception and low birthrates. In a "natural-fertility population," she reasoned, she could more clearly see the connection between the physiology of women and the strategies men and women use to exploit that physiology for their own reproductive ends.

Strassmann ended up in a remote corner of West Africa, living in close quarters with the Dogon, a traditional society whose indigenous religion of ancestor worship requires that menstruating women spend their nights at a small hut. For more than two years Strassmann kept track of the women staying at the hut, and she confirmed the menstruations by testing urine samples for the appropriate hormonal changes. In so doing, she amassed the first long-term data describing how a traditional society appropriates a physiological event—menstruation—and refracts that event through a prism of behaviors and beliefs.

What she found explicitly challenges the conclusions of earlier investigators about the cultural function of menstrual taboos. For the Dogon men, she discovered, enforcing visits to the menstrual hut serves to channel parental resources into the upbringing of their own children. But more, Strassmann, who also had training as a reproductive physiologist, proposed a new theory of why menstruation itself evolved as it did—and again, the answer is essentially a story of conserving resources. Finally, her observations pose provocative questions about women's health in industrialized societies, raising serious doubts about the tactics favored by Western medicine for developing contraceptive technology.

Menstruation is the visible stage of the ovarian cycle, orchestrated primarily by hormones secreted by the ovaries: progesterone and a family of hormones called estrogens. At the beginning of each cycle (by convention, the first day of a woman's period) the levels of the estrogens begin to rise. After about five days, as their concentrations increase, they cause the blood- and nutrient-rich inner lining of the uterus, called the endometrium, to thicken and acquire a densely branching network of blood vessels. At about the middle of the cycle, ovulation takes place, and an egg makes its way from one of the two ovaries down one of the paired fallopian tubes to the uterus. The follicle from which the egg was released in the ovary now begins to secrete progesterone as well as estrogens, and the progesterone causes the endometrium to swell and become even richer with blood vessels—in short, fully ready for a pregnancy, should conception take place and the fertilized egg become implanted.

If conception does take place, the levels of estrogens and progesterone continue to rise throughout the pregnancy. That keeps the endometrium thick enough to support the quickening life inside the uterus. When the baby is born and the new mother begins nursing, the estrogens and progesterone fall to their initial levels, and lactation hormones keep them suppressed. The uterus thus lies quiescent until frequent lactation ends, which triggers the return to ovulation.

If conception does not take place after ovulation, all the ovarian hormones also drop to their initial levels, and menstruation—the shedding of part of the uterine lining—begins. The lining is divided into three layers: a basal layer that is constantly maintained, and two superficial layers, which shed and regrow with each menstrual cycle. All mammals undergo cyclical changes in the state of the endometrium. In most mammals the sloughed-off layers are resorbed into the body if fertilization does not take place. But in some higher primates, including humans, some of the shed endometrium is not resorbed. The shed lining, along with some blood, flows from the body through the vaginal opening, a process that in humans typically lasts from three to five days.

Of course, physiological facts alone do not explain why so many human groups have infused a bodily function with symbolic meaning. And so in 1986 Strassmann found herself driving through the Sahel region of West Africa at the peak of the hot season, heading for a sandstone cliff called the Bandiagara Escarpment, in Mali. There, permanent Dogon villages of mud or stone houses dotted the rocky plateau. The menstrual huts were obvious: round, low-roofed buildings set apart from the rectangular dwellings of the rest of the village.

The Dogon are a society of millet and onion farmers who endorse polygyny, and they maintain their traditional culture despite the occasional visits of outsiders. In a few Dogon villages, in fact, tourists are fairly common, and ethnographers had frequently studied the Dogon language, religion and social structure before Strassmann's arrival. But her visit was the first time someone from the outside wanted to delve into an intimate issue in such detail.

It took Strassmann a series of hikes among villages, and long talks with male elders under the thatched-roof shelters where they typically gather, to find the appropriate sites for her research. She gained permission for her study in fourteen villages, eventually choosing two. That exceptional welcome, she thinks, emphasized the universality of her interests. "I'm working on all the things that really matter to [the Dogon]—fertility, economics—so they never questioned my motives or wondered why I would be interested in these things," she says. "It seemed obvious to them." She set up shop for the next two and a half years in a stone house in the village, with no running water or electricity. Eating the daily fare of the Dogon, millet porridge, she and a research assistant began to integrate themselves into village life, learning the language, getting to know people and tracking visits to the menstrual huts.

Following the movements of menstruating women was surprisingly easy. The menstrual huts are situated outside the walled compounds of the village, but in full view of the men's thatched-roof shelters. As the men relax under their shelters, they can readily see who leaves the huts in the morning and returns to them in the evening. And as nonmenstruating women pass the huts on their way to and from the fields or to other compounds, they too can see who is spending the night there. Strassmann found that when she left her house in the evening to take data, any of the villagers could accurately predict whom she would find in the menstrual huts.

The huts themselves are cramped, dark buildings—hardly places where a woman might go to escape the drudgery of work or to avoid an argument with her husband or a co-wife. The huts sometimes become so crowded that some occupants are forced outside—making the women even more conspicuous. Although babies and toddlers can go with their mothers to the huts, the women consigned there are not allowed to spend time with the rest of their families. They must cook with special pots, not their usual household possessions. Yet they are still expected to do their usual jobs, such as working in the fields.

Why, Strassmann wondered, would anyone put up with such conditions?

The answer, for the Dogon, is that a menstruating woman is a threat to the sanctity of religious altars, where men pray and make sacrifices for the protection of their fields, their families and their village. If menstruating women come near the altars, which are situated both indoors and outdoors, the Dogon believe that their aura of pollution will ruin the altars and bring calamities upon the village. The belief is so ingrained that the women themselves have internalized it, feeling its burden of responsibility and potential guilt. Thus violations of the taboo are rare, because a menstruating woman who breaks the rules knows that she is personally responsible if calamities occur.

Nevertheless, Strassmann still thought a more functional explanation for menstrual taboos might also exist, one closely related to reproduction. As she was well aware, even before her studies among the Dogon, people around the world have a fairly sophisticated view of how reproduction works. In general, people everywhere know full well that menstruation signals the absence of a pregnancy and the possibility of another one. More precisely, Strassmann could frame her hypothesis by reasoning as follows: Across cultures, men and women recognize that a lack of menstrual cycling in a woman implies she is either pregnant, lactating or menopausal. Moreover, at least among natural-fertility cultures that do not practice birth control, continual cycles during peak reproductive years imply to people in those cultures that a woman is sterile. Thus, even though people might not be able to pinpoint ovulation, they can easily identify whether a woman will soon be ready to conceive on the basis of whether she is menstruating. And that leads straight to Strassmann's insightful hypothesis about the role of menstrual taboos: information about menstruation can be a means of tracking paternity.

"There are two important pieces of information for assessing paternity," Strassmann notes: timing of intercourse and timing of menstruation. "By forcing women to signal menstruation, men are trying to gain equal access to one part of that critical information." Such information, she explains, is crucial to Dogon men, because they invest so many resources in their own offspring. Descent is marked through the male line; land and the food that comes from the land is passed down from fathers to sons. Information about paternity is thus crucial to a man's entire lineage. And because each man has as many as four wives, he cannot possibly track them all. So forcing women to signal their menstrual periods, or lack thereof, helps men avoid cuckoldry.

To test her hypothesis, Strassmann tracked residence in the menstrual huts for 736 consecutive days, collecting data on 477 complete cycles. She noted who was at each hut and how long each woman stayed. She also collected urine from ninety-three women over a ten-week period, to check the correlation between residence in the menstrual hut and the fact of menstruation.

The combination of ethnographic records and urinalyses showed that the Dogon women mostly play by the rules. In 86 percent of the hormonally detected menstruations, women went to the hut. Moreover, none of the tested women went to the hut when they were not menstruating. In the remaining 14 percent of the tested menstruations, women stayed home from the hut, in violation of the taboo, but some were near menopause and so not at high risk for pregnancy. More important, none of the women who violated the taboo did it twice in a row. Even they were largely willing to comply.

Thus, Strassmann concluded, the huts do indeed convey a fairly reliable signal, to men and to everyone else, about the status of a woman's fertility. When she leaves the hut, she is considered ready to conceive. When she stops going to the hut, she is evidently pregnant or menopausal. And women of prime reproductive age who visit the hut on a regular basis are clearly infertile.

It also became clear to Strassmann that the Dogon do indeed use that information to make paternity decisions. In several cases a man was forced to marry a pregnant woman, simply because everyone knew that the man had been the woman's first sexual partner after her last visit to the menstrual hut. Strassmann followed one case in which a child was being brought up by a man because he was the mother's first sexual partner after a hut visit, even though the woman soon married a different man. (The woman already knew she was pregnant by the first man at the time of her marriage, and she did not visit the menstrual hut before she married. Thus the truth was obvious to everyone, and the real father took the child.)

In general, women are cooperative players in the game because without a man, a woman has no way to support herself or her children. But women follow the taboo reluctantly. They complain about going to the hut. And if their husbands convert from the traditional religion of the Dogon to a religion that does not impose menstrual taboos, such as Islam or Christianity, the women quickly cease visiting the hut. Not that such a religious conversion quells a man's interest in his wife's fidelity: far from it. But the rules change. Perhaps the sanctions of the new religion against infidelity help keep women faithful, so the men can relax their guard. Or perhaps the men are willing to trade the reproductive advantages of the menstrual taboo for the economic benefits gained by converting to the new religion. Whatever the case, Strassmann found an almost perfect correlation between a husband's religion and his wives' attendance at the hut. In sum, the taboo is established by men, backed by supernatural forces, and internalized and accepted by women until the men release them from the belief.

But beyond the cultural machinations of men and women that Strassmann expected to find, her data show something even more fundamental—and surprising—about female biology. On average, she calculates, a woman in a natural-fertility population such as the Dogon has only about 110 menstrual periods in her lifetime. The rest of the time she will be prepubescent, pregnant, lactating or menopausal. Women in industrialized cultures, by contrast, have more than three times as many cycles: 350 to 400, on average, in a lifetime. They reach menarche (their first menstruation) earlier—at age twelve and a half, compared with the onset age of sixteen in natural-fertility cultures. They have fewer babies, and they lactate hardly at all. All those factors lead women in the industrialized world to a lifetime of nearly continuous menstrual cycling.

The big contrast in cycling profiles during the reproductive years can be traced specifically to lactation. Women in more traditional societies spend most of their reproductive years in lactation amenorrhea, the state in which the hormonal changes required for nursing suppress ovulation and inhibit menstruation. And it is not just that the Dogon bear more children (eight to nine on average); they also nurse each child on demand rather than in scheduled bouts, all through the night as well as the day, and intensely enough that ovulation simply stops for about twenty months per child. Women in industrialized societies typically do not breast-feed as intensely (or at all), and rarely breast-feed each child for as long as the Dogon women do. (The average for American women is four months.)

The Dogon experience with menstruation may be far more typical of the human condition over most of evolutionary history than is the standard menstrual experience in industrialized nations. If so, Strassmann's findings alter some of the most closely held beliefs about female biology. Contrary to what the Western medical establishment might think, it is not particularly "normal" to menstruate each month. The female body, according to Strassmann, is biologically designed to spend much more time in lactation amenorrhea than in menstrual cycling. That in itself suggests that oral contraceptives, which alter hormone levels to suppress ovulation and produce a bleeding, could be forcing a continual state of cycling for which the body is ill-prepared. Women might be better protected against reproductive cancers if their contraceptives mimicked lactation amenorrhea and depressed the female reproductive hormones, rather than forcing the continual ebb and flow of menstrual cycles.

Strassmann's data also call into question a recently popularized idea about menstruation: that regular menstrual cycles might be immunologically beneficial for women. In 1993 the controversial writer Margie Profet, whose ideas about evolutionary and reproductive biology have received vast media attention, proposed in *The Quarterly Review of Biology* that menstruation could have such an adaptive value. She noted that viruses and bacteria regularly enter the female body on the backs of sperm, and she hypothesized that the best way to get them out is to flush them out. Here, then, was a positive, adaptive role for something unpleasant, an evolutionary reason for suffering cramps each month. Menstruation, according to Profet, had evolved to rid the body of pathogens. The "antipathogen" theory was an exciting hypothesis, and it helped win Profet a MacArthur Foundation award. But Strassmann's work soon showed that Profet's ideas could not be supported because of one simple fact: under less-industrialized conditions, women menstruate relatively rarely.

Instead, Strassmann notes, if there is an adaptive value to menstruation, it is ultimately a strategy to conserve the body's resources. She estimates that maintaining the endometrial lining during the second half of the ovarian cycle takes substantial metabolic energy. Once the endometrium is built up and ready to receive a fertilized egg, the tissue requires a sevenfold metabolic increase to remain rich in blood and ready to support a pregnancy. Hence, if no pregnancy is forthcoming, it makes a lot of sense for the body to let part of the endometrium slough off and then regenerate itself, instead of maintaining that rather costly but unneeded tissue. Such energy conservation is common among vertebrates: male rhesus monkeys have shrunken testes during their non-breeding season, Burmese pythons shrink their guts when they are not digesting, and hibernating animals put their metabolisms on hold.

Strassmann also suggests that periodically ridding oneself of the endometrium could make a difference to a woman's long-term survival. Because female reproductive hormones affect the brain and other tissues, the metabolism of the entire body is involved during cycling. Strassmann estimates that by keeping hormonal [levels] low through half the cycle, a woman can save about six days' worth of energy for every four nonconceptive cycles. Such caloric conservation might have proved useful to early hominids who lived by hunting and gathering, and even today it might be helpful for women living in less affluent circumstances than the ones common in the industrialized West.

But perhaps the most provocative implications of Strassmann's work have to do with women's health. In 1994 a group of physicians and anthropologists published a paper, also in *The Quarterly Review of Biology,* suggesting that the reproductive histories and lifestyles of women in industrialized cultures are at odds with women's naturally evolved biology, and that the differences lead to greater risks of reproductive cancers. For example, the investigators estimated that women in affluent cultures may have a hundredfold greater risk of breast cancer than do women who subsist by hunting and gathering. The increased risk is probably caused not only by low levels of exercise and a high-fat diet, but also by a relatively high number of menstrual cycles over a lifetime. Repeated exposure to the hormones of the ovarian cycle—because of early menarche, late menopause, lack of pregnancy and little or no breast-feeding—is implicated in other reproductive cancers as well.

Those of us in industrialized cultures have been running an experiment on ourselves. The body evolved over millions of years to move across the landscape looking for food, to live in small kin-based groups, to make babies at intervals of four years or so and to invest heavily in each child by nursing intensely for years. How many women now follow those traditional patterns? We move little, we rely on others to get our food, and we rarely reproduce or lactate. Those culturally initiated shifts in lifestyles may pose biological risks.

Our task is not to overcome that biology, but to work with it. Now that we have a better idea of how the female body was designed, it may be time to rework our lifestyles and change some of our expectations. It may be time to borrow from our distant past or from our contemporaries in distant cultures, and treat our bodies more as nature intended.

Connection Questions

1. How does the Dogon experience with menstruation affect the identities of both men and women in that society?

2. Describe how the Dogon experience reflects both biological and social constructions.

3. What menstrual taboos exist in your cultural world?

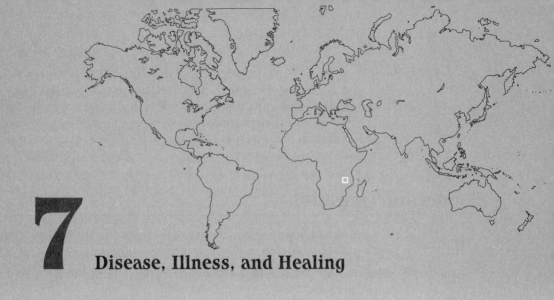

7

Disease, Illness, and Healing

Medical Anthropology: Improving Nutrition in Malawi

Sonia Patten

Applied anthropologists work in many settings. They may conduct government program evaluations, work on forest conservation projects, market or advertise products, staff rural development programs, establish foreign offices for nongovernmental organizations or corporations, or advise hospital staff, among other things. In this article, Sonia Patten describes her role as an applied medical anthropologist on a project aimed at the improvement of infant and child nutrition in the African nation of Malawi. As a medical anthropologist, her job was to collect cultural baseline data that would help to shape the program and make it appropriate to village conditions in Malawi.

Reprinted by permission from Sonia Patten, Ph.D.

Malawi—Welcome to the Warm Heart of Africa. This is the sign that greets travelers when they arrive in this southeastern African republic. The warm, open response to visitors that I have enjoyed each time I have traveled to Malawi contrasts starkly to the poverty that plagues its citizens.

Malawi is a small landlocked nation in southeast Africa that lies south of Tanzania, east of Zambia, and west of Mozambique. The country is long and thin with its axis running north and south along the Great African Rift Valley. Part of the valley holds Lake Malawi, the third largest lake in Africa, which accounts for more than 20 percent of the country's total area of 119,100 square kilometers. Malawi is one of the ten poorest countries in the world. Its economy is based predominately on agriculture, which accounts for half the gross domestic product and virtually all the exports. Cotton, tobacco, and sugar are most likely to be sold to other countries. However, despite exports, food security for both households and the nation is a chronic problem, with annual "hungry seasons" a fact of life and the specter of famine never far from people's minds. Maize, or white corn, is the staple food for the nation, and it is rare when the nation's rain-fed agriculture produces enough of it to adequately feed the population. The Malawi government faces the enormous challenges of strengthening the economy, improving educational and health facilities, and dealing with the serious environmental issues of deforestation and erosion. The country depends heavily on the International Monetary Fund, World Bank, and bilateral and multilateral donor assistance. It was a small project funded by the U.S. Agency for International Development (USAID) that brought me as a medical anthropologist to Malawi several times during the 1990s.

Medical anthropology is difficult to define because it covers such a wide scope of research and practical programming. In the broadest sense, it can be defined as the study of human health in a variety of cultural and environmental contexts. Over the past three decades, medical anthropology has become a distinct and important area within anthropology. Presently it has three major areas of emphasis. One is the study of cultural differences in health beliefs and systems of healing such as alternative therapies, shamanism, and folk concepts of disease. A second consists of biomedical studies of human adaptations to disease, including nutrition, genetics, and demography. The third is applied medical anthropology, which focuses on the application of anthropology to health-related problems and possible solutions.

Medical anthropologists often carry out research as members of interdisciplinary teams, where their main contribution is to discover a people's cultural conceptions of health, illness, and the more general cultural context within which ideas about health are situated. It was as an applied medical anthropologist that I came to be a member of such an interdisciplinary team that would work in Malawi.

In the early 1990s, I was on the faculty at one of three universities that had joined together to apply for a USAID grant under a program called University Development Linkages Program (UDLP). Two of the universities were American and one was the agricultural college that forms part of the University of

Malawi system. A major goal of the UDLP was to strengthen developing nation colleges and universities by giving them access to U.S. faculties and other American university resources. The program also sought to increase the involvement of U.S. faculty members with faculty in developing nations so that students at U.S. institutions would benefit from an internationalizing of the curriculum.

In this case, scientists from participating universities were asked to devise and implement a project that would benefit all collaborating institutions of higher education. Many teams of UDLP scientists that applied for grants designed projects intended to strengthen curricula at developing nation institutions. Our team, however, opted to design and implement a project addressing a major problem, child undernourishment in Malawi. We recognized that three out of five children in the country were undernourished. Worse, the mortality rate for children under five was 24 percent or nearly one in four. The problem was caused by the fact that children received insufficient protein and calories, which left them vulnerable to a host of infectious diseases, potential mental impairment, serious deficiency diseases such as kwashiorkor and marasmus, and premature death. This is the story of the people from two central Malawi villages and three universities as we worked to craft a program to reduce child undernourishment and increase child survival on a sustainable basis.

Faculty members who were participating in this effort represented a number of disciplines: anthropology, human nutrition, cooperative extension, animal science, veterinary medicine, and crop science. Several of the participating faculty members from Malawi had grown up in small villages, still had extended family in those villages, and were familiar with economic and cultural factors contributing to child undernourishment there. From them and from field research we learned that mothers breastfeed their babies for two to three years, which assured that the children received sufficient protein and calories during these early years. However, that changed when the children were fully weaned. The indigenous weaning food is a gruel of water and maize flour, and babies receive small amounts of it beginning at about four months of age. When mothers wean their toddlers, it is this gruel that the children eat day after day. It is a nutritionally inadequate weaning food and children soon begin to show its effects—swollen bellies, stunted growth, and increased susceptibility to malaria, measles, and other infectious diseases. The weaning food is made from the same crop, maize, that constitutes the staple food for adults, a boiled maize flour dish called *nsima*. The problem of a nutritionally inadequate weaning food is not unique to Malawi—it plagues many developing nations. In these countries there is often a high-carbohydrate food such as corn or rice that makes up as much as 90 percent of children's daily intake. If people survive into adulthood, their bodies have made an adaptation to this low-protein diet. But young children do not thrive.

As our project searched for ideas about how to create a plan for addressing child nutrition, we decided to focus on a simple approach that would use indigenous resources and be manageable at the local level. This was the introduction of a protein and calorie-rich additive, goat milk, to the local weaning food. Although goats are plentiful in Malawi villages, they are meat goats, not dairy goats. They are like walking bank accounts, to be sold when a family needs money to pay school fees for the children, health care, and rites of passage such as weddings and funerals. It would be a bold step to secure approval from male village political leaders and elders for the introduction of milk-producing goats to provide milk for young children. Dairy goats would be put directly into the hands of women, not men. Would it work? Would women be willing to learn new animal management and food handling techniques? Would they have time to carry out the additional labor that would be required? Would the goat milk be given to the children who needed it? Would husbands or brothers take the valuable animals away from the women? Would the goats and the children flourish? As time went on, we learned the answers to all these questions and more. And the village women contributed very valuable insights and suggestions that made the project a model that has been adopted elsewhere in Malawi.

The Program

Our work began with a series of planning meetings. Our goal was to create a program that would enable women to raise and keep dairy goats on a sustainable and manageable basis, and use the milk that was produced to supplement their children's diets and increase food security for their families. The plan we generated would have three parts: (1) generation of a database on the milk production and biological characteristics of goats; (2) development and implementation of demonstrations and outreach programs for distributing milk goats to rural women and teaching them how to care for the animals; and (3) formation and implementation of outreach programs for rural women so they could learn how to safely handle goat milk and use it as a regular part of the diet, especially for their children who were under five years of age. At our planning meetings we had to figure out what we were actually going to do, and in what sequence.

The animal scientists on the team knew that milk goats introduced into local villages would have to be hardy or they would die. They wanted to try out some breeding experiments using local goats and imported breeds of dairy goats to see just what kind of a crossbred doe would result in the best combination of high milk production and ability to adapt to life in the village. So they worked out a breeding scheme using local Malawi goats and imported Saanen dairy goats from South Africa, Damascus goats from Cyprus, and Anglo-Nubian goats from the U.S. The breeding experiments were carried out at the farm that the Malawi members of our team used for teaching and research.

This kind of research can't be done in a hurry. Arranging for the importation of animals is a complex process because one has to find a supplier, arrange for payment, arrange for shipment (very few airlines are willing to transport large animals internationally), work out how to feed and water the animals while they are in transit, secure permits from the Malawi Ministry of Agriculture, and quarantine the animals for a period of weeks when they arrive in country. Only then can the breeding research begin.

To our dismay, none of the imported Anglo-Nubian goats survived for very long in Malawi. And several of the Damascus goats also died. The Saanens, however, proved to be the hardier—not surprising, since they originated from relatively close by South Africa where environmental conditions were similar to those in Malawi. And when bred with local Malawi goats, the resulting cross-breeds turned out to provide substantial weekly milk yields that would be enough for the goats' kids as well as for the young children of rural families. So the team decided to import more Saanens and continue the crossbreeding program. Crossbred does would be distributed to village women and most of the crossbred bucks would be sold to support the project. As the program developed, team members discovered that some local does produced relatively high average milk yields; this finding became important as the project unfolded.

My work as the team anthropologist involved the human side of the project. With the help of team nutritionists and the extension expert, I designed a survey to collect baseline cultural information in the villages where the milk goats would be distributed. It was important to document such things as women's daily activities, the meaning and use of goats, relationships between men and women, and ways children were fed in the target villages before the milk goats were introduced. Later we would look for changes we hoped would occur after the new goats arrived and for unexpected problems.

To proceed with the social research, we selected three villages, all relatively close to the college campus in a rural setting about 25 km from the capital city of Lilongwe. To proceed, however, it was necessary to obtain permission from the people in each community. To do so we held meetings with the village headmen, men and women elders, mothers of young children who would be affected by our project, and anyone else from the village who was interested in learning about the program.

In the Central Region of Malawi where we were working, most people belong to the Chewa ethnic group. The Chewa have a matrilineal descent system and practice matrilocal residence. Thus, Chewa men and women inherit clan and lineage membership from their mothers. It is this membership that gives people the right to farm plots of land surrounding their villages. When women marry, most continue to live in the village of their birth with a group of related females—mother, maternal grandmother, mother's sisters and their children, sisters and their children, and eventually, adult daughters and their young children. When young men marry, most move to the villages of their brides. The village political leader is usually, but not always, a man. He cannot be the son of the prior headman because a son is not part of his father's matriline. Instead, he is likely to be the son of the prior headman's sister—a maternal nephew. This system creates a situation where almost all of the women and the powerful men in a village are maternal kin to one another.

To introduce the project, we had to recognize the matrilineal nature of village social organization and the need for people's approval. We met with groups of interested women and men and the headmen in two villages. We explained what we were proposing to do. We said we wanted to find out how the young children in the village were doing in terms of growth and health. Then we intended to make milk goats available to women who had children under five years old because we felt the children would benefit from goat milk in their diet. We noted that it would not cost the women any money. (Most rural women lack the means to purchase even local goats, because they cost from $30 to $50. Dairy goats would be much more expensive.) We said that women who received milk goats would be asked to return the first healthy kid, whether male or female, to the college farm and that this would constitute payment for the animal. We told them that women who took the goats would be asked to attend demonstrations to help them learn how to care for the animals, handle the milk, and feed the milk to their children. We also said that someone from the project would come to the village each week to weigh and measure the participants' children to see if goat milk in their diet was having an effect on weight and height of their youngsters.

Village women were uniformly positive about the project—they wanted to participate. But men, including the headmen, were more skeptical. They worried about the impact on social relations of such valuable animals going to women—it didn't seem appropriate—couldn't the goats be given to the men of the village? The goats were not to be sold or slaughtered, we said. They would be there for the benefit of the children, and their care would involve extra work for the women. Everyone knew that children were suffering because of malnourishment—sometimes a child would become so seriously malnourished that relatives had to take it to the district hospital for nutritional rehabilitation. This meant a three-week hospital stay with a family member right there to feed and care for the child. The cost to the family was considerable. And the death of a child was a great sorrow. So eventually the men agreed that the project should go forward. The headmen agreed that the goats should belong to the women and said they would resolve any disputes over ownership in favor of the women.

When we were ready to talk with people in a third village about the project, we learned something that quickly dissuaded us from continuing there. It seemed that there was animal theft going on in the area, and the prime suspects were a family living in the third village! Until the local system of justice had solved these crimes and dealt with the perpetrators, we could not take the risk of working in that village. Animal theft became a problem in the other two villages as well. The rural economy in Malawi has weakened in recent years because of droughts, floods, soil depletion, deforestation, erosion, low prices for commodities, and high rates of inflation. The annual hungry season, the period of time between when people consume the last of the food they have stored to the time when the next crops are harvested, used to begin in December and end in March. Now the hungry season often begins in September. People must reduce the amount of food they eat at a time when they have to carry out the heaviest agricultural labor, preparing fields and planting them when the annual rains begin. Both men and women do this work and nearly all agricultural labor is done by hand. In the depth of the hungry season, people may turn to eating maize bran, the portion of the maize kernel that they normally feed to their animals, in order to have something in their bellies to assuage the hunger pangs. Under conditions such as these, it is no surprise that theft of animals is on the rise in the countryside.

Women in the two villages who received milk goats responded vigorously to the threat of theft once a few animals had been stolen. They began to take their milk goats with them as they went to work in the fields, tethering them nearby rather than letting them range free. They built pens against the sides of their mud or brick houses, to provide shade and security. At night they brought the animals into their houses so the whole family could guard them.

Our research team hired two young women who were both native speakers of the local language, Chichewa, and who had grown up in villages. We asked them to administer the baseline survey in the two villages and to continue working on the project. They would help to distribute animals to village women and later pay weekly visits to the recipients to weigh and measure their young children. One of these young women remained with the project throughout, and is dedicated to working with the villagers. She has been a key to the success of our work.

The baseline survey of households with children under five years of age revealed some interesting and useful information. Women headed 30 percent of the households; there was no adult male regularly living with them. Almost 75 percent of the women were nonliterate. A total of 35.4 percent of the children were underweight for their age and 57.7 percent were stunted (short for age). These figures are close to the national averages for a preharvest season, i.e., the hungry season. A surprising finding was that children in female-headed households were less likely to be undernourished or stunted. We can only speculate about why this was the case. Perhaps it has to do with groups of related women sharing resources in the interest of their children's well being.

We gave women who participated in the baseline survey the opportunity to volunteer to receive a milk goat, with the understanding that they would attend demonstrations that taught ways to manage the animals and keep them healthy, how to milk goats, how to keep the milk from spoiling, and how to add it to their children's food. We also pointed out that they would have to return first-born kids to project personnel so the does could eventually be distributed to other women, but that all kids born after that would be theirs to keep. The female goats would increase their flock of milk-producers, and the males could be sold to give the women much-needed cash. All women who received milk goats would also be provided with a bucket for milking, a pan for cooking, and a measuring cup to help them track milk production.

The program proved popular. Very quickly the project had more participants than it could accommodate, and we had to create a waiting list. We gave priority to those women who had children under five that were most seriously undernourished. Other women on the waiting list agreed to this. We also provided animals to some grandmothers who were raising young grandchildren orphaned when their parents died of AIDS. Care for AIDS orphans has become a major problem in Malawi, and is reflected at the village level. It is common to see women, already struggling to care for immediate family members, stressed to the maximum as they undertake to feed and house children left behind by relatives who have succumbed to the disease.

Team members designed and began to present demonstrations for village women on goat management, goat health, milking, safe milk handling, and incorporation of milk in their children's food. Recipes using local ingredients and goat milk were developed and tested in the home economics kitchens at the college, and taste-tested by the women participants and their children at the village-based demonstrations. The recipes that passed the taste test were routinely used by the women; those that didn't were rejected.

When the women received their animals, all of the does were either pregnant or already had young kids. This is when project field assistants began their weekly visits to the villages. During each visit, the participating women gathered in a central area of the village with their children. Each woman would have her child or children weighed in a sling scale that was suspended from a tree branch. Once a month, team members measured the upper arm circumference and height of the children. The fact of high child mortality was brought home to me in a very graphic way during this process when some women initially objected to having their children's height measured because they thought it was too much like measuring the children for coffins. A few women persisted in their objection. In these cases, our field assistants could only estimate observable changes in height. The field assistants also asked women about the general health of their children during the previous week, the milk production of their goats, and the health of their goats. If a goat was ill, the field assistant arranged for a veterinary assistant or the team member who was a veterinarian to travel to the village and examine the animal. If there was a significant health problem with a child, the field assistant notified faculty team members who would then take the information to the nearest clinic where they could arrange transport of the woman and child to a hospital if that was called for. Almost all the women who received animals were committed to caring for them and using the milk for their children. Ninety-eight percent of the recipients returned the first kid to the project. This is an astonishingly high rate of return and it implies that rural women would be very good risks for other kinds of so-called "payback schemes" that make local efforts to improve economic security sustainable.

We were gratified to see that those children who began to receive even small amounts of goat milk as an ingredient in their daily diets showed steady weight and height gains even when they were sick. In time, however, we began to see children hit growth plateaus or even lose ground temporarily. We learned from village women themselves why this was happening. Women who made up village committees approached the project team with a proposal for a solution.

They told us that their milk goats had to have at least two kids before they could get a second high-yield doe, and this meant that there were periods of time when no milk was available for their children. The women asked if we could teach them how to grow soybeans. They were all familiar with soybean flour as a food for undernourished children because this is what they received when they took their malnourished children to maternal and child health clinics for treatment. Their plan was to grow soybeans and grind them into flour to feed their children when no goat milk was available.

Our project team went back to the drawing board and figured out how to incorporate this new effort. The team purchased soybean seed and distributed 5 kg of it to each woman in the two villages. The village headmen approved of this effort and in some instances designated land for use by those women who needed it. Malawi team members developed and presented demonstrations on how to grow and process soybeans. The women agreed to pay back the 5 kg of seed after their first harvest, again a way to perpetuate the program over time and make it sustainable, and all did so. Women have now completed three or four successful growing seasons with soybeans, and are many are growing and storing enough beans to see them through the periods of time when their does produce no milk. They also save enough seed for the next planting season.

It also became clear after a short period of time that we would have to change the goat crossbreeding program. The college farm could not breed enough hardy milk goats to keep up with the demand. The animal scientists on our team looked for local Malawi goats that were the highest milk producers and these, when pregnant or with a kid, were distributed to women on the waiting list. Simultaneously, plans were made to build buck stations in each of the villages and to provide each station with a Saanen or crossbred buck to breed with local goats. Village headmen oversaw the building efforts and other men and women helped to feed and water the buck. When a doe comes into heat, the owner can bring it to the station to be inseminated. In this way the Saanen genes for high milk production spread more rapidly into the village flocks. The villagers know that their bucks must be exchanged for others about every three years in order to avoid inbreeding.

I returned to Malawi for a short visit in the summer of 2004 and found that many positive features of the project were still in place. In discussions with groups of women who had received dairy goats, I learned that two-thirds of them still had their original project animals. The remaining third had lost their original animals to disease or injury, but not before the goats had delivered offspring that survived. Only one woman had sold her animal before it had given her viable kids; this is tantamount to a farmer selling or eating her seed! But the woman's situation was quite difficult. Her husband was seriously ill and could not assist with farm work, and as a consequence she had been unable to raise sufficient maize to provide for household subsistence. She was desperate for cash in order to purchase food, and it was out of this desperation that she sold her milk goat.

Several women had a sufficient number of animals that they were able to meet the nutritional needs of their young children and sell surplus goats, primarily to NGOs planning to launch similar efforts to address child malnutrition. For the most part, money earned in this way was used to buy commercial fertilizer in order to increase the maize harvest. Cooking oil, salt, and clothing were other items commonly purchased with these earnings. The loss of animals to theft had decreased due to the introduction of a community policing effort. Professional police have trained villagers to take turns patrolling the village and its surrounding area at night in order to discourage thieves, and it seemed to be working. But another danger had presented itself. Because the 2004 harvest was not a good one due to erratic rains, people were anxious about their food reserves, most knowing that they would run out long before the next harvest. One result of this is that domesticated dogs (every household has a watchdog) are not fed adequate amounts of cooked maize bran or leftover cooked maize flour. They are hungry, and they have begun running across the fields in packs, attacking kids and young goats belonging to people from villages other than their own. Some people have lost valuable kids in this way and were considering tethering kids while the does free range. Normally tethering occurs only during the rainy season after planting has taken place. There is the possibility that marauding dogs will be shot, but this raises the likelihood of inter-village conflict.

Of the four village buck stations erected as part of the project, three were in good repair and the bucks well cared for. The fourth was somewhat rundown and needed refurbishing. And it was clear that the buck needed better care. After some discussion and investigation, it became apparent that the headman had declared the buck was his personal property and only his relatives could use its services—anyone else would have to pay him a fee if they wished to bring their animals to the buck. Not surprisingly, people did not take well to this proclamation. They more or less boycotted the buck station, which meant that most of the care of the animal fell to the elderly headman and his wife. The station was repaired, the animal was provided with nutritional supplements, the household was provided with a new bucket for the dedicated purpose of bringing water to the buck, and the headman was informed that the buck would die or be returned to the college if it did not receive better care. In the end, it became clear that a miscommunication had occurred between the headman and project personnel, leading the headman to conclude that he was now free to charge for use of the buck station. By the time I left Malawi, the misunderstanding had apparently been cleared up. College personnel will continue to check on the well being of this valuable animal—it would be a great loss to the village if it were to die or be removed.

During group and individual discussions with women, everyone acknowledged the value of goat milk as a component of their children's diets. I was told that, since the milk had become available in the villages, no child had become so seriously malnourished that he or she had to be taken to the hospital for nutritional rehabilitation. This was a real change from an earlier point in time, and a hallmark of success for all of our efforts, researchers and villagers, to promote the health of children.

Conclusion

Our project team designed and tested a locally sustainable approach to alleviate infant and child malnourishment in rural Malawi. Data on changes in the participating children's weights, heights, and upper arm circumferences show that relatively small amounts of goat milk included in the regular diet make a substantial difference in promoting normal growth in children. Results from a rapid appraisal survey that I helped to design indicate that the project is highly valued by rural women. This is confirmed by key village women and by the fact that more women than project resources would permit sought to join the program. Presently some Malawi nongovernmental organizations (NGOs) have introduced similar efforts in other parts of the country. Several district hospitals that provide rehabilitation for severely malnourished children have established flocks of milk goats on their grounds and use the milk as an important part of the rehabilitation treatment. The agricultural college plans to offer training to Malawians and people from other southern African nations who are interested in replicating the program. And the project villages will be demonstration sites for trainees who want to see how the project works "on the ground."

It was important to have an anthropologist on the project team. As the team anthropologist, I participated in every phase of the project, including management duties at times when it was necessary to keep our efforts on schedule. I was responsible for providing an ethnographic account of local culture and using this information to help shape how we could present the program to villagers. I was not trained to manage goat breeding or conduct some of the health measurements, but I could point out how I thought villagers would respond to our plans and to suggest how best to make them full participants in project planning and implementation. It is easy for people from any society to believe that those who are from elsewhere still see the world in the same way they do. Since cultures differ (Americans, for example, find it difficult to understand the ramifications of a matrilineal descent system) anthropologists can translate information about such differences in ways that are useful to other members of interdisciplinary teams. Thus, we can shape programs to fit local conditions and help with cross-cultural communication. That is what I think happened in Malawi.

Connection Questions

1. In the framework of critical medical anthropology, what are the structural causes of child malnutrition in Malawi?

2. What is applied medical anthropology, and what role does it play in the programs described by Sonia Patten to improve child nutrition in Malawi?

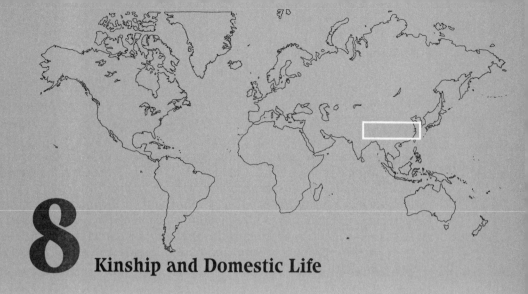

8 Kinship and Domestic Life

Life without Fathers or Husbands

Clifford Geertz

*Cross-cultural comparison is a basic feature of the anthropological enter-
prise and a source of evidence for many explanations put forward by authors
reprinted in this book. For example, some anthropologists argue that
hunter/gathers lack warfare. By comparing ethnographies of hunter/gatherer
groups and looking for the absence or presence of warlike activity, the assertion can be tested and, if necessary, modified.*

*This article provides comparative evidence for another general asser-
tion about human behavior and social organization. A long-held view in anthropology is that marriage, the socially approved union between two people,
is a feature of all societies. Marriage, anthropologists assert, leads to the formation of a basic domestic unit, the nuclear family, creates systems of descent that confer group identity, allies kinship groups with one another, and
provides for the legitimate birth and nurturing of children.*

But is this universally true? This article, by Clifford Geertz, reviews the work of Chinese anthropologist, Cia Hua.[1] Based on extended fieldwork among a Chinese tribal group, the Na, Hua describes a matrilineal society that lacks marriage entirely. Women and their children live with brothers and other close matrilineal kin in the same household. Men make appointments to "visit" women in their houses (several ways are described here), arriving late at night and leaving just before dawn. Men and women are likely to sleep with many members of the opposite sex during their lifetimes and do not form permanent relationships. Despite this unusual arrangement, Na society has successfully survived for centuries, until now that is. Under intense pressure from the Chinese government to marry in the "approved" way, the system is breaking down.

Love and marriage, love and marriage
Go together like a horse and carriage
Dad was told by mother
You can't have one without the other
—"Love and Marriage," Sammy
Cahn and Jimmy van Heusen[2]

Not everywhere.

Among the Na, a tribal people hidden away in the Yongning hills of Yunnan province in southern China and the subject of the French-trained Chinese anthropologist Cai Hua's provocative new monograph, there is no marriage, in fact or word. Mothers exist, as do children, but there are no dads. Sexual intercourse takes place between casual, opportunistic lovers, who develop no broader, more enduring relations to one another. The man "visits," usually furtively, the woman at her home in the middle of the night as impulse and opportunity appear, which they do with great regularity. Almost everyone of either sex has multiple partners, serially or simultaneously; simultaneously usually two or three, serially as many as a hundred or two. There are no nuclear families, no in-laws, no stepchildren. Brothers and sisters, usually several of each, reside together, along with perhaps a half-dozen of their nearer maternal relatives, from birth to death under one roof—making a living, keeping a household, and raising the sisters' children.

The incest taboo is of such intensity that not only may one not sleep with opposite sex members of one's own household, one cannot even allude to sexual

---

[1]This article represents a review of Cia Hua, *A Society without Fathers or Husbands: The Na of China,* translated from the French by Asti Hustvedt (New York: Zone Books, 2001). All quotes included in the article are taken from this book.

[2]*Love and Marriage* by Sammy Cahn and Jimmy Van Husen. Copyright © 1955 (renewed) by Cahn Music Co., and Barton Music Corp. All rights reserved; used by permission of Hal Leonard.

matters in their presence. One may not curse where they can hear, or sit with them in the same row at the movies, lest an emotional scene appear on the screen. As paternity is socially unrecognized, and for the most part uncertain, fathers may happen, now and again, to sleep with daughters. A man is free to sleep with his mother's brother's daughter, who is not considered any kind of relative, not even a "cousin." There is no word for bastard, none for promiscuity, none for infidelity; none, for that matter, for incest, so unthinkable is it. Jealousy is infra dig:

> "You know, Luzo [who is nineteen] has not had a lot of [lovers], but he has made many visits [his friend said]. This is because he only goes to the homes of beauties. In particular, he goes to visit Seno, a pretty girl in our village. Do you want to go [visit her] at her house?" he asked me.
>
> "No! If I go there, Luzo will be jealous," I answered.
>
> "How could I be jealous!" [Luzo] responded. "You can ask whomever you want. You will see that . . . we don't know how to be jealous."
>
> "He's right!" his friend interjected. And to explain himself he added: "Girls [are available] to everyone. Whoever wants to can visit them. There is nothing to be jealous about."

Obviously, this is an interesting place for an anthropologist—especially for an anthropologist brought up on that King Charles's head of his profession, "kinship theory."

There are two major variants of such theory, "descent theory" and "alliance theory," and the Na, Hua says, fit neither of them. In the first, associated with the name of the British anthropologist A. R. Radcliffe-Brown and his followers, the "nuclear," "basic," or "elementary" family—a man, his wife, and their children—"founded as it is on natural requirements," is universal, and "forms the hard core around which any social organization revolves." The relationship between parents and children, "filiation," is critical, and out of it are developed various "jural," that is, normative, rules of descent which group certain sets of relatives together against others: lineages, clans, kindreds, and the like. "Families can be compared to threads which it is the task of nature to warp in order that the social fabric can develop."

In the alliance model, deriving in the main from the French anthropologist, and Hua's mentor, Claude Lévi-Strauss, "the institutionalized exchange of women" between families "by the alliance of marriage [is taken] to be the central point of kinship." The universality of the incest taboo, "a natural phenomenon," necessitates marriage and the creation of the "transversal [that is, affinal or 'in-law'] networks of alliances [that] engender all social organization."

Since the Na have no matrimonial relationship they falsify both theories. They neither form elementary families out of which a filiative social fabric can be spun, nor, though they have a variety of the incest taboo (an odd variety, in that with its father-daughter twist it does not exclude all primary relatives), do they form twined and expandable affinal networks, or indeed any networks of "in-laws" at all. "From now on," Hua proclaims at the end of his book, "marriage can no longer be considered the only possible institutionalized mode of sexual behavior." The Na "visit" demonstrates that

> Marriage, affinity, alliance of marriage, family, [usually considered] essential to anthropology, . . . seem absent from this culture. The Na case attests to the fact that marriage and the family (as well as the Oedipus complex) can no longer be considered universal, neither logically nor historically.

This is a little grand, for there are other "institutionalized modes of sexual behavior"—concubinage, prostitution, wife-borrowing—just about everywhere, and whether the Oedipus complex is universal or not, or even whether it exists at all, is not dependent upon marital arrangements. But clearly, "the visit" is an unusual, perhaps though one never knows what is coming next out of Papua, the Amazon, or Central Asia—a unique institution sustaining a most unusual "kinship system," its existence often regarded as impossible. It is a system in which the facts of reproduction (though recognized—the Na know where babies come from) are incidental and all ties are (conceived to be) "blood ties"— the entire house can be called consanguineous.

The Na "visit," for all its fluidity, opportunism, and apparent freedom from moral or religious anxiety, is as well outlined a social institution, as deeply embedded in a wider social structure, as marriage is elsewhere. (The Na are Tibetan-style Buddhists, nearly a third of the adult men being monks, whose sexual practices, a handful of Lhasa-bound celibates aside, are the same as those of laymen.) This is clear from the exact and explicit terminology that marks it out:

> Society calls a man and a woman who set up this kind of sexual relationship *nana sésé hing,* which means people in a relationship of furtive meetings; the man and the woman discreetly call each other *açia* ["discreetly" because of the "incest" taboo against public references to sexuality where opposite sex consanguines may hear them]. The term *açia* is made up of the diminutive prefix *a* and the root *çia.* The Na add *a* to names and proper nouns to indicate intimacy, affection, friendship, and respect; *çia,* when used as a noun, means lover. The same word is used for both sexes, and as a verb it means literally to lie down and figuratively to mate, to sleep and to tempt. *Açia* means lover.
>
> A Na saying depicts those who are *açia* very well: . . . It is not enough to say that we are *çia* for it to be so, sleeping together once makes (us) *çia.*

The enactment of such a relationship shows the same detailed cultural patterning: it is not a matter of brute and unfettered physical desire, but of a modeled, almost balletic self-control. The rendezvous takes place in the bedroom of the woman around midnight. (A bit earlier in the winter, Hua says, a bit later in the summer.) The man comes in near-perfect quietness, does what he does (Hua is wholly silent about what that might be and about how the cries of love are muffled), and leaves at cockcrow, creeping as stealthily back to his own house. As men and women enjoy "complete equality" and are "in daily contact, in town, in the workplace, and elsewhere," either can make the first advance and either may accept or refuse:

> A girl might say to a boy, "Come stay at my house tonight." The boy might then respond, "Your mother is not easygoing." And then the girl might say, "She won't scold you. Come secretly in the middle of the night." If the boy accepts, he says, "Okay." If the boy refuses, he says, "I don't want to come. I'm not going to come over to sleep." In this case, no matter what the girl says, nothing will change his mind.
>
> When the man takes the initiative . . . he often uses the expression "I'll come to your house tonight, okay?," to which the woman responds with a smile or by saying, "Okay." Some come straight out and ask "Do you want to be my *açia?*" If a woman refuses . . . , she can use a ready-made formula: "No, it is not possible. I already have one for tonight." In that case, the man will not insist.

There are other, more oblique ways of making one's wishes known. One can snatch away some personal object—a scarf, a pack of cigarettes—from the desired partner. If he or she does not protest, the tryst is on. One can shout from a distance, "Hey, hey, do you want to trade something?" If you get a "hey, hey" back, you exchange belts and fix an appointment. These days, Chinese movies—shown virtually every night, though they are imperfectly understood by the Tibeto-Burmese-speaking Na—are a particularly favored setting for putting things in motion:

> The young men and women purchase tickets and wait in front of the theater, getting to know each other. . . . One man can offer several women a ticket, just as one woman can offer a ticket to more than one man. Once a ticket is handed over, the man and woman move away from each other and only get back together inside the theater. During the film, the viewers talk loudly, often drowning out the sound from the speakers. If they have had a good time during the movie and reached an agreement, they leave discreetly to spend an amorous night together.

The "amorous night" itself may be a one-time thing. Or it may be repeated at shorter or longer intervals over the course of months or years. It may be begun, broken off for awhile, then begun again. It may be stopped altogether at any time by either party, usually without prior notice or much in the way of explanation. It does not, in short, involve any sort of exclusive and permanent "horse and carriage" commitment. But it, too, is, for all its fluidity and seeming negligence, carefully patterned—framed and hemmed in by an elaborate collection of cultural routines, a love-nest ethic.

When the *amant* arrives at the *amante*'s house, usually after having climbed over a fence or two and thrown a bone to the guard dog, he will give some sort of signal of his presence—toss pebbles on the roof, crouch at the woman's bedroom window (Hua says that every man in a village complex—four or five hundred people—knows the location of every woman's bedroom), or, if he is confident of being received or has been there often, simply knock on the front door. "In a household where there are women of the age to receive visitors [there may be several such on one night, and even a woman may have, in turn, more than one visitor], every evening after nightfall, the men of the house will not open the front door."

Usually, the woman who is waiting will herself open the door and the two will creep wordlessly off to her bedroom. If the wrong woman opens the door— a sister or a cousin, or perhaps even one of those "not easygoing" mothers—this causes little embarrassment: the man simply proceeds to the right woman's bedroom. During the encounter, the lovers must whisper "so that nothing will reach the ears of the woman's relatives, above all the men (especially uncles and great-uncles)."

No one can force anyone else in these matters. The woman can always, and at any time, refuse the man's entreaties and send him packing. A woman may never, in any case, visit a man; so if she is scorned she is just out of luck. A legend accounts for this virtually unique exception to rigorous symmetry of the system:

> When humanity originated, no one knew how to regulate visits. Abaodgu, the god in charge of setting all the rules, proposed the following test: he ordered that a man be shut up in a house and that a woman be sent to join him. To reach the man, the woman had to pass through nine doors. At dawn, she had reached the seventh door. Then Abaodgu tested the man, who succeeded in passing through three doors. . . . Abaodgu [concluded] that women were too passionate [to do] the visiting. . . . The men [would have to] visit the women.

Hua goes on to trace out, methodically and in remorseless detail, the variations, the social ramifications, and the ethnographical specifics of all this, worried, not without reason, that if he does not make his arguments over and over again and [retell] every last fact he has gathered in four periods of fieldwork (1985, 1986, 1988–1989, 1992) his account will not be believed.

He describes two other, special and infrequent "modalities" of sexual encounter—"the conspicuous visit" and "cohabitation." In the conspicuous visit, which always follows upon a series of furtive visits, the effort to conceal the relationship is abandoned ("vomited up," as the idiom has it), mainly because the principals have grown older, perhaps tired of the pretense and folderol, and everyone knows about them anyway.

In cohabitation, an even rarer variant, a household that is short of women by means of which to produce children or of men to labor for it in its fields will adopt a man or woman from a household with a surplus to maintain its reproductive or economic viability, the adopted one becoming a sort of permanent conspicuous visitor (more or less: these arrangements often break up too). Among chiefly families, called *zhifu*, a Chinese word for "regional governor," successive relationships are established over several generations, leading to a peculiar household alternation of chiefship and a greater restriction on who may mate with whom. . . .

After centuries of resistance to efforts to bring it into line with what is around it—that is, Han propriety—[the Na] cosmos is now apparently at last dissolving. The pressures on the Na to shape up and mate morally like normal human beings have been persistent and unremitting. As early as 1656, the Manchurian Qing, troubled by succession problems among "barbarian" tribes, decreed that the chiefs of such tribes, including the Na, must marry in the standard way and produce standard sons, grandsons, and cousins to follow them legitimately into office.

The extent to which this rule was enforced varied over time with the strengths and interests of the various dynasties. But the intrusion of Han practices—virilocality (by which married couples live near the husband's parents), patrifiliation (making kinship through fathers central), polygynous marriage (i.e., involving several wives), written genealogies, and "ancestor worship" (the Na cast the ashes of their dead unceremoniously across the hillsides)—into the higher reaches of Na society provided an alternative cultural model, a model that the Na, for the most part, contrived to keep at bay. Members of chiefly families, and some of the wealthy commoners and resident immigrants, began to marry to preserve their estates and to secure a place in the larger Chinese society. But most of the population proceeded as before, despite being continuously reviled as "primitive," "depraved," "backward," "licentious," "unclean," and ridden with sexual disease. (The last was, and is, more or less true. "More than 50 percent of Na adults have syphilis . . . a significant percentage of the women are sterile . . . people are deformed. . . . The . . . population is stagnating.")

This cultural guerrilla war, with edicts from the center and evasions from the periphery, continued fitfully for nearly three hundred years, until the arrival of the Communists in the 1950s rendered matters more immediate.[3] The Party considered the tradition of the visit "a 'backward and primitive custom' . . . contraven[ing] the matrimonial legislation of the People's Republic of China . . . [and disrupting] productiveness at work because the men think of nothing but running off to visit someone." The Party's first move against the tradition was a regulation designed to encourage nuclear family formation by distributing land to men who would set up and maintain such a family. When this failed to have any effect at all ("the government could not understand how it was possible that Na men did not want to have their own land"), it moved on, during the Great Leap Forward, to a full press effort to "encourage monogamy" through a licensing system, an effort "guided" by the recommendation of two groups of ethnologists, who insisted that, "with planning," Na men and women could be led toward setting up families as economic units and raising their children together. Though this was a bit more successful—in Hua's "sample" seven

---

[3]The Communists of course came to power in 1949, but the Na area remained essentially Kuomintang country until 1956, when the Party installed its own local government, placing Han commissars in the region and effectively ending the traditional chiefship system.

couples officially married—it too soon ran out of steam in the face of Na indifference to the sanctions involved.

The small carrot and the little stick having failed to produce results, the Party proceeded in the period of the Cultural Revolution (1966–1969) to get real about the problem. Dedicated to the national project of "sweeping out the four ancients" (customs, habits, morality, culture), the People's Commune of Yongning pronounced it "shameful not to know who one's genitor is" and imposed marriage by simple decree on any villager involved in a conspicuous visit relationship. But this too failed. As soon as the cadres departed, the couples broke up.

Finally, in 1974, the provincial governor of Yunnan, declaring that "the reformation of this ancient matrimonial system comes under the framework of the class struggle in the ideological domain and therefore constitutes a revolution in the domain of the superstructure" (one can almost hear the collective Na, "*Huh?*"), made it the law that: (1) everyone under fifty in a relationship "that has lasted for a long time" must officially marry forthwith at commune headquarters; (2) every woman who has children must publically state who their genitor is, cart him off to headquarters, and marry him; (3) those who divorce without official sanction will have their annual grain ration suspended; (4) any child born out of wedlock will also not get a ration and must be supported by his genitor until age eighteen; and, (5) visiting, furtive or conspicuous, was forbidden.

This, supported by nightly meetings of the local military brigade and some collusive informing, seemed finally to work—after a fashion, and for a while:

> [The] District government sent a Jeep filled with marriage licenses to the People's Commune of Yongning. Ten and twenty at a time, couples were rounded up in the villages . . . and a leader would take their fingerprints on the marriage form and hand them each a marriage license. . . . [When] the day [for the ceremony] came, horse-drawn carriages were sent into the villages to provide transportation for the "newlyweds" to [Party] headquarters. . . . They each received a cup of tea, a cigarette, and several pieces of candy, and then everybody participated in a traditional dance. The government called this "the new way of getting married."

It was new enough, but for the Na it was ruinous. "No other ethnic group in China underwent as deep a disruption as the Na did during the Cultural Revolution," Hua writes in a rare show of feeling. "To understand the trouble this reform caused in Na society, it is enough to imagine a reform in our society, but with the reverse logic":

> During that period [one of Hua's informants said], the tension was so high that our thoughts never strayed from this subject. No one dared to make a furtive visit. Before, we were like roosters. We took any woman we could catch. We went to a woman's house at least once a night. But, with that campaign, we got scared. We

did not want to get married and move into someone else's house, and as a result, we no longer dared to visit anyone. Because of this, we took a rest for a few years.

After the accession of Deng Xiaoping in 1981, the more draconian of these measures—the denial of rations, the exposure of genitors—were softened or suspended, and emphasis shifted toward "educational," that is, assimilationist approaches. In particular, the expansion of the state school system, where "all the textbooks are impregnated with Han ideas and values," is leading to rapid and thorough Sinicization of the Na. Today—or, anyway, in 1992—the school, assisted by movies and other "modern" imports, is accomplishing what political pressure could not: the withering away of "Na-ism":

> When students graduate from middle school, they must complete a form that includes a column requesting information on their civil status. Unable to fill in the blank asking for the name of their father, they suddenly become aware they do not have a father, while their classmates from other ethnic backgrounds do. Some of the Na students, usually the most brilliant ones, find a quiet spot where they can cry in private. . . . The message [of the school] is clear. . . . There is only one culture that is legitimate, and that is Han culture.

In China, as elsewhere, it is not licentiousness that powers most fear. Nor even immorality. It is difference.

Connection Questions

1. Describe the unilineal descent of the Na society and explain its special features.

2. What rule of exclusion is evident in Na culture?

3. Given Miller's description of various forms of households, how would you categorize that of the Na?

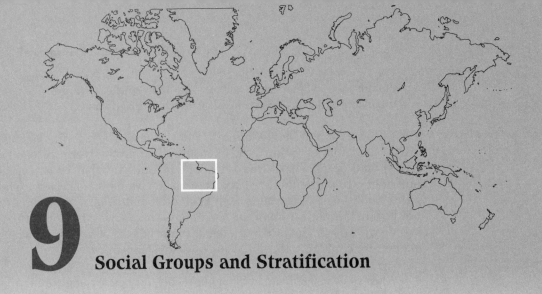

9

Social Groups and Stratification

Mixed Blood

Jeffrey M. Fish

Many Americans believe that people can be divided into races. For them, races are biologically defined groups. Anthropologists, on the other hand, have long argued that U.S. racial groups are American cultural construc-tions; they represent the way Americans classify people rather than a geneti-cally determined reality. In this article, Jeffrey Fish demonstrates the cultural basis of race by comparing how races are defined in the United States and Brazil. In America, a person's race is determined not by how he or she looks, but by his or her heritage. A person will be classified as black, for example, if one of his or her parents is classified that way no matter what the person looks like. In Brazil, on the other hand, people are classified into a series of tipos *on the basis of how they look. The same couple may have children clas-sified into three or four different* tipos *based on a number of physical mark-ers such as skin color and nose shape. As a result, Fish's daughter, who has brown skin and whose mother is Brazilian, can change her race from black in the United States to* moreno *(brunette), a category just behind* branca *(blond) in Brazil, by simply taking a plane there.*

Last year my daughter, who had been living in Rio de Janeiro, and her Brazilian boyfriend paid a visit to my cross-cultural psychology class. They had agreed to be interviewed about Brazilian culture. At one point in the interview I asked her, "Are you black?" She said, "Yes." I then asked him the question, and he said "No."

"How can that be?" I asked. "He's darker than she is."

Psychologists have begun talking about race again. They think that it may be useful in explaining the biological bases of behavior. For example, following publication of *The Bell Curve,* there has been renewed debate about whether black–white group differences in scores on IQ tests reflect racial differences in intelligence. (Because this article is about race, it will mainly use racial terms, like black and white, rather than cultural terms, like African-American and European-American.)

The problem with debates like the one over race and IQ is that psychologists on both sides of the controversy make a totally unwarranted assumption: that there is a biological entity called "race." If there were such an entity, then it would at least be possible that differences in behavior between "races" might be biologically based.

Before considering the controversy, however, it is reasonable to step back and ask ourselves "What is race?" If, as happens to be the case, race is not a biologically meaningful concept, then looking for biologically based racial differences in behavior is simply a waste of time.

The question "What is race?" can be divided into two more limited ones. The answers to both questions have long been known by anthropologists, but seem not to have reached other social or behavioral scientists, let alone the public at large. And both answers differ strikingly from what we Americans think of as race.

The first question is "How can we understand the variation in physical appearance among human beings?" It is interesting to discover that Americans (including researchers, who should know better) view only a part of the variation as "racial," while other equally evident variability is not so viewed.

The second question is "How can we understand the kinds of racial classifications applied to differences in physical appearance among human beings?" Surprisingly, different cultures label these physical differences in different ways. Far from describing biological entities, American racial categories are merely one of numerous, very culture-specific schemes for reducing uncertainty about how people should respond to other people. The fact that Americans believe that Asians, blacks, Hispanics, and whites constitute biological entities called races is a matter of cultural interest rather than scientific substance. It tells us something about American culture—but nothing at all about the human species.

The short answer to the question "What is race?" is: There is no such thing. Race is a myth. And our racial classification scheme is loaded with pure fantasy.

Let's start with human physical variation. Human beings are a species, which means that people from anywhere on the planet can mate with others from anywhere else and produce fertile offspring. (Horses and donkeys are two different species because, even though they can mate with each other, their offspring—mules—are sterile.)

Our species evolved in Africa from earlier forms and eventually spread out around the planet. Over time, human populations that were geographically separated from one another came to differ in physical appearance. They came by these differences through three major pathways: mutation, natural selection, and genetic drift. Since genetic mutations occur randomly, different mutations occur and accumulate over time in geographically separated populations. Also, as we have known since Darwin, different geographical environments select for different physical traits that confer a survival advantage. But the largest proportion of variability among populations may well result from purely random factors; this random change in the frequencies of already existing genes is known as genetic drift.

If an earthquake or disease kills off a large segment of a population, those who survive to reproduce are likely to differ from the original population in many ways. Similarly, if a group divides and a subgroup moves away, the two groups will, by chance, differ in the frequency of various genes. Even the mere fact of physical separation will, over time, lead two equivalent populations to differ in the frequency of genes. These randomly acquired population differences will accumulate over successive generations along with any others due to mutation or natural selection.

A number of differences in physical appearance among populations around the globe appear to have adaptive value. For example, people in the tropics of Africa and South America came to have dark skins, presumably, through natural selection, as protection against the sun. In cold areas, like northern Europe or northern North America, which are dark for long periods of time, and where people covered their bodies for warmth, people came to have light skins—light skins make maximum use of sunlight to produce vitamin D.

The indigenous peoples of the New World arrived about 15,000 years ago, during the last ice age, following game across the Bering Strait. (The sea level was low enough to create a land bridge because so much water was in the form of ice.) Thus, the dark-skinned Indians of the South American tropics are descended from light-skinned ancestors, similar in appearance to the Eskimo. In other words, even though skin color is the most salient feature thought by Americans to be an indicator of race—and race is assumed to have great time depth—it is subject to relatively rapid evolutionary change.

Meanwhile, the extra ("epicanthic") fold of eyelid skin, which Americans also view as racial, and which evolved in Asian populations to protect the eye against the cold, continues to exist among South American native peoples because its presence (unlike a light skin) offers no reproductive disadvantage. Hence, skin color and eyelid form, which Americans think of as traits of different races, occur together or separately in different populations.

Like skin color, there are other physical differences that also appear to have evolved through natural selection—but which Americans do not think of as racial. Take, for example, body shape. Some populations in very cold climates, like the Eskimo, developed rounded bodies. This is because the more spherical an object is, the less surface area it has to radiate heat. In contrast, some populations in very hot climates, like the Masai, developed lanky bodies. Like the tubular pipes of an old-fashioned radiator, the high ratio of surface area to volume allows people to radiate a lot of heat.

In terms of American's way of thinking about race, lanky people and rounded people are simply two kinds of whites or blacks. But it is equally reasonable to view light-skinned people and dark-skinned people as two kinds of "lankys" or "roundeds." In other words, our categories for racial classification of people arbitrarily include certain dimensions (light versus dark skin) and exclude others (rounded versus elongated bodies).

There is no biological basis for classifying race according to skin color instead of body form—or according to any other variable, for that matter. All that exists is variability in what people look like—and the arbitrary and culturally specific ways different societies classify that variability. There is nothing left over that can be called race. This is why race is a myth.

Skin color and body form do not vary together: Not all dark-skinned people are lanky; similarly, light-skinned people may be lanky or rounded. The same can be said of the facial features Americans think of as racial—eye color, nose width (actually, the ratio of width to length), lip thickness ("evertedness"), hair form, and hair color. They do not vary together either. If they did, then a "totally white" person would have very light skin color, straight blond hair, blue eyes, a narrow nose, and thin lips; a "totally black" person would have very dark skin color, black tight curly hair, dark brown eyes, a broad nose, and thick lips; those in between would have—to a correlated degree—wavy light brown hair, light brown eyes, and intermediate nose and lip forms.

While people of mixed European and African ancestry who look like this do exist, they are the exception rather than the rule. Anyone who wants to can make up a chart of facial features (choose a location with a diverse population, say, the New York City subway) and verify that there are people with all possible admixtures of facial features. One might see someone with tight curly blond hair, light skin, blue eyes, broad nose, and thick lips—whose features are half "black" and half "white." That is, each of the person's facial features occupies one end or the other of a supposedly racial continuum, with no intermediary forms (like wavy light brown hair). Such people are living proof that supposedly racial features do not vary together.

Since the human species has spent most of its existence in Africa, different populations in Africa have been separated from each other longer than East Asians or Northern Europeans have been separated from each other or from Africans. As a result, there is remarkable physical variation among the peoples of Africa, which goes unrecognized by Americans who view them all as belonging to the same race.

In contrast to the very tall Masai, the diminutive stature of the very short Pygmies may have evolved as an advantage in moving rapidly through tangled forest vegetation. The Bushmen of the Kalahari desert have very large ("steatopygous") buttocks, presumably to store body fat in one place for times of food scarcity, while leaving the rest of the body uninsulated to radiate heat. They also have "peppercorn" hair. Hair in separated tufts, like tight curly hair, leaves space to radiate the heat that rises through the body to the scalp; straight hair lies flat and holds in body heat, like a cap. By viewing Africans as constituting a single race, Americans ignore their greater physical variability, while assigning racial significance to lesser differences between them.

Although it is true that most inhabitants of northern Europe, east Asia, and central Africa look like Americans' conceptions of one or another of the three purported races, most inhabitants of south Asia, southwest Asia, north Africa, and the Pacific islands do not. Thus, the 19th century view of the human species as comprised of Caucasoid, Mongoloid, and Negroid races, still held by many Americans, is based on a partial and unrepresentative view of human variability. In other words, what is now known about human physical variation does not correspond to what Americans think of as race.

In contrast to the question of the actual physical variation among human beings, there is the question of how people classify that variation. Scientists classify things in scientific taxonomies—chemists' periodic table of the elements, biologists' classification of life forms into kingdoms, phyla, and so forth.

In every culture, people also classify things along culture-specific dimensions of meaning. For example, paper clips and staples are understood by Americans as paper fasteners, and nails are not, even though, in terms of their physical properties, all three consist of differently shaped pieces of metal wire. The physical variation in pieces of metal wire can be seen as analogous to human physical variation; and the categories of cultural meaning, like paper fasteners versus wood fasteners, can be seen as analogous to races. Anthropologists refer to these kinds of classifications as folk taxonomies.

Consider the avocado—is it a fruit or a vegetable? Americans insist it is a vegetable. We eat it in salads with oil and vinegar. Brazilians, on the other hand, would say it is a fruit. They eat it for dessert with lemon juice and sugar.

How can we explain this difference in classification?

The avocado is an edible plant, and the American and Brazilian folk taxonomies, while containing cognate terms, classify some edible plants differently. The avocado does not change. It is the same biological entity, but its folk classification changes, depending on who's doing the classifying.

Human beings are also biological entities. Just as we can ask if an avocado is a fruit or a vegetable, we can ask if a person is white or black. And when we ask race questions, the answers we get come from folk taxonomies, not scientific ones. Terms like "white" or "black" applied to people—or "vegetable" or "fruit" applied to avocados—do not give us biological information about people or avocados. Rather, they exemplify how cultural groups (Brazilians or Americans) classify people and avocados.

Americans believe in "blood," a folk term for the quality presumed to be carried by members of so-called races. And the way offspring—regardless of their physical appearance—always inherit the less prestigious racial category of mixed parentage is called "hypo-descent" by anthropologists. A sentence thoroughly intelligible to most Americans might be, "Since Mary's father is white and her mother is black, Mary is black because she has black 'blood.'" American researchers who think they are studying racial differences in behavior would, like other Americans, classify Mary as black—although she has just as much white "blood."

According to hypo-descent, the various purported racial categories are arranged in a hierarchy along a single dimension, from the most prestigious ("white"), through intermediary forms ("Asian"), to the least prestigious ("black"). And when a couple come from two different categories, all their children (the "descent" in "hypo-descent") are classified as belonging to the less prestigious category (thus, the "hypo"). Hence, all the offspring of one "white" parent and one "black" parent—regardless of the children's physical appearance—are called "black" in the United States.

The American folk concept of "blood" does not behave like genes. Genes are units which cannot be subdivided. When several genes jointly determine a trait, chance decides which ones come from each parent. For example, if eight genes determine a trait, a child gets four from each parent. If a mother and a father each have the hypothetical genes BBBBWWWW, then a child could be born with any combination of B and W genes, from BBBBBBBB to WWWWWWWW. In contrast, the folk concept "blood" behaves like a uniform and continuous entity. It can be divided in two indefinitely—for example, quadroons and octoroons are said to be people who have one-quarter and one-eighth black "blood," respectively. Oddly, because of hypo-descent, Americans consider people with one-eighth black "blood" to be black rather than white, despite their having seven-eighths white "blood."

Hypo-descent, or "blood," is not informative about the physical appearance of people. For example, when two parents called black in the United States have a number of children, the children are likely to vary in physical appearance. In the case of skin color, they might vary from lighter than the lighter parent to darker than the darker parent. However, they would all receive the same racial classification—black—regardless of their skin color.

All that hypo-descent tells you is that, when someone is classified as something other than white (e.g., Asian), at least one of his or her parents is classified in the same way, and that neither parent has a less prestigious classification (e.g., black). That is, hypo-descent is informative about ancestry—specifically, parental classification—rather than physical appearance.

There are many strange consequences of our folk taxonomy. For example, someone who inherited no genes that produce "African"-appearing physical features would still be considered black if he or she has a parent classified as black. The category "passing for white" includes many such people. Americans have the curious belief that people who look white but have a parent classified as black are "really" black in some biological sense, and are being deceptive if they present themselves as white. Such examples make it clear that race is a social rather than a physical classification.

From infancy, human beings learn to recognize very subtle differences in the faces of those around them. Black babies see a wider variety of black faces than white faces, and white babies see a wider variety of white faces than black faces. Because they are exposed only to a limited range of human variation, adult members of each "race" come to see their own group as containing much wider variation than others. Thus, because of this perceptual learning, blacks see greater physical variation among themselves than among whites, while whites see the opposite. In this case, however, there is a clear answer to the question of which group contains greater physical variability. Blacks are correct.

Why is this the case?

Take a moment. Think of yourself as an amateur anthropologist and try to step out of American culture, however briefly.

It is often difficult to get white people to accept what at first appears to contradict the evidence they can see clearly with their own eyes—but which is really the result of a history of perceptual learning. However, the reason that blacks view themselves as more varied is not that their vision is more accurate. Rather, it is that blacks too have a long—but different—history of perceptual learning from that of whites (and also that they have been observers of a larger range of human variation).

The fact of greater physical variation among blacks than whites in America goes back to the principle of hypo-descent, which classifies all people with one black parent and one white parent as black. If they were all considered white, then there would be more physical variation among whites. Someone with one-eighth white "blood" and seven-eighths black "blood" would be considered white; anyone with any white ancestry would be considered white. In other words, what appears to be a difference in biological variability is really a difference in cultural classification.

Perhaps the clearest way to understand that the American folk taxonomy of race is merely one of many—arbitrary and unscientific like all the others—is to contrast it with a very different one, that of Brazil. The Portuguese word that in the Brazilian folk taxonomy corresponds to the American "race" is "*tipo*." *Tipo*, a cognate of the English word "type," is a descriptive term that serves as a kind of shorthand for a series of physical features. Because people's physical features vary separately from one another, there are an awful lot of tipos in Brazil.

Since tipos are descriptive terms, they vary regionally in Brazil—in part reflecting regional differences in the development of colloquial Portuguese, but in part because the physical variation they describe is different in different regions. The Brazilian situation is so complex I will limit my delineation of tipos to some of the main ones used in the city of Salvador, Bahia, to describe people whose physical appearance is understood to be made up of African and European features. (I will use the female terms throughout; in nearly all cases the male term simply changes the last letter from *a* to *o*.)

Proceeding along a dimension from the "whitest" to the "blackest" tipos, a *loura* is whiter-than-white, with straight blond hair, blue or green eyes, light skin color, narrow nose, and thin lips. Brazilians who come to the United States think that a *loura* means a "blond" and are surprised to find that the American term refers to hair color only. A *branca* has light skin color, eyes of any color, hair of any color or form except tight curly, a nose that is not broad, and lips that are not thick. *Branca* translates as "white," though Brazilians of this *tipo* who come to the United States—especially those from elite families—are often dismayed to find that they are not considered white here, and, even worse, are viewed as Hispanic despite the fact that they speak Portuguese.

A *morena* has brown or black hair that is wavy or curly but not tight curly, tan skin, a nose that is not narrow, and lips that are not thin. Brazilians who come to the United States think that a *morena* is a "brunette," and are surprised to find that brunettes are considered white but *morenas* are not. Americans have difficulty classifying *morenas,* many of whom are of Latin American origin: Are they black or Hispanic? (One might also observe that *morenas* have trouble with Americans, for not just accepting their appearance as a given, but asking instead "Where do you come from?" "What language did you speak at home?" "What was your maiden name?" or even, more crudely, "What *are* you?")

A *mulata* looks like a *morena,* except with tight curly hair and a slightly darker range of hair colors and skin colors. A *preta* looks like a *mulata,* except with dark brown skin, broad nose, and thick lips. To Americans, *mulatas* and *pretas* are both black, and if forced to distinguish between them would refer to them as light-skinned blacks and dark-skinned blacks, respectively.

If Brazilians were forced to divide the range of tipos, from *loura* to *preta,* into "kinds of whites" and "kinds of blacks" (a distinction they do not ordinarily make), they would draw the line between *morenas* and *mulatas;* whereas Americans, if offered only visual information, would draw the line between *brancas* and *morenas.*

The proliferation of tipos, and the difference in the white–black dividing line, do not, however, exhaust the differences between Brazilian and American folk taxonomies. There are tipos in the Afro-European domain that are considered to be neither black nor white—an idea that is difficult for Americans visiting Brazil to comprehend. A person with tight curly blond (or red) hair, light skin, blue (or green) eyes, broad nose, and thick lips, is a *sarará.* The opposite features—straight black hair, dark skin, brown eyes, narrow nose, and thin lips—are those of a *cabo verde. Sarará* and *cabo verde* are both tipos that are considered by Brazilians in Salvador, Bahia, to be neither black nor white.

When I interviewed my American daughter and her Brazilian boyfriend, she said she was black because her mother is black (even though I am white). That is, from her American perspective, she has "black blood"—though she is a *morena* in Brazil. Her boyfriend said that he was not black because, viewing himself in terms of Brazilian tipos, he is a *mulato* (not a *preto*).

There are many differences between the Brazilian and American folk taxonomies of race. The American system tells you about how people's parents are classified but not what they look like. The Brazilian system tells you what they look like but not about their parents. When two parents of intermediate appearance have many children in the United States, the children are all of one race; in Brazil they are of many tipos.

Americans believe that race is an immutable biological given, but people (like my daughter and her boyfriend) can change their race by getting on a plane and going from the United States to Brazil—just as, if they take an avocado with them, it changes from a vegetable into a fruit. In both cases, what changes is not the physical appearance of the person or avocado, but the way they are classified.

I have focused on the Brazilian system to make clear how profoundly folk taxonomies of race vary from one place to another. But the Brazilian system is just one of many. Haiti's folk taxonomy, for example, includes elements of both ancestry and physical appearance, and even includes the amazing term (for foreigners of African appearance) *un blanc noir*—literally, "a black white." In the classic study *Patterns of Race in the Americas*, anthropologist Marvin Harris gives a good introduction to the ways in which the conquests by differing European powers of differing New World peoples and ecologies combined with differing patterns of slavery to produce a variety of folk taxonomies. Folk taxonomies of race can be found in many—though by no means all—cultures in other parts of the world as well.

The American concept of race does not correspond to the ways in which human physical appearance varies. Further, the American view of race ("hypo-descent") is just one among many folk taxonomies, [none] of which correspond to the facts of human physical variation. This is why race is a myth and why races as conceived by Americans (and others) do not exist. It is also why differences in behavior between "races" cannot be explained by biological differences between them.

When examining the origins of IQ scores (or other behavior), psychologists sometimes use the term "heritability"—a statistical concept that is not based on observations of genes or chromosomes. It is important to understand that questions about heritability of IQ have nothing to do with racial differences in IQ. "Heritability" refers only to the relative ranking of individuals *within* a population, under given environmental conditions, and not to differences *between* populations. Thus, among the population of American whites, it may be that those with high IQs tend to have higher-IQ children than do those with low IQs. Similarly, among American blacks, it may be that those with high IQs also tend to have higher-IQ children.

In both cases, it is possible that the link between the IQs of parents and children may exist for reasons that are not entirely environmental. This heritability of IQ *within* the two populations, even if it exists, would in no way contradict the average social advantages of American whites as a group compared to the average social disadvantages of American blacks as a group. Such differences in social environments can easily account for any differences in the average test scores *between* the two groups. Thus, the heritability of IQ *within* each group is irrelevant to understanding differences *between* the groups.

Beyond this, though, studies of differences in behavior between "populations" of whites and blacks, which seek to find biological causes rather than only social ones, make a serious logical error. They assume that blacks and whites are populations in some biological sense, as sub-units of the human species. (Most likely, the researchers make this assumption because they are American and approach race in terms of the American folk taxonomy.)

In fact, though, the groups are sorted by a purely social rule for statistical purposes. This can easily be demonstrated by asking researchers how they know that the white subjects are really white and the black subjects are really black. There is no biological answer to this question, because race as a biological category does not exist. All that researchers can say is, "The tester classified them based on their physical appearance," or "Their school records listed their race," or otherwise give a social rather than biological answer.

So when American researchers study racial differences in behavior, in search of biological rather than social causes for differences between socially defined groups, they are wasting their time. Computers are wonderful machines, but we have learned about "garbage in/garbage out." Applying complex computations to bad data yields worthless results. In the same way, the most elegant experimental designs and statistical analyses, applied flawlessly to biologically meaningless racial categories, can only produce a very expensive waste of time.

As immigrants of varied physical appearance come to the United States from countries with racial folk taxonomies different from our own, they are often perplexed and dismayed to find that the ways they classify themselves and others are irrelevant to the American reality. Brazilians, Haitians, and others may find themselves labeled by strange, apparently inappropriate, even pejorative terms, and grouped together with people who are different from and unreceptive to them. This can cause psychological complications (a Brazilian immigrant—who views himself as white—being treated by an American therapist who assumes that he is not).

Immigration has increased, especially from geographical regions whose people do not resemble American images of blacks, whites, or Asians. Intermarriage is also increasing, as the stigma associated with it diminishes. These two trends are augmenting the physical diversity among those who marry each other—and, as a result, among their children. The American folk taxonomy of race (purportedly comprised of stable biological entities) is beginning to change to accommodate this new reality. After all, what race is someone whose four grandparents are black, white, Asian, and Hispanic?

Currently, the most rapidly growing census category is "Other," as increasing numbers of people fail to fit available options. Changes in the census categories every 10 years reflect the government's attempts to grapple with the changing self-identifications of Americans—even as statisticians try to maintain the same categories over time in order to make demographic comparisons. Perhaps they will invent one or more "multiracial" categories, to accommodate the wide range of people whose existence defies current classification. Perhaps they will drop the term "race" altogether. Already some institutions are including an option to "check as many as apply," when asking individuals to classify themselves on a list of racial and ethnic terms.

Thinking in terms of physical appearance and folk taxonomies helps to clarify the emotionally charged but confused topics of race. Understanding that different cultures have different folk taxonomies suggests that we respond to the question "What race is that person?" not by "Black" or "White," but by "Where?" and "When?"

Connection Questions

1. What is the difference between the way "race" is defined in the United States and Brazil?

2. How are "race" and ethnicity related?

3. How does racial stratification impact social inequality? Describe an example of this found in the Miller text.

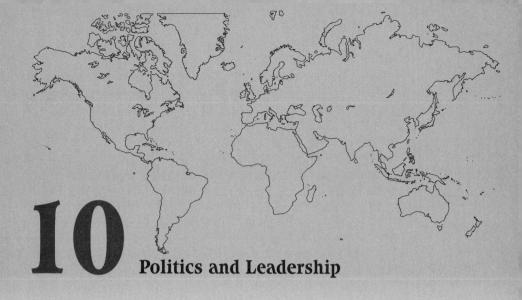

10

Politics and Leadership

Life without Chiefs

Marvin Harris

It may come as a surprise to most Americans, but there were, and in a few cases still are, societies in the world that lack formal political structure. Instead of presidents, mayors, senators, and directors of homeland security, there are headmen, big men, and chiefs who lead by their ability to persuade and impress without the authority to make *people act. In this article, Marvin Harris traces the evolution of political leadership, associating* headmen *with small hunting and gathering societies marked by reciprocal exchange, and* big men *with slightly larger horticultural societies that employ redistributive exchange. Chiefs also occupied the center of redistribution systems but their societies were larger and chiefs could inherit their positions. He concludes that human biological inheritance was shaped by a hunter-gatherer existence; there is nothing inherited about the political formalism and social inequality that characterize large state societies.*

"Was There Life without Chiefs?" from *Our Kind* by Marvin Harris.

Can humans exist without some people ruling and others being ruled? To look at the modern world, you wouldn't think so. Democratic states may have done away with emperors and kings, but they have hardly dispensed with gross inequalities in wealth, rank, and power.

However, humanity hasn't always lived this way. For about 98 percent of our existence as a species (and for four million years before then), our ancestors lived in small, largely nomadic hunting-and-gathering bands containing about 30 to 50 people apiece. It was in this social context that human nature evolved. It has been only about ten thousand years since people began to settle down into villages, some of which eventually grew into cities. And it has been only in the last two thousand years that the majority of people in the world have not lived in hunting-and-gathering societies. This brief period of time is not nearly sufficient for noticeable evolution to have taken place. Thus, the few remaining foraging societies are the closest analogues we have to the "natural" state of humanity.

To judge from surviving examples of hunting-and-gathering bands and villages, our kind got along quite well for the greater part of prehistory without so much as a paramount chief. In fact, for tens of thousands of years, life went on without kings, queens, prime ministers, presidents, parliaments, congresses, cabinets, governors, and mayors—not to mention the police officers, sheriffs, marshals, generals, lawyers, bailiffs, judges, district attorneys, court clerks, patrol cars, paddy wagons, jails, and penitentiaries that help keep them in power. How in the world did our ancestors ever manage to leave home without them?

Small populations provide part of the answer. With 50 people per band or 150 per village, everybody knew everybody else intimately. People gave with the expectation of taking and took with the expectation of giving. Because chance played a great role in the capture of animals, collection of wild foodstuffs, and success of rudimentary forms of agriculture, the individuals who had the luck of the catch on one day needed a handout on the next. So the best way for them to provide for their inevitable rainy day was to be generous. As expressed by anthropologist Richard Gould, "The greater the amount of risk, the greater the extent of sharing." Reciprocity is a small society's bank.

In reciprocal exchange, people do not specify how much or exactly what they expect to get back or when they expect to get it. That would besmirch the quality of that transaction and make it similar to mere barter or to buying and selling. The distinction lingers on in societies dominated by other forms of exchange, even capitalist ones. For we do carry out a give-and-take among close kin and friends that is informal, uncalculating, and imbued with a spirit of generosity. Teenagers do not pay cash for their meals at home or for the use of the family car, wives do not bill their husbands for cooking a meal, and friends give each other birthday gifts and Christmas presents. But much of this is marred by the expectation that our generosity will be acknowledged with expression of thanks.

Where reciprocity really prevails in daily life, etiquette requires that generosity be taken for granted. As Robert Dentan discovered during his fieldwork among the Semai of Central Malaysia, no one ever says "thank you" for the meat received from another hunter. Having struggled all day to lug the carcass of a pig home through the jungle heat, the hunter allows his prize to be cut up into exactly equal portions, which he then gives away to the entire group. Dentan explains that to express gratitude for the portion received indicates that you are the kind of ungenerous person who calculates how much you give and take: "In this context, saying 'thank you' is very rude, for it suggests, first, that one has calculated the amount of a gift and, second, that one did not expect the donor to be so generous." To call attention to one's generosity is to indicate that others are in debt to you and that you expect them to repay you. It is repugnant to egalitarian peoples even to suggest that they have been treated generously.

Canadian anthropologist Richard Lee tells how, through a revealing incident, he learned about this aspect of reciprocity. To please the !Kung, the "bushmen" of the Kalahari desert, he decided to buy a large ox and have it slaughtered as a present. After days of searching Bantu agricultural villages for the largest and fattest ox in the region, he acquired what appeared to be a perfect specimen. But his friends took him aside and assured him that he had been duped into buying an absolutely worthless animal. "Of course, we will eat it," they said, "but it won't fill us up—we will eat and go home to bed with stomachs rumbling." Yet, when Lee's ox was slaughtered, it turned out to be covered with a thick layer of fat. Later, his friends explained why they had said his gift was valueless, even though they knew better than he what lay under the animal's skin.

"Yes, when a young man kills much meat he comes to think of himself as a chief or a big man, and he thinks of the rest of us as his servants or inferiors. We can't accept this. We refuse one who boasts, for someday his pride will make him kill somebody. So we always speak of his meat as worthless. This way we cool his heart and make him gentle."

Lee watched small groups of men and women returning home every evening with the animals and wild fruits and plants that they had killed or collected. They shared everything equally, even with campmates who had stayed behind and spent the day sleeping or taking care of their tools and weapons.

"Not only do families pool that day's production, but the entire camp—residents and visitors alike—shares equally in the total quantity of food available," Lee observed. "The evening meal of any one family is made up of portions of food from each of the other families resident. There is a constant flow of nuts, berries, roots, and melons from one family fire-place to another, until each person has received an equitable portion. The following morning a different combination of foragers moves out of camp, and when they return late in the day, the distribution of foodstuffs is repeated."

In small, prestate societies, it was in everybody's best interest to maintain each other's freedom of access to the natural habitat. Suppose a !Kung with a lust for power were to get up and tell his campmates, "From now on, all this land and everything on it belongs to me. I'll let you use it but only with my permission and on the condition that I get first choice of anything you capture, collect, or grow." His campmates, thinking that he had certainly gone crazy, would pack up their few belongings, take a long walk, make a new camp, and resume their usual life of egalitarian reciprocity. The man who would be king would be left by himself to exercise a useless sovereignty.

The Headman: Leadership, Not Power

To the extent that political leadership exists at all among band-and-village societies, it is exercised by individuals called headmen. These headmen, however, lack the power to compel others to obey their orders. How can a leader be powerless and still lead?

The political power of genuine rulers depends on their ability to expel or exterminate disobedient individuals and groups. When a headman gives a command, however, he has no certain physical means of punishing those who disobey. So, if he wants to stay in "office," he gives few commands. Among the Eskimo, for instance, a group will follow an outstanding hunter and defer to his opinion with respect to choice of hunting spots. But in all other matters, the leader's opinion carries no more weight than any other man's. Similarly, among the !Kung, each band has its recognized leaders, most of whom are males. These men speak out more than others and are listened to with a bit more deference. But they have no formal authority and can only persuade, never command. When Lee asked the !Kung whether they had headmen—meaning powerful chiefs—they told him, "Of course we have headmen! In fact, we are all headmen. Each one of us is headman over himself."

Headmanship can be a frustrating and irksome job. Among Indian groups such as the Mehinacu of Brazil's Zingu National Park, headmen behave something like zealous scoutmasters on overnight cookouts. The first one up in the morning, the headman tries to rouse his companions by standing in the middle of the village plaza and shouting to them. If something needs to be done, it is the headman who starts doing it, and it is the headman who works harder than anyone else. He sets an example not only for hard work but also for generosity: After a fishing or hunting expedition, he gives away more of his catch than anyone else does. In trading with other groups, he must be careful not to keep the best items for himself.

In the evening, the headman stands in the center of the plaza and exhorts his people to be good. He calls upon them to control their sexual appetites, work hard in their gardens, and take frequent baths in the river. He tells them not to sleep during the day or bear grudges against each other.

Coping with Freeloaders

During the reign of reciprocal exchange and egalitarian headmen, no individual, family, or group smaller than the band or village itself could control access to natural resources. Rivers, lakes, beaches, oceans, plants and animals, the soil and subsoil were all communal property.

Among the !Kung, a core of people born in a particular territory say that they "own" the water holes and hunting rights, but this has no effect on the people who happen to be visiting and living with them at any given time. Since !Kung from neighboring bands are related through marriage, they often visit each other for months at a time and have free use of whatever resources they need without having to ask permission. Though people from distant bands must make a request to use another band's territory, the "owners" seldom refuse them.

The absence of private possession in land and other vital resources means that a form of communism probably existed among prehistoric hunting and collecting bands and small villages. Perhaps I should emphasize that this did not rule out the existence of private property. People in simple band-and-village societies own personal effects such as weapons, clothing, containers, ornaments, and tools. But why should anyone want to steal such objects? People who have a bush camp and move about a lot have no use for extra possessions. And since the group is small enough that everybody knows everybody else, stolen items cannot be used anonymously. If you want something, better to ask for it openly, since by the rules of reciprocity such requests cannot be denied.

I don't want to create the impression that life within egalitarian band-and-village societies unfolded entirely without disputes over possessions. As in every social group, nonconformists and malcontents tried to use the system for their own advantage. Inevitably there were freeloaders, individuals who consistently took more than they gave and lay back in their hammocks while others did the work. Despite the absence of a criminal justice system, such behavior eventually was punished. A widespread belief among band-and-village peoples attributes death and misfortune to the malevolent conspiracy of sorcerers. The task of identifying these evildoers falls to a group's shamans, who remain responsive to public opinion during their divinatory trances. Well-liked individuals who enjoy strong support from their families need not fear the shaman. But quarrelsome, stingy people who do not give as well as take had better watch out.

From Headman to Big Man

Reciprocity was not the only form of exchange practiced by egalitarian band-and-village peoples. Our kind long ago found other ways to give and take. Among them the form of exchange known as redistribution played a crucial role in creating distinctions of rank during the evolution of chiefdoms and states.

Redistribution occurs when people turn over food and other valuables to a prestigious figure such as a headman, to be pooled, divided into separate portions, and given out again. The primordial form of redistribution was probably keyed to seasonal hunts and harvests, when more food than usual became available.

True to their calling, headmen-redistributors not only work harder than their followers but also give more generously and reserve smaller and less desirable portions for themselves than for anyone else. Initially, therefore, re-distribution strictly reinforced the political and economic equality associated with reciprocal exchange. The redistributors were compensated purely with ad-miration and in proportion to their success in giving bigger feasts, in person-ally contributing more than anybody else, and in asking little or nothing for their effort, all of which initially seemed an innocent extension of the basic prin-ciple of reciprocity.

But how little our ancestors understood what they were getting themselves into! For if it is a good thing to have a headman give feasts, why not have sev-eral headmen give feasts? Or, better yet, why not let success in organizing and giving feasts be the measure of one's legitimacy as a headman? Soon, where conditions permit, there are several would-be headmen vying with each other to hold the most lavish feasts and redistribute the most food and other valu-ables. In this fashion there evolved the nemesis that Richard Lee's !Kung infor-mants had warned about: the youth who wants to be a "big man."

A classic anthropological study of big men was carried out by Douglas Oliver among the Siuai, a village people who live on the South Pacific island of Bougainville, in the Solomon Islands. In the Siuai language, big men were known as *mumis*. Every Siuai boy's highest ambition was to become a *mumi*. He began by getting married, working hard, and restricting his own con-sumption of meats and coconuts. His wife and parents, impressed with the se-riousness of his intentions, vowed to help him prepare for his first feast. Soon his circle of supporters widened and he began to construct a clubhouse in which his male followers could lounge about and guests could be entertained and fed. He gave a feast at the consecration of the clubhouse; if this was a suc-cess, the circle of people willing to work for him grew larger still, and he began to hear himself spoken of as a mumi. Larger and larger feasts meant that the mumi's demands on his supporters became more irksome. Although they grumbled about how hard they had to work, they remained loyal as long as their mumi continued to maintain and increase his renown as a "great provider."

Finally the time came for the new mumi to challenge the older ones. He did this at a *muminai* feast, where both sides kept a tally of all the pigs, coconut pies, and sago-almond puddings given away by the host mumi and his follow-ers to the guest mumi and his followers. If the guests could not reciprocate with a feast as lavish as that of the challengers, their mumi suffered a great social humiliation, and his fall from mumihood was immediate.

At the end of a successful feast, the greatest of mumis still faced a lifetime of personal toil and dependence on the moods and inclinations of his follow-ers. Mumihood did not confer the power to coerce others into doing one's bid-ding, nor did it elevate one's standard of living above anyone else's. In fact, because giving things away was the essence of mumihood, great mumis con-sumed less meat and other delicacies than ordinary men. Among the Kaoka, another Solomon Islands group, there is the saying, "The giver of the feast takes the bones and the stale cakes; the meat and the fat go to the others." At one great feast attended by 1,100 people, the host mumi, whose name was Soni, gave away thirty-two pigs and a large quantity of sago-almond puddings. Soni himself and some of his closest followers went hungry. "We shall eat Soni's renown," they said.

From Big Man to Chief

The slide (or ascent?) toward social stratification gained momentum wherever extra food produced by the inspired diligence of redistributors could be stored while awaiting muminai feasts, potlatches, and other occasions of redistribution. The more concentrated and abundant the harvest and the less perishable the crop, the greater its potential for endowing the big man with power. Though others would possess some stored-up foods of their own, the redistributor's stores would be the largest. In times of scarcity, people would come to him, expecting to be fed; in return, he could call upon those who had special skills to make cloth, pots, canoes, or a fine house for his own use. Eventually, the redistributor no longer needed to work in the fields to gain and surpass bigman status. Management of the harvest surpluses, a portion of which continued to be given to him for use in communal feasts and other communal projects (such as trading expeditions and warfare), was sufficient to validate his status. And, increasingly, people viewed this status as an office, a sacred trust, passed on from one generation to the next according to the rules of hereditary succession. His dominion was no longer a small, autonomous village but a large political community. The big man had become a chief.

Returning to the South Pacific and the Trobriand Islands, one can catch a glimpse of how these pieces of encroaching stratification fell into place. The Trobrianders had hereditary chiefs who held sway over more than a dozen villages containing several thousand people. Only chiefs could wear certain shell ornaments as the insignia of high rank, and it was forbidden for commoners to stand or sit in a position that put a chief's head at a lower elevation. British anthropologist Bronislaw Malinowski tells of seeing all the people present in the village of Bwoytalu drop from their verandas "as if blown down by a hurricane" at the sound of a drawn-out cry warning that an important chief was approaching.

Yams were the Trobrianders' staff of life; the chiefs validated their status by storing and redistributing copious quantities of them acquired through donations from their brothers-in-law at harvest time. Similar "gifts" were received by husbands who were commoners, but chiefs were polygynous and, having as many as a dozen wives, received many more yams than anyone else. Chiefs placed their yam supply on display racks specifically built for this purpose next to their houses. Commoners did the same, but a chief's yam racks towered over all the others.

This same pattern recurs, with minor variations, on several continents. Striking parallels were seen, for example, twelve thousand miles away from the

Trobrianders, among chiefdoms that flourished throughout the southeastern region of the United States—specifically among the Cherokee, former inhabitants of Tennessee, as described by the eighteenth-century naturalist William Bartram.

At the center of the principal Cherokee settlements stood a large circular house where a council of chiefs discussed issues involving their villages and where redistributive feasts were held. The council of chiefs had a paramount who was the principal figure in the Cherokee redistributive network. At the harvest time a large crib, identified as the "chief's granary," was erected in each field. "To this," explained Bartram, "each family carries and deposits a certain quantity according to his ability or inclination, or none at all if he so chooses." The chief's granaries functioned as a public treasury in case of crop failure, a source of food for strangers or travelers, and as military store. Although every citizen enjoyed free access to the store, commoners had to acknowledge that it really belonged to the supreme chief, who had "an exclusive right and ability . . . to distribute comfort and blessings to the necessitous."

Supported by voluntary donations, chiefs could now enjoy lifestyles that set them increasingly apart from their followers. They could build bigger and finer houses for themselves, eat and dress more sumptuously, and enjoy the sexual favors and personal services of several wives. Despite these harbingers, people in chiefdoms voluntarily invested unprecedented amounts of labor on behalf of communal projects. They dug moats, threw up defensive earthen embankments, and erected great log palisades around their villages. They heaped up small mountains of rubble and soil to form platforms and mounds on top of which they built temples and big houses for their chief. Working in teams and using nothing but levers and rollers, they moved rocks weighing fifty tons or more and set them in precise lines and perfect circles, forming sacred precincts for communal rituals marking the change of seasons.

If this seems remarkable, remember that donated labor created the megalithic alignments of Stonehenge and Carnac, put up the great statues on Easter Island, shaped the huge stone heads of the Olmec in Vera Cruz, dotted Polynesia with ritual precincts set on great stone platforms, and filled the Ohio, Tennessee, and Mississippi valleys with hundreds of large mounds. Not until it was too late did people realize that their beautiful chiefs were about to keep the meat and fat for themselves while giving nothing but bones and stale cakes to their followers.

In the End

As we know, chiefdoms would eventually evolve into states, states into empires. From peaceful origins, humans created and mounted a wild beast that ate continents. Now that beast has taken us to the brink of global annihilation.

Will nature's experiment with mind and culture end in nuclear war? No one knows the answer. But I believe it is essential that we understand our past before we can create the best possible future. Once we are clear about the roots of human nature, for example, we can refute, once and for all, the notion that it is a biological imperative for our kind to form hierarchical groups. An observer viewing human life shortly after cultural takeoff would easily have concluded that our species was destined to be irredeemably egalitarian except for distinctions of sex and age. That someday the world would be divided into aristocrats and commoners, masters and slaves, billionaires and homeless beggars would have seemed wholly contrary to human nature as evidenced in the affairs of every human society then on Earth.

Of course, we can no more reverse the course of thousands of years of cultural evolution than our egalitarian ancestors could have designed and built the space shuttle. Yet, in striving for the preservation of mind and culture on Earth, it is vital that we recognize the significance of cultural takeoff and the great difference between biological and cultural evolution. We must rid ourselves of the notion that we are an innately aggressive species for whom war is inevitable. We must reject as unscientific claims that there are superior and inferior races and that the hierarchical divisions within and between societies are the consequences of natural selection rather than of a long process of cultural evolution. We must struggle to gain control over cultural selection through objective studies of the human condition and the recurrent process of history. Not only a more just society, but our very survival as a species may depend on it.

Connection Questions

1. What is the difference among headmen, big men, and chiefs according to Harris?

2. How do these positions resemble leadership roles in your society?

3. What is political anthropology?

4. How do outside forces affect the political organization of a society?

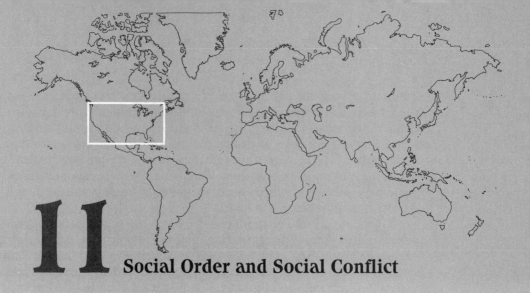

II Social Order and Social Conflict

Notes from an Expert Witness

Barbara Joans

North Americans increasingly live in a multicultural society that can easily generate disputes based on cross-cultural misunderstanding. As a result, anthropologists who had never thought of working outside the teaching profession have been called on to testify in cases that involve expert knowledge about a culture. But some anthropologists have found that their broad training in anthropology's four fields and their preparation in ethnographic research methods enables them to serve as expert witnesses in cases that don't require prior knowledge of a particular culture. Instead, they come to the task with anthropological tools that permit them to develop appropriate testimony. This is what happened to the author of this article, Barbara Joans. She describes three cases where she served as an expert witness: a dispute between a welfare agency and Bannock-Shoshoni women, a civil case between a Plains Indian family and a funeral home over the mistaken cremation of a relative, and a child custody case pitting the anthropologist against a court-appointed psychologist. Joans relates how she was able to use her training in anthropological linguistics, ethnographic interviewing, ethnohistorical research, and the ability to spot cultural difference and ethnocentrism to discover evidence and prepare court briefs. Her experience illustrates the unique legal role anthropologists can play in an increasingly multicultural society.

In December 1978, a lawyer from the Idaho Legal Aid Society contacted me for help. He was representing six Bannock-Shoshoni women who were accused of withholding financial information while receiving supplemental security income (SSI). By that point in my life, I had settled on a career as an academic. My goal was to teach anthropology in a college or university, and that was what I was doing at Idaho State University in Pocatello when the lawyer approached me. I had not thought too much about the practical application of cultural anthropology although I knew that some anthropologists had always applied their academic knowledge. For example, several had advised the U.S. Government about societies the military would encounter during World War II and others were (and still are) involved in the design of overseas development programs following the War. Instead, the lure of the discipline for me had been its power to understand cultural groups in their own terms. Like most new graduate anthropologists in those days, my goal was to teach students how to acquire this cross-cultural perspective.

Although my career as an academic anthropologist is still primary—I teach college students and am the director of a museum—my perspective on the usefulness of anthropology changed when I accepted the lawyer's invitation. I was to become an expert witness and discover that my training as a cultural anthropologist, as well as in anthropology's other fields (anthropological linguistics, archaeology, and biological anthropology), was a practical asset in court. This, it turned out, was especially true because so many disputes that reach court involve cross-cultural misunderstandings that lead to conflict. Since that time I have served as an expert witness in several cases where anthropological training and perspective proved useful. Let me discuss three of them: the original case mentioned above about alleged income fraud in Pocatello, a dispute among American Indians over the disposal of the dead, and a child custody case in California.

Problems in Pocatello

One thousand Bannock-Shoshoni Indians live on the Fort Hall Indian reservation located about 10 miles from the southeast Idaho city of Pocatello. Life on the reservations is hard. Although the land is mostly desert, residents scrape out a meager living by farming. Some also make pottery and jewelry, which they sell to nearby townspeople. A few of the Indians rent part of their land to local Anglos for a small annual income.

It was this rent income that got six Bannock-Shoshoni women, all over sixty years old, in trouble with the Pocatello Social Services. The women were eligible for supplemental security income (SSI), which was distributed by the agency. SSI rules stated that recipients had to declare all their income each year to ensure their eligibility. The agency claimed that the women had failed to declare their land rent money in 1978 and therefore had to return their SSI income, which amounted to about $2,000 for each of them. The women, who had no way to pay this amount, claimed they didn't know they had to include the rent income in the annual statement, and the dispute ended up in court.

The issue before the court seemed clear. Had the Indian women understood what was expected of them? Finding a way to answer this question became my main task and language seemed to be the key. Although not a fully trained linguist, I did have "four-fields" training in anthropology as a graduate student. One of those fields is anthropological-linguistics, so I felt capable of using language as the criterion for cultural understanding in the Pocatello case. Because all the verbal exchanges between the Bannock-Shoshoni women and the SSI staff members had taken place in English (the rules regarding SSI were explained in English to the women at a community lunch meeting on the reservation), and the women normally spoke Bannock or Shoshoni as their everyday language, I chose the women's comprehension of English as an index of their general cultural understanding. If the Indian women had sufficiently understood the English used to explain SSI requirements to them, then the Pocatello Social Service people would have a justified claim. If the women's understanding of English was incomplete, the defense could make a good case for misunderstanding.

Even without any evidence I could have made the argument in court that because English was not the defendants' native language, they had been unable to understand the SSI rules. The prosecution would have countered, however, that the women could easily be observed carrying on conversations in English, which meant they could understand the rules, but flaunted them. I clearly needed a way to determine the women's *level* of English comprehension, not just their ability to speak it to some extent. To do this, I created a three-part system to test the English language sophistication of the Indian women.

Level one consisted of everyday common speech. For example, I asked questions in English such as "Are you hungry? Are you cold? How are you feeling?" From their answers, it was clear that all the women could understand English at this level.

Level two was more complex. Could they joke in English and understand the double-entendres, the mixed meanings, and the puns associated with jokes. Because they often joked about the behavior of Pocatello officials in their own language, I presented them with jokes in English about the same individuals. At this level, only one woman was able to follow my conversation and "get" what was funny about what I was saying.

Level three involved an understanding of the rules and regulations governing Indian lives and the ability to articulate rules in English. Even the woman who was able to joke about Pocatello officials in English could not articulate the government rules using that language. Although she could describe *reservation* rules using English, she could not use it successfully to explain the regulations presented to them in English by non-Indian Pocatello officials.

In short, all six Bannock Shoshoni women could speak and understand an everyday brand of English. One of them could even handle the nuances of joking in English. It was this ability that had lead Pocatello officials to *assume* the women could comprehend SSI rules written and stated in English. But my research revealed and my testimony would state that none of them understood governmental English. The "crime," I concluded, was clearly a case of cross-cultural misunderstanding based on lack of language competence and the women's failure to declare their rent income was, therefore, unintended.

I presented this evidence and my conclusions in court, and was gratified when the women were cleared of any misconduct. More than that, the case managed to effect some permanent change in the dealings between Pocatello officials and the Bannock-Shoshoni. From then on, both Bannock and Shoshoni languages had to be used in conjunction with English at all agency-related meetings. To prevent future misunderstandings, interpreters now had to be present at all times. For the first time in Idaho, variant cultural language patterns and cultural understandings were accepted in court as determinants of behavior. The Indian women had their day in court and had won. They also gained control over their economic resources.

The Unfortunate Cremation

The second case involved a civil suit. Several years ago I was hired to be an expert witness in a dispute between a Northwestern Plains Indian family and a funeral home. Once again, the dispute revolved around lack of communication and cultural differences. In this case the primary issue was the way the body of an American Indian should be treated. Several family members of a fairly typical Plains Indian group living in Northwestern United States faced a difficult situation. A deceased family member who had lived far away from home for over fifty years died and was, by mistake, wrongfully cremated. The family was furious. The employees at the funeral home where the cremation took place were remorseful. They had followed instructions to cremate the body given to them based on hospital records and these turned out to be wrong.

When members of the deceased family found out what had happened, they claimed that according to their religion, cremation was an abomination. Citing their Indian beliefs, the family feared that the dead man would never be able to find his homeland again and so would never rest in peace. They sued the funeral home for substantial damages.

The funeral service personnel were apologetic and contrite but the deed had been done. They could not take it back. From their perspective there had been a mistake, but one that was innocent and that did not warrant the large financial penalty sought by the family. Indeed, if the family won the award they were asking, it would bankrupt the business.

There was a second complication. It was not possible to verify with certainty that the ashes residing at the funeral home were entirely those of the deceased, because they may have been mixed with those of several other people. Given this situation, the deceased's family also claimed they should be compensated because no proper Plains Indian rituals and end-of-life ceremonies could ever be performed.

I was retained as an expert witness to evaluate several matters. Were the plaintiff's assertions about cremation commensurate with their traditional Indian beliefs? Did the fact that the deceased had left home many years before and was out of touch with family members matter in Indian society? Could funeral rites and disposal of the remains be accomplished under Indian custom if someone was cremated?

Most of my inquiry involved the methods of ethnohistory. To find out if cremation was ever used as an acceptable end-of-life ceremony, I collected information about both traditional and modern American Indian views concerning the care of the dead. Library research, rather than participant observation and linguistic analysis, was the main mode of inquiry. In the course of my research, I discovered three important facts: Under certain though admittedly unusual circumstances, cremation had occurred in Indian society. I also learned that there are many ways that Indians conduct funeral ceremonies and that these can be done even in the absence of *any* physical remains. Finally, I discovered that under traditional circumstances, Indian family members would not go fifty years without seeing important relatives. The deceased, himself, had defied Indian cultural norms.

This led me to ask some important questions. Since so much time had elapsed between family visits, was the grief expressed by family members genuine? Second, given the fact that family members (as it turned out) had not known where the deceased had been living, had his cremation genuinely offended the family's sense of tribal tradition or were they simply seeking revenge? And was the suit simply a way to make money? Finally, although the family was indeed injured, was their litigation also a way to deflect the pain and guilt associated with a lifetime of family avoidance and neglect toward the deceased?

In the end, my report resulted in an out-of-court settlement. Research indicated that fifty years was a long time for family members to stay out of touch. It also indicated that historically, tribal warriors who died far from home in battle were often cremated and that Plains Indians had held proper memorial services over their ashes. The differing parties read the report, the anthropological brief, considered the analysis, and decided to settle out of court. They used the anthropological brief as a guideline for resolving their differences and deciding on a fair settlement for all involved. The family received a sizable settlement and the funeral establishment was able to stay in business.

Coming to this settlement was not easy for the Indian family. They had to acknowledge that for their Indian Nation, fifty years was a long time to go between visits, especially since they had not been in touch with, nor tried to contact the deceased during that time. They also had to recognize that they had deliberately disregarded tribal history and traditions.

To reach this point in negotiations, family members had to experience and accept a number of attitudinal changes. First was to recognize that there were alternative forms of ceremonial burial and to acknowledge that ash, even mixed and impure ash remains, could be used in ceremonial ways. They also had to accept that they could still orchestrate memorial services and participate in traditional Plains Indian rituals in spite of the fact that the bodily remains were in the form of ash. With attitudinal change, they could recognize that cremation was not totally foreign to their traditions. Finally, family members had to recognize that they were and still are a people who have a wide variety of acceptable customs and that they still hold within themselves the ability to create new customs, new patterns, and use cultural adaptability to perform a fitting final ceremony for their deceased relative.

Child Custody: Anthropology versus Psychology

The third case, which involved a child custody dispute, illustrates a different issue: whether or not an anthropological brief that looks at differences in cultural values and expectations can be considered expert testimony along with expert opinion prepared by a psychologist. Unlike the cases described above, which involved American Indians and thus more obvious cross-cultural contrast and a clearer legitimate need for anthropological opinion, the welfare of a child within mainstream U.S. culture is a different matter and psychologists have regularly played the central role in such matters. Psychology is a long-established human science in the United States and psychological explanations appeal to culturally individualistic North Americans. Child psychologists have produced decades of research on child socialization and its impact on young, growing personalities. Anthropologists, on the other hand, are concerned more with the shared cultural rules of child training and the broader social contexts in which children are raised, a point of view that I was to present in a California courtroom in the context of a bitterly contested child custody case.

In 1994, I was hired by the child's father's counsel to act as an expert witness in family court. Both father and mother were battling for custody of their two-year-old daughter. The father wanted shared custody; the mother wanted complete custody. The mother, just divorced from the child's father and again pregnant, was planning both her second marriage and her departure from the United States. Her new family would be living abroad. The father was fighting not only for joint custody, but for the ability to continue being part of his child's life.

As is the issue in many child custody disputes, the case hinged on the adequacy of child care and parental effectiveness. The father, through a previous court order, had had temporary custody. Now he was asking for shared custody. In keeping with her new life, the mother wanted sole custody of the infant. This would enable her to move abroad.

The court-appointed psychologist conducted visits to the homes of both parents, and on the basis of his observations judged the mother to be the better parent. The mother's home was, at the time of his visit, child-free, because she did not have immediate custody and there were no other children living with her. She was offering, however, what would become a nuclear family arrangement complete with stay-at-home mother, new husband, and about-to-be-born half-sibling. Her uncluttered child-free home was described, in the psychologist's report, as elegant and spacious.

My anthropological approach was different. I also based my expert opinion on home visits, but in the anthropological tradition, on visits that lasted many hours for many days in both parental settings. On the basis of my observations, I judged the father to be an excellent parent. He lived close to his own parents and siblings. He hired a full-time nanny who daily brought the child to her cousin's home for play. The grandparents played an important custodial role. In short, it was like the extended families observed by anthropologists in many societies, fully operational and amazingly functional. The child was thriving.

But these observations were unimportant to the psychiatrist. He observed that the father's home was cluttered and furnished with aging, scratched furniture. The fact that the furniture was old, comfortable, and extremely child-friendly impressed him as a sign of careless housekeeping and sloppy home management rather than child-comfortable and user-friendly. On the other hand, he perceived the mother's then-childless home as a model of good taste; a clean and orderly environment ideal for child raising. And ethnicity and class probably played roles in his view as well. The mother, with an upper middle class home and Anglo-heritage appeared to him to provide a better environment than the one offered by the father, with his working-class Italian ancestry. The psychiatrist concluded on these bases that the mother would be the best parent for her little daughter.

Psychologists, like other social scientists, are neither neutral nor value-free. They, like the rest of the social science professional community, carry their socialization as Americans within. As a result, they rarely challenge U.S. evaluations of class-based behavior and values, or family structure. This is reflected in their evaluations of who will make the most suitable parents in custody cases. Major among these stereotypes, and clearly within the psychologist's court report, was the belief that the *nuclear family* is superior to other kinds of arrangements and that the mother–child bond is always the primary one.

As an anthropologist I also view the maternal bond as crucial, but not the only one of significance. In my evaluation of the father's home, I was struck by the significance of the child's social relationships. These were forged within a wholesome and happy multi-generational *extended family*. The family not only shared ritual events, such as birthdays, anniversaries, and national holidays together, they participated together in important, small, everyday proceedings as well. For example, all the cousins had milk and dessert daily at a big, wooden, scratched, and worn kitchen table. In contrast, the mother, pregnant with her husband-to-be's child, could at best offer her daughter space in a carefully manicured house as part of a blended family where she might eventually become the family stepchild. Taken to another country, it would be probable that the little girl would never see her father or extended kin again. Visiting her abroad would present a nearly insurmountable barrier for a working-class family.

Anthropologists go into situations with a cross-cultural focus, one that is broadened by exposure to countless descriptions of different cultural contexts. They know that many societies are organized around extended families, and that children can thrive under these conditions. They also know that neatness and cleanliness in the North American sense does not necessarily guarantee successful child-raising in the context of U.S. nuclear families.

Participant observation requires that we look at the total environment, both physical and social, and the specific family circumstances to make judgments about child welfare. By approaching people with this inclusive perspective, it is often possible to get answers to questions that at first we had not thought to ask. In the child custody case, I observed the broader picture of the child's living situation, one that included the human as well as the economic content, and discovered a smooth, well-functioning extended family that had been thriving for generations. I presented my findings in a carefully written document to the court.

. . . In order to be taken seriously by the court, lawyers, and the judge, and to maximize the impact of my testimony, I had to look the professional part. . . . Unfortunately, professional dress and my credentials as an anthropologist were not enough. My anthropological brief, written as a court document, summarized my findings and examined how and why my analysis differed from the psychologist's. The brief also contained questions to be asked and answered in court, thus allowing me to reveal my own analysis of the situation. I was able to provide the court with a fresh perspective on the diversity of U.S. patterns of family life. I was also able to confirm that the nuclear family represents only one type of American family and frequently not the most common one.

Regrettably, the judge, while allowing my testimony, did not allow my brief to be entered into the court records. He permitted my research bibliography and *vita* to be submitted as evidence of competency, but refused the anthropological brief under the grounds that it would violate an initial court agreement that stipulated there would be only one social science professional (i.e., the court-appointed psychologist) permitted to submit a written evaluation. My inability to have my cultural analysis accepted as a written brief clearly weakened the father's case.

The judge took all the papers minus my brief home to consider his verdict, relying only on his recollection of what I had said in court. From the beginning, the admissibility of an anthropological perspective was suspect in his eyes. He had cross-examined me and my credentials for over an hour before he permitted my testimony. But in the end, he considered the psychologist the "real" expert on child welfare.

Even though the judge permitted my testimony, it is clear to me that anthropology has a long way to go before courts treat our field with the same kind of respect afforded psychology. Yet, in spite of the defeat, anthropology did establish a foothold in a professional courtroom setting. This foothold had previously belonged, at least in California, mainly to psychologists. Anthropological analysis was finally seen as appropriate to use in child custody issues. The community of lawyers, once the judge ruled that I could speak, apparently looked favorably on the entrance of another professional into their domain. Unfortunately, being unable to have my anthropological brief accepted as case appropriate analysis lost, for my client, the critical writings that might have won a more favorable decision. We lost the decision.

These days, over half of the anthropologists who are granted PhDs find careers entirely outside the academic setting. They work for environmental consulting firms, advertising agencies, government bureaus, and manufacturing companies among others. But it is also clear that in today's multicultural world, anthropological expertise has become increasingly useful and important in the settlement of disputes and that even full-time academics such as myself can play a significant role in the legal arena.

Connection Questions

1. According to Miller, what is social control, and what are the two major instruments of social control?

2. How are these present in the case of the Bannock-Soshoni women?

3. What aspect of the author's anthropological training was especially useful in the dispute between the Plains Indian family and the funeral home?

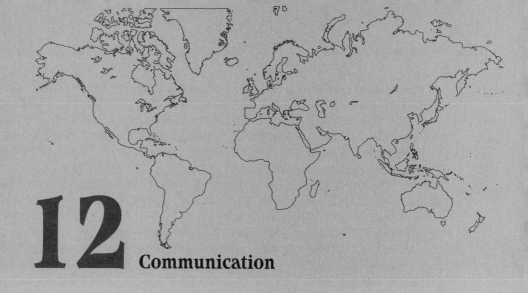

12 Communication

The Sapir-Whorf Hypothesis: Worlds Shaped by Words

David S. Thomson

For many people, language mirrors reality. Words are labels for what we sense; they record what is already there. This view, which is another manifestation of what we have called naive realism, *is clearly challenged by previous selections in this book. Members of different societies may not share cultural categories; words from one language often cannot be translated directly into another. In the 1930s, a young linguist named Benjamin Lee Whorf took the objection to the "words label reality" assertion one step further by arguing that words and grammatical structure actually shape reality. This piece by David Thomson describes Whorf's theory, shows how linguists have evaluated it, and applies it in modified form to the use of words, euphemisms, and doublespeak in the modern United States.*

The scene is the storage room at a chemical plant. The time is evening. A night watchman enters the room and notes that it is partially filled with gasoline drums. The drums are in a section of the room where a sign says "Empty Barrels." The watchman lights a cigarette and throws the still-hot match into one of the empty barrels.

The result: an explosion.

The immediate cause of the explosion, of course, was the gasoline fumes that remained in the barrels. But it could be argued that a second cause of the explosion was the English language. The barrels were empty of their original contents and so belonged under the empty sign. Yet they were not empty of everything—the fumes were still present. English has no word—no single term—that can convey such a situation. Containers in English are either empty or they are not; there is no word describing the ambiguous state of being empty and yet not empty. There is no term in the language for "empty but not quite" or "empty of original contents but with something left over." There being no word for such an in-between state, it did not occur to the watchman to think of the explosive fumes.

This incident is hypothetical, but the questions about language it raises are real. The example of the gasoline drums often was cited by Benjamin Lee Whorf to illustrate a revolutionary theory he had about language. Whorf was an unusual man who combined two careers, for he was both a successful insurance executive and a brilliant (and largely self-taught) linguistic scholar. Language, he claimed, may be shaped by the world, but it in turn shapes the world. He reasoned that people can think about only those things that their language can describe or express. Without the words or structures with which to articulate a concept, that concept will not occur. To turn the proposition around, if a language is rich in ways to express certain sorts of ideas, then the speakers of that language will habitually think along those linguistic paths. In short, the language that humans speak governs their view of reality; it determines their perception of the world. The picture of the universe shifts from tongue to tongue.

The originator of this startling notion came from an intellectually active New England family. Whorf's brother John became an artist of note and his brother Richard a consummately professional actor. Benjamin's early bent was not for drawing or acting but photography, especially the chemistry that was involved in developing pictures, and this interest may have influenced his choice of the Massachusetts Institute of Technology, where he majored in chemical engineering. After he was graduated from M.I.T. he became a specialist in fire prevention and in 1919 went to work for the Hartford Fire Insurance Company. His job was to inspect manufacturing plants, particularly chemical plants, that the Hartford insured to determine whether they were safe and thus good insurance risks. He quickly became highly skilled at his work. "In no time at all," wrote C. S. Kremer, then the Hartford's board chairman, "he became in my opinion as thorough and fast a fire prevention inspector as there ever has been."

Whorf was a particularly acute chemical engineer. On one occasion he was refused admittance to inspect a client's building because, a company official maintained, a secret process was in use here. "You are making such-and-such a product?" asked Whorf. "Yes," said the official. Whorf pulled out a pad and scribbled the formula of the supposedly secret process, adding coolly, "You couldn't do it any other way." Needless to say, he was allowed to inspect the building. Whorf rose in the Hartford hierarchy to the post of assistant secretary of the company in 1940. But then in 1941 his health, never strong, gave way, and he died at the early age of forty-four.

While Whorf was becoming a successful insurance executive, he was also doing his revolutionary work in linguistics. He started by studying Hebrew but then switched to Aztec and other related languages of Mexico. Later he deciphered Maya inscriptions, and tried to reconstruct the long-lost language of the ancient Maya people of Mexico and Central America. Finally he tackled the complexities of the still-living language of the Hopi Indians of Arizona. He published his findings in respected anthropological and linguistic journals, earning the praise and respect of scholars in the two fields—all without formal training in linguistic science. As his fame as a linguist spread, the Hartford obligingly afforded him vacations and leaves to travel to the Southwest in pursuit of the structure and lexicon of the Hopi. He also put in countless hours in the Watkinson Library in Connecticut, a rich repository of Mexican and Indian lore.

It was primarily his study of Hopi that impelled Whorf toward his revolutionary ideas. He was encouraged and aided by the great cultural anthropologist and linguist of Yale, Edward Sapir, and the idea that language influences a person's view of the world is generally known as the Sapir-Whorf hypothesis. Whorf formulated it a number of times, but perhaps his clearest statement comes from his 1940 essay "Science and Linguistics": "The background linguistic system (in other words, the grammar) of each language is not merely a reproducing instrument for voicing ideas but rather is itself the shaper of ideas. . . . We dissect nature along lines laid down by our native language. The categories and types that we isolate from the world of phenomena we do not find there because they stare every observer in the face; on the contrary, the world is presented in a kaleidoscopic flux of impressions which has to be organized by our minds—and this means largely by the linguistic systems in our minds."

These ideas developed from Whorf's study of the Hopi language. He discovered that it differs dramatically from languages of the Indo-European family such as English or French, particularly in its expression of the concept of time. English and its related languages have three major tenses—past, present, and future ("it was," "it is," "it will be")—plus the fancier compound tenses such as "it will have been." Having these tenses, Whorf argued, encourages Europeans and Americans to think of time as so many ducks in a row. Time past is made up of uniform units of time—days, weeks, months, years—and the future is similarly measured out. This division of time is essentially artificial, Whorf said, since people can only experience the present. Past and future are only abstractions, but Westerners think of them as real because their language virtually forces them to do so. This view of time has given rise to the fondness in Western cultures for diaries, records, annals, histories, clocks, calendars, wages paid by the hour or day, and elaborate timetables for the use of future time. Time is continually quantified. If Westerners set out to build a house they establish a deadline; the work will be completed at a specified time in the future, such as May 5 or October 15.

Hopis do not behave this way; when they start to weave a mat they are not concerned about when it will be completed. They work on it desultorily, then quit, then begin again; the finished product may take weeks. This casual progress is not laziness but a result of the Hopi's view of time—one symptom of the fact that their language does not have the past, present, and future tenses. Instead it possesses two modes of thought: the objective, that is, things that exist now, and the subjective, things that can be thought about and therefore belong to a state of becoming. Things do not become in terms of a future measured off in days, weeks, months. Each thing that is becoming has its own individual life rhythms, growing or declining or changing in much the same manner as a plant grows, according to its inner nature. The essence of Hopi life, therefore, Whorf said, is preparing in the present so that those things that are capable of becoming can in fact come to pass. Thus weaving a mat is preparing a mat to become a mat; it will reach that state when its nature so ordains—whenever that will be.

This view of the future is understandable, Whorf noted, in an agricultural people whose welfare depends on the proper preparing of earth and seeds and plants for the hoped-for harvest. It also helps explain why the Hopi have such elaborate festivals, rituals, dances, and magic ceremonies: All are intended to aid in the mental preparation that is so necessary if the crops, which the Hopi believe to be influenced by human thought, are to grow properly. This preparing involves "much visible activity," Whorf said, "introductory formalities, preparing of special food . . . intensive sustained muscular activity like running, racing, dancing, which is thought to increase the intensity of development of events (such as growth of crops), mimetic and other magic preparations based on esoteric theory involving perhaps occult instruments like prayer sticks, prayer feathers, and prayer meal, and finally the great cyclic ceremonies and dances, which have the significance of preparing rain and crops." Whorf went on to note that the very noun for *crop* is derived from the verb that means "to prepare." *Crop* therefore is in the Hopi language literally "the prepared." Further, the Hopi prayer pipe, which is smoked as an aid in concentrating good thoughts on the growing fields of corn and wheat, is named *na'twanpi*, "instrument of preparing."

The past to the Hopi, Whorf believed, is also different from the chronological time sense of the speakers of Indo-European languages. The past is not a uniform row of days or weeks to the Hopi. It is rather an undifferentiated stream in which many deeds were done that have accumulated and prepared the present and will continue to prepare the becoming that is ahead. Everything is connected, everything accumulates. The past is not a series of events, separated and completed, but is present in the present.

To Whorf these striking differences in the Hopi language and sense of time implied that the Hopi live almost literally in another world from the speakers of Indo-European languages. The Hopi language grew out of its speakers' peculiar circumstances: As a geographically isolated agricultural people in a land where rainfall was scanty, they did the same things and prayed the same prayers year after year and thus did not need to have past and future tenses. But the language, once it had developed, perpetuated their particular and seemingly very different world view.

Many linguists and anthropologists who have worked with American Indians of the Southwest have been convinced that Whorf's theories are by and large correct. Other linguists are not convinced, however, and through the years since Whorf's death they have attacked his proposals. The controversy is unlikely to be settled soon, if ever. One of the problems is the difficulty of setting up an experiment that would either prove or disprove the existence of correlations between linguistic structure and nonlinguistic behavior. It would be fruitless to go about asking people of various cultures their opinions as to whether the language they spoke had determined the manner in which they thought, had dictated their view of the world. Nobody would be able to answer such a question, for a people's language is so completely embedded in their consciousness that they would be unable to conceive of any other way of interpreting the world.

Despite the near impossibility of proving or disproving Whorf's theory, it will not go away but keeps coming back, intriguing each succeeding generation of linguists. It is certainly one of the most fascinating theories created by the modern mind. It is comparable in some ways to Einstein's theory of relativity. Just as Einstein said that how people saw the phenomena of the universe was relative to their point of observation, so Whorf said that a people's world view was relative to the language they spoke.

And demonstrations of Whorf's ideas are not entirely lacking. They come mainly from studies of color—one of the very few aspects of reality that can be specified by objective scientific methods and also is rather precisely specified by people's naming of colors. In this instance it is possible to compare one person's language, expressing that person's view of the world, with another's language for exactly the same characteristic of the world. The comparison can thus reveal different views that are linked to different descriptions of the same reality. English-speakers view purple as a single relatively uniform color; only if pressed and then only with difficulty will they make any attempt to divide it into such shades as lavender and mauve. But no English-speaker would lump orange with purple; to the users of English, those colors are completely separate, for no single word includes both of them. If other languages made different distinctions in the naming of color—if lavender and mauve were always separate, never encompassed by a word for purple, or if orange and purple were not distinguished but were called by a name that covered both—then it would seem that the users of those languages interpreted those colors differently.

Such differences in color-naming, it turns out, are fairly widespread. Linguist H. A. Gleason compared the color spectrum as described by English-speaking persons to the way it was labeled by speakers of Bassa, a language spoken in Liberia, and by speakers of Shona, spoken in Rhodesia. English-speaking people, when seeing sunlight refracted through a prism, identify by name at least six colors—purple, blue, green, yellow, orange, and red. The speakers of Shona, however, have only three names for the colors of the spectrum. They group orange, red, and purple under one name. They also lump blue and green-blue under one of their other color terms and use their third word to identify yellow and the yellower hues of green. The speakers of Bassa are similarly restricted by a lack of handy terms for color, for they have only two words for the hues of the spectrum.

Gleason's observations prompted psychologists to perform an experiment that also showed the influence words can have on the way colors are handled intellectually and remembered. It was an ingenious and complex experiment with many checks and double checks of the results, but in essence it boiled down to something like this: English-speaking subjects were shown a series of color samples—rather like the little "chips" provided by a paint store to help customers decide what color to paint the living room. The subjects were then asked to pick out the colors they had seen from a far larger array of colors. It turned out that they could more accurately pick out the right colors from the larger selection when the color involved had a handy, ordinary name like "green." The subjects had difficulty with the ambiguous, in-between colors such as off-purples and misty blues. In other words, a person can remember a color better if that person's language offers a handy label for it, but has trouble when the language does not offer such a familiar term. Again the human ability to differentiate reality seemed to be affected by the resources offered by language.

Richness of linguistic resource undoubtedly helps people to cope with subtle gradations in the things they deal with every day. The Hanunóo people of the Philippine Islands have different names for ninety-two varieties of rice. They can easily distinguish differences in rice that would be all but invisible to English-speaking people, who lump all such grains under the single word *rice*. Of course, English-speakers can make distinctions by resorting to adjectives and perhaps differentiate long-grain, brown rice from small-grain, yellow rice, but surely no European or American would, lacking the terms, have a sufficiently practiced eye to distinguish ninety-two varieties of rice. Language is essentially a code that people use both to think and to communicate. As psychologist Roger Brown sums up the rice question: "Among the Hanunóo, who have names for ninety-two varieties of rice, any one of those varieties is highly codable in the array of ninety-one other varieties. The Hanunóo have a word for it and so can transmit it efficiently and presumably can recognize it easily. Among speakers of English one kind of rice among ninety-one other kinds would have very low codability."

Brown goes on to suppose that the Hanunóo set down in New York would be baffled by the reality around them partly because they would then be the ones lacking the needed words. "If the Hanunóo were to visit the annual Automobile Show in New York City, they would find it difficult to encode distinctively any particular automobile in that array. But an American having such lexical resources as *Chevrolet, Ford, Plymouth, Buick, Corvette, hard-top, convertible, four-door, station wagon,* and the like could easily encode ninety-two varieties."

The very existence of so many different languages, each linked to a distinctive culture, is itself support of a sort for Whorf's hypothesis. At least since the time of the Tower of Babel, no single tongue has been shared by all the people of the world. Many attempts have been made to invent an international language, one so simply structured and easy to learn it would be used by everyone around the globe as a handy adjunct to their native speech. Yet even the most successful of these world languages, Esperanto, has found but limited acceptance.

There are international languages, however, to serve international cultures. The intellectual disciplines of music, dance, and mathematics might be considered specialized cultures; each is shared by people around the world, and each has an international language, used as naturally in Peking as in Paris. English is a world language in certain activities that straddle national boundaries, such as international air travel; it serves for communications between international flights and the ground in every country—a Lufthansa pilot approaching Athens talks with the airport control tower neither in German nor in Greek but in English.

The trouble with most attempts to lend credence to the Sapir-Whorf hypothesis is that, while they indicate connections between culture and language, they do not really prove that a language shaped its users' view of the world. Just because the speakers of Shona have only three main distinctions of color does not mean that their "world view" is all that different from that of the English-speaker who has more convenient color terms. Shona speakers obviously see all the colors in the rainbow that English-speakers see. Their eyes are physiologically the same. Their comparative poverty of words for those colors merely means that it is harder for them to talk about color. Their "code" is not so handy; the colors' codability is lower.

Critics also point out that Whorf may have mistaken what are called dead metaphors for real differences in the Hopi language. All languages are loaded with dead metaphors—figures of speech that have lost all figurative value and are now just familiar words. The word "goodbye" is a dead metaphor. Once it meant "God be with you," but in its contracted form it conjures up no thought or picture of God. If a Whorfian linguist who was a native speaker of Hopi turned the tables and analyzed English he might conclude that English-speakers were perpetually thinking of religion since this everyday word incorporates a reference to God—a ridiculous misreading of a term that has lost all of its original religious significance. In like fashion, perhaps Whorf was reading too much into the Hopi lexicon and grammar, seeing significances where there were none.

The argument about how far Whorf's ideas can be stretched has gone on for several decades and promises to go on for several more. Most psychologists believe that all people see pretty much the same reality; their languages merely have different words and structures to approximate in various idiosyncratic ways a picture of that reality. And yet the experts accept what might be called modified Whorfism—a belief in the power of language to affect, if not to direct, the perception of reality. If a language is rich in terms for certain things or ideas—possesses extensive codability for them—then the people speaking that language can conceive of, and talk about, those things or ideas more conveniently. If different languages do not give their speakers entirely different world views, they certainly influence thinking to some degree.

Even within the Indo-European family of languages, some tongues have words for concepts that other tongues lack. German is especially rich in philosophical terms that have no exact counterparts in English, French, Italian—or any known language. One is *Weltschmerz*, which combines in itself meanings that it takes three English phrases to adequately convey—"weariness of life," "pessimistic outlook," and "romantic discontent." Another German word that has no direct translation is *Weltanschauung*. To approximate its meaning in English requires a number of different terms—"philosophy of life," "world outlook," "ideology"—for all of these elements are included in the German word. *Weltanschauung* is untranslatable into any single English term. It represents an idea for which only German has a word. Possessing the convenient term, German writers can develop this idea more easily than the users of other languages, and thus explore its ramifications further.

Even when a word from one language may seem to be easily translatable into another, it often is not really equivalent. The French term *distingué* would appear to translate easily enough into the English *distinguished*. But the French use their word in ways that no English-speaker would ever employ for *distinguished*. A Frenchman might reprimand his son by saying that his impolite behavior was not *distingué* or he might tell his wife that a scarf she has worn out to dinner is charmingly *distingué*. The word does not mean "distinguished" as English-speakers employ the term, but something more like "suitable," or "appropriate," or "in keeping with polite standards." It is simply not the same word in the two languages no matter how similar the spelling. It represents a different idea, connoting a subtle difference in mental style.

In some cases the existence of a word leads users of it down tortured logical paths toward dead ends. The common word *nothing* is one example. Since there is a word for the concept, points out philosopher George Pitcher, it tempts people to think that "nothing" is a real entity, that somehow it exists, a palpable realm of not-being. It has in fact led a number of philosophers, including the twentieth-century French thinker Jean-Paul Sartre, to spend a great deal of effort speculating about the nature of "nothing." The difficulty of this philosophic dilemma is indicated by a typical Sartre sentence on the subject: "The Being by which Nothingness arrives in the world must nihilate. Nothingness in its Being, and even so it still runs the risk of establishing Nothingness as a transcendent in the very heart of immanence unless it nihilates Nothingness in its being in connection with its own being." Sartre could hardly have gotten himself tangled up in such agonized prose had French lacked a noun for *le neant*, nothing, and the value to human welfare of his attempt to explain is open to question.

The power of language to influence the world can be seen not only in comparisons of one tongue to another, but also within a single language. The way in which people use their native tongue—choosing one term over another to express the same idea or action, varying structures or phrases for different situations—has a strong effect on their attitudes toward those situations. Distasteful ideas can be made to seem acceptable or even desirable by careful choices of words, and language can make actions or beliefs that might otherwise be considered correct appear to be obsolescent or naive. Value judgments of many kinds can be attached to seemingly simple statements. Shakespeare may have believed that "a rose by any other name would smell as sweet," but he was wrong, as other theatrical promoters have proved repeatedly. A young English vaudevillian known as Archibald Leach was a minor comedian until he was given the more romantic name of Cary Grant. The new name did not make him a star, but it did create an atmosphere in which he could demonstrate his talent, suggesting the type of character he came to exemplify.

If the power of a stage name to characterize personality seems of relatively minor consequence in human affairs, consider the effect of a different sort of appellation: "boy." It was—and sometimes still is—the form of address employed by whites in the American South in speaking to black males of any age. This word, many authorities believe, served as an instrument of subjugation. It implied that the black was not a man but a child, someone not mature enough to be entrusted with responsibility for himself, let alone authority over others. His inferior position was thus made to seem natural and justified, and it could be enforced without compunction.

Characterizing people by tagging them with a word label is a world-wide practice. Many peoples use a single word to designate both themselves and the human race. "The Carib Indians, for example, have stated with no equivocation, 'We alone are people,'" reported anthropologist Jack Conrad. "Similarly, the ancient Egyptians used the word *romet* (men) only among themselves and in no case for strangers. The Lapps of Scandinavia reserve the term 'human being' for those of their own kind, while the Cherokee Indians call themselves *Ani-Yunwiya*, which means 'principal people.' The Kiowa Indians of the Southwest are willing to accept other peoples as human, but the very name, *Kiowa*, meaning 'real people,' shows their true feeling." The effect of reserving a term indicating "human" to one group is far-reaching. It alters the perception of anyone from outside that group. He is not called "human," and need not be treated as human. Like an animal, he can be entrapped, beaten, or even killed with more or less impunity. This use of a word to demote whole groups from the human class is often a wartime tactic—the enemy is referred to by a pejorative name to justify killing him.

While language can be twisted to make ordinarily good things seem bad, it can also be twisted in the opposite direction to make bad things seem good or run-of-the-mill things better than they really are. The technique depends on the employment of euphemisms, a term derived from the Greek for "words of good omen." A euphemism is roundabout language that is intended to conceal something embarrassing or unpleasant. Some classes of euphemism—little evasions that people use every day—are inoffensive enough. It is when such cloudy doubletalk invades the vital areas of politics and foreign affairs that it becomes perilous.

A large and commonly used—and relatively harmless—class of euphemism has to do with bodily functions. Many people shy away from frank talk about excretion or sex; in fact, many of the old, vivid terms—the four-letter words—are socially taboo. So people for centuries have skirted the edge of such matters, inventing a rich vocabulary of substitute terms. Americans offered turkey on Thanksgiving commonly say "white meat" or "dark meat" to announce their preference. These terms date back to the nineteenth century when it was considered indelicate to say "breast" or "leg." *Toilet,* itself a euphemism coined from the French *toilette* ("making oneself presentable to the outside world"), long ago became tainted and too graphic for the prudish. The list of euphemistic substitutes is almost endless, ranging from the commonplace *washroom, bathroom,* and *restroom* (whoever rests in a restroom?) to *john, head,* and *Chic Sale* in the United States, and in England the *loo. Loo* may be derived from a mistaken English pronunciation of the French *l'eau,* water. Or it may be a euphemism derived from a euphemism. The French, with Gallic delicacy, once commonly put the number 100 on bathroom doors in hotels. It is easy to see how an English person might have mistaken the number for the word *loo.* Meanwhile, ladies in restaurants have adopted "I'm going to powder my nose" or, in England, where it once cost a penny to use public toilets, "I'm going to spend a penny."

Another generally harmless use of euphemistic language is the practice, especially notable in the United States, of giving prestigious names to more-or-less ordinary trades. As H. L. Mencken pointed out in *The American Language,* his masterly examination of English as spoken in the United States, ratcatchers are fond of calling themselves "exterminating engineers" and hairdressers have long since showed a preference for "beautician." The *-ician* ending, in fact, has proved very popular, doubtless because it echoes "physician" and thus sounds both professional and scientific. In the late nineteenth century undertakers had already begun to call themselves "funeral directors," but starting in 1916 ennobled themselves even further by battening on the newer euphemistic coinage, "mortician." Meanwhile a tree trimmer became a "tree surgeon" (that love of medicine again) and a press agent became a "publicist" or, even more grandly, a "public relations counsel."

Americans (and the English, too) not only chose high-sounding euphemisms for their professions but also gave new and gaudy names to their places of business. Thus pawn shops became "loan offices," saloons became "cocktail rooms," pool halls became "billiard parlors," and barber shops "hairstyling salons."

Purists might say that such shading or blunting of the stark truth leads to moral decay, but it is difficult to see why anybody should be the worse for allowing women to excuse themselves by pleading that they must powder their noses. There are euphemisms, however, that are clearly anything but harmless. These are evasive, beclouding phraseologies that hide truths people must clearly perceive if they are to govern themselves intelligently and keep a check on those in positions of power. Slick phrases, slippery evasions—words deliberately designed to hide unpleasant truth rather than reveal it—can so becloud political processes and so easily hide mistaken policies that the entire health of a nation is imperiled.

The classic treatise on the political misuse of language in modern times is the 1946 essay "Politics and the English Language" by the British writer George Orwell. "In our time, political speech and writing are largely the defence of the indefencible," Orwell said. "Thus political language has to consist largely of euphemism, question-begging and sheer cloudy vagueness." He concluded, "Such phraseology is needed if one wants to name things without calling up mental pictures of them. . . . When there is a gap between one's real and one's declared aims, one turns as it were instinctively to long words and exhausted idioms, like a cuttlefish squirting out ink."

Orwell supplied numerous examples to buttress his charges. "Defenceless villages are bombarded from the air, the inhabitants driven out into the countryside, the cattle machine-gunned, the huts set on fire with incendiary bullets: this is called *pacification*." He went on to observe that in Stalin's Russia people were "imprisoned for years without trial or shot in the back of the neck or sent to die of scurvy in Arctic lumber camps: this is called *elimination of unreliable elements*."

Orwell, who died at the age of forty-six in 1950, did not live to collect even more deplorable distortions of language. The French clothed their brutal war in Algeria with a veil of euphemism; the North Koreans accused the South Koreans of "aggression" when the North invaded the South. The United States invented a whole lexicon of gobbledygook to disguise the horror of the war in Vietnam: "protective reaction strike" (the bombing of a Vietnamese village); "surgical bombing" (the same as protective reaction strike); "free-fire zone" (an area in which troops could shoot anything that moved, including helpless villagers); "new life hamlet" (a refugee camp for survivors of a surgical bombing).

Perhaps the most appalling use of this type of euphemism was the word employed by the Nazis for their program to exterminate all of Europe's Jews. The word is *Endlösung*, which means final solution. Behind that verbal façade the Nazis gassed, burned, shot, or worked to death some six million Jews from Germany, France, Poland, and other conquered parts of Europe. Hitler and Gestapo chief Himmler often employed the euphemism among themselves, and it was always used in official records—but not necessarily to preserve secrecy for purposes of state security. Apparently the euphemism shielded the Nazis from themselves. Openly brutal and murderous as they were, they could not face up to the horrible reality of what they were doing, and they had to hide it in innocuous language.

Such distortion of language can do more than disguise truth. It can turn truth around, so that the idea conveyed is the opposite of actuality. After the USSR savagely crushed the Hungarian rebellion in 1956 the Soviet aggression was made to seem, in the twisted language used by other Communist dictatorships, an expression of friendship. The Peking radio commented after the rebellion was put down: "The Hungarian people can see that Soviet policy toward the people's democracies is truly one of equality, friendship, and mutual assistance, not of conquest, aggression, and plunder."

The possibility that such topsy-turvy language might ultimately make the world topsy-turvy—an ironic demonstration of the fundamental truth of Benjamin Lee Whorf's insights—was raised in a dramatic way by George Orwell. His novel *1984*, a chilling and convincing description of life in a totalitarian society, shows how language might destroy reality. In the imaginary nation of Oceania the official language is Newspeak, which is intended to facilitate "doublethink," the ability to accept simultaneously ideas contradicting each other. The Oceania state apparatus includes a Ministry of Truth, its headquarters building emblazoned with three slogans: "WAR IS PEACE"; "FREEDOM IS SLAVERY"; "IGNORANCE IS STRENGTH." There are also other ministries, Orwell explained: "The Ministry of Peace, which concerned itself with war; the Ministry of Love, which maintained law and order." Anyone who would use language this way, Orwell made clear, denies the meaning of his or her words. He or she has lost touch with reality and substituted for it an emptiness concealed in sounds that once had meaning.

There is another threat to language besides the intentional twisting of words by demagogues and others who would control people's thoughts. It is less obvious, but a danger nevertheless: simple imprecision, slovenliness, mindlessness in the use of the language. It seems a small matter that English-speakers increasingly confuse *uninterested* with *disinterested*, for example. But these words do not mean the same thing. *Disinterested* means impartial, not taking sides. *Uninterested* means lacking in interest, bored. A judge should be *disinterested* but never *uninterested*. Many such changes result from the inevitable evolution of language as it changes over the years, but the change can be a loss. The slow erosion of distinctions, visible in much writing, audible in many conversations, makes language imprecise and thus clumsy and ineffective as communication.

Among the symptoms of such erosion are stock phrases that people mindlessly repeat, substituting noise for thought. Everyone has heard speechmakers use such clichés as "having regard to," "play into the hands of," "in the interest of," "no axe to grind." Although this brief list is drawn from Orwell's essay of 1946 these exhausted clichés are still heard. Such verbal dead limbs do not distort thought but rather tend to obliterate it in a cloud of meaninglessness. "The slovenliness of our language makes it easier for us to have foolish thoughts," wrote Orwell. And ultimately, as has been pointed out by commentator Edwin

Newman in his book *Strictly Speaking,* "Those for whom words have lost their value are likely to find that ideas have also lost their value."

Connection Questions

1. Miller describes two models for the relationship between language and culture. What are they?

2. Give two examples from the Thomson article that reflect how grammar can shape the perceptions of people in a specific culture.

3. Provide examples of ways in which language affects thought from your own experience.

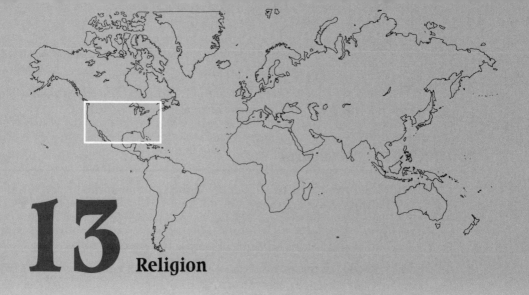

13 Religion

Baseball Magic

George Gmelch

Americans pride themselves on their scientific approach to life and problem solving. But as George Gmelch demonstrates in this article, U.S. baseball players, much like people in many parts of the world, also turn to supernatural forces to ensure success. Following the pioneering analysis of Trobriand magic by Bronislaw Malinowski, Gmelch shows that, like Trobriand Islanders, baseball players use magic, including ritual, taboos, and fetishes, to manage the anxiety generated by unpredictable events that challenge human control.

On each pitching day for the first three months of a winning season, Dennis Grossini, a pitcher on a Detroit Tiger farm team, arose from bed at exactly 10:00 A.M. At 1:00 P.M. he went to the nearest restaurant for two glasses of iced tea and a tuna fish sandwich. When he got to the ballpark at 3:00 P.M., he put on the sweatshirt and jock he wore during his last winning game; one hour before the game he chewed a wad of Beech-Nut chewing tobacco. After each pitch during the game he touched the letters on his uniform and straightened his cap after each ball. Before the start of each inning he replaced the pitcher's rosin bag next

Reprinted by permission of George Gmelch.

to the spot where it was the inning before. And after every inning in which he gave up a run, he washed his hands.

When I asked which part of his ritual was most important, he said, "You can't really tell what's most important so it all becomes important. I'd be afraid to change anything. As long as I'm winning, I do everything the same."

Trobriand Islanders, according to anthropologist Bronislaw Malinowski, felt the same way about their fishing magic. Trobrianders fished in two different settings: in the *inner lagoon* where fish were plentiful and there was little danger, and on the *open sea* where fishing was dangerous and yields varied widely. Malinowski found that magic was not used in lagoon fishing, where men could rely solely on their knowledge and skill. But when fishing on the open sea, Trobrianders used a great deal of magical ritual to ensure safety and increase their catch.

Baseball, America's national pastime, is an arena in which players behave remarkably like Malinowski's Trobriand fishermen. To professional ballplayers, baseball is more than a game, it is an occupation. Because their livelihoods depend on how well they perform, many use magic in an attempt to control the chance that is built into baseball. There are three essential activities of the game: pitching, hitting, and fielding. In the first two, chance can play a surprisingly important role. The pitcher is the player least able to control the outcome of his efforts. He may feel great and have good stuff warming up in the bullpen and then get in the game and get clobbered. He may make a bad pitch and see the batter miss it for a strike or see it hit hard but right into the hands of a fielder for an out. Conversely, his best pitch may be blooped for a base hit. He may limit the opposing team to just a few hits yet lose the game, and he may give up many hits and win. And the good and bad luck don't always average out over the course of a season. For instance, this past season Jeriome Robertson gave up 1.4 more runs per game than his teammate Tim Redding but had a better win–loss record. Robertson went 15–9, while Redding was only 10–14. Both pitched for the same team—the Houston Astros—which meant they had the same fielders behind them. Regardless of how well a pitcher performs, the outcome of the game also depends upon the proficiency of his teammates, the ineptitude of the opposition, and luck.

Hitting, which many observers call the single most difficult task in the world of sports, is also full of uncertainty. Unless it's a home run, no matter how hard the batter hits the ball, fate determines whether it will go into a waiting glove or find a gap between the fielders. The uncertainty is compounded by the low success rate of hitting: the average hitter gets only one hit in every four trips to the plate, while the very best hitters average only one hit in every three trips. Fielding, which we will return to later, is the one part of baseball where chance does not play much of a role.

How does the risk and uncertainty in pitching and hitting affect players? How do they try to control the outcomes of their performance? These are questions that I first became interested in many years ago both as a ballplayer and as an anthropology student. I had devoted much of my youth to baseball, and played professionally as a first baseman in the Detroit Tiger organization in the 1960s. It was shortly after the end of one baseball season that I took an anthropology course called "Magic, Religion, and Witchcraft." As I listened to my professor describe the magical rituals of the Trobriand Islanders, it occurred to me that what these so-called "primitive" people did wasn't all that different from what my teammates and I did for luck and confidence at the ballpark.

Routines and Rituals

The most common way players attempt to reduce chance and their feelings of uncertainty is to develop a daily routine—a course of action which is regularly followed. Talking about the routines of ballplayers, Pittsburgh Pirates' coach Rich Donnelly said:

> They're like trained animals. They come out here [ballpark] and everything has to be the same, they don't like anything that knocks them off their routine. Just look at the dugout and you'll see every guy sitting in the same spot every night. It's amazing, everybody in the same spot. And don't you dare take someone's seat. If a guy comes up from the minors and sits here, they'll say, "Hey, Jim sits here, find another seat." You watch the pitcher warm up and he'll do the same thing every time. . . . You got a routine and you adhere to it and you don't want anybody knocking you off it.

Routines are comforting; they bring order into a world in which players have little control. And sometimes practical elements in routines produce tangible benefits, such as helping the player concentrate. But some of what players do goes beyond mere routine. These actions become what anthropologists define as *ritual*—prescribed behaviors in which there is no empirical connection between the means (e.g., tapping home plate three times) and the desired end (e.g., getting a base hit). Because there is no real connection between the two, rituals are not rational. Sometimes they are quite irrational. Similar to rituals are the nonrational beliefs that form the basis of taboos and fetishes, which players also use to bring luck to their side. But first let's take a close look at rituals.

Baseball rituals are infinitely varied. Most are personal, performed by individuals rather than by a team or group. Most are done in an unemotional manner, in much the same way players apply pine tar to their bats to improve the grip or dab eye black on their upper cheeks to reduce the sun's glare. A ballplayer may ritualize any activity that he considers important or somehow linked to good performance. Recall the variety of things that Dennis Grossini does, from specific times for waking and eating to foods and dress. Jason Bere of the White Sox listens to the same song on his Walkman before he pitches. Atlanta Brave Denny Neagle goes to a movie on days he is scheduled to start. Baltimore Oriole Glenn Davis used to chew the same gum every day during hitting streaks, saving it under his cap. Astros Infielder Julio Gotay always played with a cheese sandwich in his back pocket (he had a big appetite, so there might also have been a measure of practicality here). Wade Boggs of the Red Sox ate chicken before every game during his career, and that was just one of many elements in his pre- and postgame routine, which also included leaving his house for the ballpark at precisely the same time each day (1:47 for a 7:05 game).

Many hitters go through a series of preparatory rituals before stepping into the batter's box. These include tugging on their caps, touching their uniform letters or medallions, crossing themselves, and swinging, tapping, or bouncing the bat on the plate a prescribed number of times. Consider Cubs shortstop Nomar Garciaparra. After each pitch he steps out of the batters box, kicks the dirt with each toe, adjusts his right batting glove, adjusts his left batting glove, and touches his helmet before getting back into the box. Mike Hargrove, former Cleveland Indian first baseman, had so many time-consuming elements in his batting ritual that he was nicknamed "the human rain delay." Both players believe their batting rituals helped them regain their concentration after each pitch. But others wondered if the two had become prisoners of their superstitions. Another ritual associated with hitting is tagging a base when leaving and returning to the dugout between innings. Some players don't "feel right" unless they tag a specific base on each trip between dugout and field. One of my teammates added some complexity to his ritual by tagging third base on his way to the dugout only after the third, sixth, and ninth innings.

Players who have too many or particularly bizarre rituals risk being labeled as flakes, and not just by teammates but by fans and the media as well. For example, Mets pitcher Turk Wendell's eccentric rituals, which include wearing a necklace of teeth from animals he has killed, made him a cover story subject in the *New York Times Sunday Magazine*.

Baseball fans observe a lot of this ritual behavior, such as pitchers smoothing the dirt on the mound before each new batter, never realizing its importance to the player. The one ritual many fans do recognize, largely because it's a favorite of TV cameramen, is the "rally cap"—players in the dugout folding their caps and wearing them bill up in hopes of sparking a rally.

Most rituals grow out of exceptionally good performances. When a player does well, he seldom attributes his success to skill alone; he knows that his skills don't change much from day to day. So, then, what was different about today that can explain his three hits? He may attribute his success, in part, to an object, a food he ate, not having shaved, a new shirt he bought that day, or just about any behavior out of the ordinary. By repeating those behaviors, the player seeks to gain control over his performance, to bring more good luck. Outfielder John White explained how one of his rituals started:

> I was jogging out to centerfield after the national anthem when I picked up a scrap of paper. I got some good hits that night and I guess I decided that the paper had

something to do with it. The next night I picked up a gum wrapper and had another good night at the plate. . . . I've been picking up paper every night since.

When outfielder Ron Wright played for the Calgary Cannons he shaved his arms once a week. It all began two years before when after an injury he shaved his arm so it could be taped, and then hit three homers. Now he not only has one of the smoothest swings in the minor leagues, but two of the smoothest forearms. Wade Boggs' routine of eating chicken before every game began when he was a rookie in 1982 and noticed a correlation between multiple-hit games and poultry plates (his wife has 40 chicken recipes). One of Montreal Expo farmhand Mike Saccocio's rituals also concerned food: "I got three hits one night after eating at Long John Silver's. After that when we'd pull into town, my first question would be, "Do you have a Long John Silver's?" Unlike Boggs, Saccocio abandoned his ritual and looked for a new one when he stopped hitting well.

When in a slump, most players make a deliberate effort to change their routines and rituals in an attempt to shake off their bad luck. One player tried taking different routes to the ballpark, another tried sitting in a different place in the dugout, another shaved his head, and several reported changing what they ate before the game. Years ago, some of my teammates rubbed their hands along the handles of the bats protruding from the bat bin in hopes of picking up some power or luck from the bats of others. I had one manager who would rattle the bat bin when the team was not hitting well, as if the bats were in a stupor and could be aroused by a good shaking.

Taboo

Taboos (the word comes from a Polynesian term meaning prohibition) are the opposite of rituals. These are things you shouldn't do. Breaking a taboo, players believe, leads to undesirable consequences or bad luck. Most players observe at least a few taboos, such as never stepping on the white foul lines. A few, like Nomar Garciaparra, leap over the entire basepath. One teammate of mine would never watch a movie on a game day, despite the fact that we played nearly every day from April to September. Another teammate refused to read anything before a game because he believed it weakened his batting eye.

Many taboos take place off the field, out of public view. On the day a pitcher is scheduled to start, he is likely to avoid activities he believes will sap his strength and detract from his effectiveness. Some pitchers avoid eating certain foods, others will not shave on the day of a game, refusing to shave again as long as they are winning. Early in one season Oakland's Dave Stewart had six consecutive victories and a beard by the time he lost.

Taboos usually grow out of exceptionally poor performances, which players, in search of a reason, attribute to a particular behavior. During my first season of pro ball I ate pancakes before a game in which I struck out three times. A few weeks later I had another terrible game, again after eating pancakes. The result was a pancake taboo: I never again ate pancakes during the season. Pitcher Jason Bere has a taboo that makes more sense in dietary terms: after eating a meatball sandwich and not pitching well, he swore off them for the rest of the season.

While most taboos are idiosyncratic, there are a few that all ballplayers hold and that do not develop out of individual experience or misfortune. These form part of the culture of baseball, and are sometimes learned as early as Little League. Mentioning a no-hitter while one is in progress is a well-known example.

Fetishes

Fetishes are charms, material objects believed to embody supernatural power that can aid or protect the owner. Good-luck charms are standard equipment for some ballplayers. These include a wide assortment of objects from coins, chains, and crucifixes to a favorite baseball hat. The fetishized object may be a new possession or something a player found that coincided with the start of a streak and which he holds responsible for his good fortune. While playing in the Pacific Coast League, Alan Foster forgot his baseball shoes on a road trip and borrowed a pair from a teammate. That night he pitched a no-hitter, which he attributed to the shoes. Afterwards he bought them from his teammate and they became a fetish. Expo farmhand Mark LaRosa's rock has a different origin and use:

> I found it on the field in Elmira after I had gotten bombed. It's unusual, perfectly round, and it caught my attention. I keep it to remind me of how important it is to concentrate. When I am going well I look at the rock and remember to keep my focus. The rock reminds me of what can happen when I lose my concentration.

For one season Marge Schott, former owner of the Cincinnati Reds, insisted that her field manager rub her St. Bernard "Schotzie" for good luck before each game. When the Reds were on the road, Schott would sometimes send a bag of the dog's hair to the field manager's hotel room. Religious medallions, which many Latino players wear around their necks and sometimes touch before going to the plate or mound, are also fetishes, though tied to their Roman Catholicism. Also relating to their religion, some players make the sign of the cross or bless themselves before every at bat (a few like Pudge Rodriguez do so before every pitch), and a few point to the heavens after hitting a home run.

Some players regard certain uniform numbers as lucky. When Ricky Henderson came to the Blue Jays in 1993, he paid teammate Turner Ward $25,000 for the right to wear number 24. Don Sutton got off cheaper. When he joined the Dodgers he convinced teammate Bruce Boche to give up number 20 in exchange for a new set of golf clubs. Oddly enough, there is no consensus about the effect of wearing number 13. Some players shun it, while a few request it. When Jason Giambi arrived with the Oakland A's his favorite number 7 was already taken, so he settled for 16 (the two numbers add up to 7). When he signed with the Yankees, number 7 (Mickey Mantle's old number) was retired and 16 was taken, so he settled for 25 (again, the numbers add up to 7).

Number preferences emerge in different ways. A young player may request the number of a former star, sometimes hoping that it will bring him the same success. Or he may request a number he associates with good luck. Colorado Rockies' Larry Walker's fixation with the number 3 has become well known to baseball fans. Besides wearing 33, he takes three practice swings before stepping into the box, he showers from the third nozzle, sets his alarm for three minutes past the hour and he was married on November 3 at 3:33 P.M.[1] Fans in ballparks all across America rise from their seats for the seventh-inning stretch before the home club comes to bat because the number 7 is lucky, although the specific origin of this tradition has been lost.

Clothing, both the choice and the order in which it is put on, combine elements of both ritual and fetish. Some players put on the part of their uniform in a particular order. Expos farmhand Jim Austin always puts on his left sleeve, left pants leg, and left shoe before the right. Most players, however, single out one or two lucky articles or quirks of dress for ritual elaboration. After hitting two home runs in a game, for example, ex-Giant infielder Jim Davenport discovered that he had missed a buttonhole while dressing for the game. For the remainder of his career he left the same button undone. Phillies' Len Dykstra would discard his batting gloves if he failed to get a hit in a single at-bat. In a hitless game, he might go through four pair of gloves. For outfielder Brian Hunter the focus is shoes: "I have a pair of high tops and a pair of low tops. Whichever shoes don't get a hit that game, I switch to the other pair." At the time of our interview, he was struggling at the plate and switching shoes almost every day. For Birmingham Baron pitcher Bo Kennedy the arrangement of the different pairs of baseball shoes in his locker is critical:

> I tell the clubbies [clubhouse boys] when you hang stuff in my locker don't touch my shoes. If you bump them move them back. I want the Ponys in front, the turfs to the right, and I want them nice and neat with each pair touching each other. . . . Everyone on the team knows not to mess with my shoes when I pitch.

During hitting or winning streaks players may wear the same clothes day after day. Once I changed sweatshirts midway through the game for seven consecutive nights to keep a hitting streak going. Clothing rituals, however, can become impractical. Catcher Matt Allen was wearing a long sleeve turtle neck shirt on a cool evening in the New York-Penn League when he had a three-hit game. "I kept wearing the shirt and had a good week," he explained. "Then the weather got hot as hell, 85 degrees and muggy, but I would not take that shirt off. I wore it for another ten days—catching—and people thought I was crazy." Former Phillies, Expos, Twins, and Angels manager Gene Mauch never washed

---

[1]Lee Allen, "The Superstitions of Baseball Players," *New York Folklore Quarterly* 20, no. 20 (1964): 98–109.

his underwear or uniform after a win. Perhaps taking a ritual to the extreme, Leo Durocher, managing the Brooklyn Dodgers to a pennant in 1941, spent three and a half weeks in the same gray slacks, blue coat, and knitted blue tie. Losing can produce the opposite effect, such as the Oakland A's players who went out and bought new street clothes in an attempt to break a 14-game losing streak.

Baseball's superstitions, like most everything else, change over time. Many of the rituals and beliefs of early baseball are no longer observed. In the 1920s–30s sportswriters reported that a player who tripped en route to the field would often retrace his steps and carefully walk over the stumbling block for "insurance." A century ago players spent time on and off the field intently looking for items that would bring them luck. To find a hairpin on the street, for example, assured a batter of hitting safely in that day's game. A few managers were known to strategically place a hairpin on the ground where a slumping player would be sure to find it. Today few women wear hairpins—a good reason the belief has died out. In the same era, Philadelphia Athletics manager Connie Mack hoped to ward off bad luck by employing a hunchback as a mascot. Hall of Famer Ty Cobb took on a young black boy as a good luck charm, even taking him on the road during the 1908 season. It was a not uncommon then for players to rub the head of a black child for good luck.

To catch sight of a white horse or a wagon-load of barrels were also good omens. In 1904 the manager of the New York Giants, John McGraw, hired a driver with a team of white horses to drive past the Polo Grounds around the time his players were arriving at the ballpark. He knew that if his players saw white horses, they would have more confidence and that could only help them during the game. Belief in the power of white horses survived in a few backwaters until the 1960s. A gray-haired manager of a team I played for in Drummondville, Quebec, would drive around the countryside before important games and during the playoffs looking for a white horse. When he was successful, he would announce it to everyone in the clubhouse.

One belief that appears to have died out recently is a taboo about crossed bats. Some of my Latino teammates in the 1960s took it seriously. I can still recall one Dominican player becoming agitated when another player tossed a bat from the batting cage and it landed on top of his bat. He believed that the top bat might steal hits from the lower one. In his view, bats contained a finite number of hits. It was once commonly believed that when the hits in a bat were used up no amount of good hitting would produce any more. Hall of Famer Honus Wagner believed each bat contained only 100 hits. Regardless of the quality of the bat, he would discard it after its 100th hit. This belief would have little relevance today, in the era of light bats with thin handles—so thin that the typical modern bat is lucky to survive a dozen hits without being broken. Other superstitions about bats do survive, however. Position players on the Class A Asheville Tourists would not let pitchers touch or swing their bats, not even to warm up. Poor-hitting players, as most pitchers are, were said to pollute or weaken the bats.

Uncertainty and Magic

The best evidence that players turn to rituals, taboos, and fetishes to control chance and uncertainty is found in their uneven application. They are associated mainly with pitching and hitting—the activities with the highest degree of chance—and not fielding. I met only one player who had any ritual in connection with fielding, and he was an error-prone shortstop. Unlike hitting and pitching, a fielder has almost complete control over the outcome of his performance. Once a ball has been hit in his direction, no one can intervene and ruin his chances of catching it for an out (except in the unlikely event of two fielders colliding). Compared with the pitcher or the hitter, the fielder has little to worry about. He knows that in better than 9.7 times out of 10 he will execute his task flawlessly. With odds like that there is little need for ritual.

Clearly, the rituals of American ballplayers are not unlike those of the Trobriand Islanders studied by Malinowski many years ago.[2] In professional baseball, fielding is the equivalent of the inner lagoon while hitting and pitching are like the open sea.

While Malinowski helps us understand how ballplayers respond to chance and uncertainty, behavioral psychologist B. F. Skinner sheds light on why personal rituals get established in the first place.[3] With a few grains of seed Skinner could get pigeons to do anything he wanted. He merely waited for the desired behavior (e.g., pecking) and then rewarded it with some food. Skinner then decided to see what would happen if pigeons were rewarded with food pellets regularly, every fifteen seconds, regardless of what they did. He found that the birds associate the arrival of the food with a particular action, such as tucking their head under a wing or walking in clockwise circles. About ten seconds after the arrival of the last pellet, a bird would begin doing whatever it associated with getting the food and keep doing it until the next pellet arrived. In short, the pigeons behaved as if their actions made the food appear. They learned to associate particular behaviors with the reward of being given seed.

Ballplayers also associate a reward—successful performance—with prior behavior. If a player touches his crucifix and then gets a hit, he may decide the gesture was responsible for his good fortune and touch his crucifix the next time he comes to the plate. Unlike pigeons, however, most ballplayers are quicker to change their rituals once they no longer seem to work. Skinner found that once a pigeon associated one of its actions with the arrival of food or water, only sporadic rewards were necessary to keep the ritual going. One pigeon, believing that hopping from side to side brought pellets into its feeding cup, hopped ten thousand times without a pellet before finally giving up. But, then,

[2]Bronislaw Malinowski, *Magic, Science and Religion and Other Essays* (Glencoe, IL: Free Press, 1948).

[3]B. F. Skinner, *Behavior of Organisms: An Experimental Analysis* (New York: Appleton Century, 1938).

didn't Wade Boggs eat chicken before every game, through slumps and good times, for seventeen years?

Obviously the rituals and superstitions of baseball do not make a pitch travel faster or a batted ball find the gaps between the fielders, nor do the Trobriand rituals calm the seas or bring fish. What both do, however, is give their practitioners a sense of control, and with that, added confidence. And we all know how important that is. If you really believe eating chicken or hopping over the foul lines will make you a better hitter, it probably will.

Connection Questions

1. Based on the definitions in Miller, describe the kind(s) of ritual exhibited in the Gmelch article.

2. How is religion distinguished from magic in the Miller text?

3. What are some examples from your culture of magical behavior or thinking?

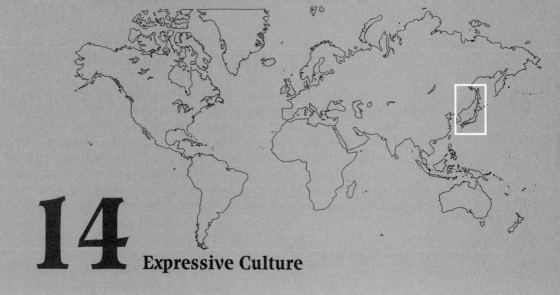

14

Expressive Culture

Japanese Hip-Hop and the Globalization of Popular Culture

Ian Condry

By now, anyone who travels the world knows that something is afoot. Hilton, Sheraton, Radisson, and other national chain look-alike hotels grace downtown districts in most major international cities. African cab drivers deliver embarking airline passengers to historic "American" districts in our nation's capital. Tourists eat in a Chinese restaurant located in Cusco, high in the Andes. Faxes and e-mails flash around the world in seconds. Clothing and hairstyles look similar from one country to the next. But does this global "sameness" related to population movement, transnational companies, and

Reprinted by permission of Waveland Press, Inc., from Ian Condry, "Japanese Hip-Hop and the Globalization of Popular Culture" from *Urban Life*. (Long Grove, IL: Waveland Press, Inc., 2002). All rights reserved.

cross-cultural borrowing mean that a single world culture is emerging? In some ways, perhaps, yes, but in many ways borrowed culture is hybridized by a process of localization. When new cultural forms arrive, they are often understood and modified by local cultural perspectives. And often their appearance stimulates the creation of new cultural forms. Anthropologists have a long tradition of investigating beliefs, social organization, and events at the local level, so the process of hybridization and cultural creation "on the ground" is where they can make the greatest contribution to an understanding of globalization.

This is a point made by Ian Condry in this selection. Using the example of hip-hop, originally a North American contribution to pop culture, he shows how this entertainment form has been adapted to the club scene in metropolitan Tokyo. Sporting typical—in most cases American-like—clothing and hairstyles, crowds of Japanese young people jam all-night clubs to hear hip-hop performers do their stuff. But they continue to do this in a Japanese fashion, using the musical form as a way to express their presence as young individuals in traditionally group-oriented, age-ranked Japanese society.

Introduction

Japanese hip-hop, which began in the 1980s and continues to develop today, is an intriguing case study for exploring the globalization of popular culture. Hip-hop is but one example among many of the transnational cultural styles pushed by entertainment and fashion industries, pulled by youth eager for the latest happening thing, and circulated by a wide range of media outlets eager to draw readers and to sell advertising. In Tokyo, a particular combination of local performance sites, artists, and fans points to ways that urban areas are crucibles of new, hybrid cultural forms. Hip-hop was born in the late 1970s in New York City as a form of street art: rapping on sidewalk stoops, outdoor block parties with enormous sound systems, graffiti on public trains, and breakdancing in public parks. In its voyage to Japan, the street ethic of hip-hop remains, but it is performed most intensely in all-night clubs peppered around Tokyo. This paper examines these nightclubs as an urban setting that helps us grasp the cultural dynamics of Japanese hip-hop. In particular, the interaction between artist-entrepreneurs and fans in live shows demonstrates how "global" popular culture is still subject to important processes of localization.

Anthropologists have a special role in analyzing such transnational forms because of their commitment to extended fieldwork in local settings. Ethnography aims to capture the cultural practices and social organization of a people. This offers a useful way of seeing how popular culture is interwoven with everyday life. Yet there is a tension between ethnography and globalization, because in many ways they seem antithetical to each other. While ethnography attempts to evoke the distinctive texture of local experience, globalization is often seen as erasing local differences. An important analytical challenge for today's media-saturated world is finding a way to understand how local culture interacts with such global media flows.

On one hand, it seems as if locales far removed from each other are becoming increasingly the same. It is more than a little eerie to fly from New York to Tokyo and see teenagers in both places wearing the same kinds of fashion characteristic of rap fans: baggy pants with boxers on display, floppy hats or baseball caps, and immaculate space-age Nike sneakers. In Tokyo stores for youth, rap music is the background sound of choice. Graffiti styled after the New York City aerosol artists dons numerous walls, and breakdancers can be found in public parks practicing in the afternoon or late at night. In all-night dance clubs throughout Tokyo, Japanese rappers and DJs take to the stage and declare that they have some "extremely bad shit" (*geki yaba shitto*)—meaning "good music"—to share with the audience. For many urban youth, hip-hop is the defining style of their era. In 1970s Japan, the paradigm of high school cool was long hair and a blistering solo on lead guitar. Today, trendsetters are more likely to sport "dread" hair and show off their scratch techniques with two turntables and a mixer. In the last few years, rap music has become one of the best-selling genres of music in the United States and around the world as diverse youth are adapting the style to their own messages and contexts.

But at the same time, there are reasons to think that such surface appearances of sameness disguise differences at some deeper level. Clearly, cultural setting and social organization have an impact on how movies and television shows are viewed. Yet if we are to understand the shape of cultural forms in a world that is increasingly connected by global media and commodity flows, we must situate Japanese rappers in the context of contemporary Japan. When thinking about how hip-hop is appropriated, we must consider, for example, that most Japanese rappers and fans speak only Japanese. Many of them live at home with their parents, and they all went through the Japanese education system. Moreover, even if the origin of their beloved music genre is overseas, they are caught up in social relations that are ultimately quite local, animated primarily by face-to-face interactions and telephone calls. So while these youth see themselves as "hip-hoppers" and "B-Boys" and "B-Girls," and associate themselves with what they call a "global hip-hop culture," they also live in a day-to-day world that is distinctly Japanese.

For those interested in studying the power of popular culture, there is also a more practical question of research methods. How does a lone researcher go about studying something as broad and unwieldy as the globalization of mass culture? One of the tenets of anthropological fieldwork is that you cannot understand a people without being there, but in the case of a music genre, where is "there"? In the fall of 1995, I began a year and a half of fieldwork in Tokyo, and the number of potential sites was daunting. There were places where the music was produced: record companies, recording studios, home studios, and even on commuter trains with handheld synthesizers. There were places where the music was promoted: music magazines, fashion magazines, TV and radio shows, night-clubs, and record stores. There was the interaction between musicians and fans at live shows, or in mediated form on cassettes, CDs, and 12-inch LPs. To make matters worse, rap music is part of the larger category of "hip-hop." Hip-hop encompasses not only rap, but also breakdance, DJ, graffiti, and fashion. The challenge was to understand the current fascination among Japanese youth with hip-hop music and style, while also considering the role of money-making organizations. How does one situate the experiential pleasures within the broader structures of profit that produce mass culture?

As I began interviewing rappers, magazine writers, and record company people, I found a recurring theme that provided a partial answer. Everyone agreed that you cannot understand Japanese rap music without going regularly to the clubs. Clubs were called the "actual site" *(genba)* of the Japanese rap scene.[1] It was there that rappers performed, DJs learned which songs elicit excitement in the crowd, and breakdancers practiced and competed for attention. In what follows, I would like to suggest that an effective tool for understanding the globalization of popular culture is to consider places like Japanese hip-hop nightclubs in terms of what might be called "genba globalism." By using participant–observation methods to explore key sites that are a kind of media crossroads, we can observe how globalized images and sounds are performed, consumed, and then transformed in an ongoing process. I use the Japanese term "genba" to emphasize that the processing of such global forms happens through the local language and in places where local hip-hop culture is produced. In Japanese hip-hop, these clubs are important not only as places where fans can see live shows and hear the latest releases from American and Japanese groups, but also as places for networking among artists, writers, and record company people. In this essay, I would like to point out some of the advantages of considering key sites as places to understand the cross-cutting effects of globalization. To get a sense of what clubs are about, let's visit one.

Going to Harlem on the Yamanote Line

A visit to Tokyo's Harlem is the best place to begin a discussion of Japanese hip-hop. Opened in the summer of 1997, Harlem is one of many all night dance clubs, but as the largest club solely devoted to hip-hop and R&B, it has become the flagship for the Japanese scene (at least, at the time of this writing in February 2001). Nestled in the love hotel area of the Shibuya section of Tokyo, Harlem is representative of the otherworldliness of clubs as well as their location within the rhythms and spaces of mainstream Japan.

---

[1]The word *"genba"* is made up of the characters "to appear" and "place," and it is used to describe a place where something actually happens, like the scene of an accident or of a crime, or a construction site. In the hip-hop world the term is used to contrast the intense energy of the club scene with the more sterile and suspect marketplace.

If we were visiting the club, we would most likely meet at Shibuya train station around midnight because the main action seldom gets started before 1 A.M. Most all-night revelers commute by train, a practice that links Tokyo residents in a highly punctual dance. The night is divided between the last train (all lines stop by 1 A.M. at the latest) and the first train of the morning (between 4:30 and 5 A.M.). The intervening period is when clubs (*kurabu*) are most active.[2] Shortly after midnight, Shibuya station is the scene for the changing of the guard: those heading home, running to make their connections for the last train, and those like us heading out, dressed up, and walking leisurely because we will be spending all night on the town. The magazine stands are closing. Homeless men are spread out on cardboard boxes on the steps leading down to the subways. The police observe the masses moving past each other in the station square towards their respective worlds. Three billboard-size TVs looming overhead, normally spouting pop music videos and snowboard ads during the day, are now dark and silent. The throngs of teenagers, many in their school uniforms, that mob Shibuya during afternoons and all weekend have been replaced by a more balanced mix of college students, "salarymen" and "career women," and of course more than a few B-Boys and B-Girls—the hip-hop enthusiasts in baggy pants and headphones. The sidewalks are splashed with light from vending machines—cigarettes, soda, CDs, beer (off for the night), and "valentine call" phone cards. A few drunken men are being carried by friends or lie in their suits unconscious on the sidewalk.

To get to Harlem, we walk uphill along Dôgenzaka Avenue toward a corner with a large neon sign advertising a capsule hotel, where businessmen who have missed their last train can sleep in coffin-like rooms. We pass disposable lamppost signs and phone booth stickers advertising various sex services. An elderly man in the back of a parked van is cooking and selling *takoyaki* (octopus dumplings) to those with the late-night munchies. The karaoke box establishments advertise cheaper rates at this hour. Turning right at a Chinese restaurant, we move along a narrow street packed with love hotels, which advertise different prices for "rest" or "stay." In contrast to the garish yellow sign advertising the live music hall, On-Air East, about fifty meters ahead, a nondescript door with a spiffy, long-haired bouncer out front is all that signals us that Harlem is inside. It seems there are always a couple of clubbers out front talking on their tiny cell phones. Up the stairs, past a table filled with flyers advertising upcoming hip-hop events, we pay our ¥3000 each (around $25, which may seem expensive, but is only about half again as much as a movie ticket). We move into the circulating and sweaty mass inside.

Traveling to a club instills a sense of moving against the mainstream in time and space. Others are going home to bed as the clubber heads out. When

---

[2]Hip-hop is not the only style for club music. Techno, House, Reggae, Jungle/Drum 'n' Bass, and so on, are some of the other popular club music styles. Live music tends to be performed earlier in the evening, usually starting around 7 P.M., and finishing in time for the audience to catch an evening train home. In contrast to "clubs," "discos" must by law close by 1 A.M.

the clubber returns home in the morning, reeking of smoke and alcohol, the train cars hold early-bird workers as well. So the movement to and from the club, often from the distant suburbs, gives clubbers a sense of themselves as separate, flaunting their leisure, their costumes, and their consumer habits. During the course of my year-and-a-half of fieldwork, between the fall of 1995 and the spring of 1997, I went to over a hundred club events around Tokyo and I began to see that clubs help one understand not only the pleasures of rap in Japan, but also the social organization of the scene and the different styles that have emerged. This becomes clear as you spend time inside the clubs.

Inside the Club

Inside the club, the air is warm and thick, humid with the breath and sweat of dancing bodies. Bone-thudding bass lines thump out of enormous speakers. There is the scratch-scratch of a DJ doing his turntable tricks, and the hum of friends talking, yelling really, over the sound of the music. The lighting is subdued, much of it coming from a mirrored ball slowly rotating on the ceiling. The fraternity house smell of stale beer is mostly covered up by the choking cigarette haze, but it is best not to look too closely at what is making the floor alternately slippery and sticky. The darkness, low ceiling, black walls, and smoky murk create a space both intimate and claustrophobic. Almost everyone heads for the bar as soon as they come in. An important aspect of clubbing is the physical experience of the music and crowded setting.

Harlem is a larger space than most of the Tokyo clubs, and can hold upwards of one thousand people on a crowded weekend night. On the wall behind the DJ stage, abstract videos, *anime* clips, or edited Kung Fu movies present a background of violence and mayhem, albeit with an Asian flavor. Strobe lights, steam, and moving spotlights give a strong sense of the space, and compound the crowded, frenetic feeling imposed by the loud music. The drunken revelry gives clubs an atmosphere of excitement that culminates with the live show and the following freestyle session. But an important part of clubbing is also the lull before and after the show, when one circulates among the crowd, flirting, networking, gossiping, or simply checking out the scene. Clubs are a space where the diffuse network of hip-hop fans comes together in an elusive effort to have fun. To the extent that a "community" emerges in the hip-hop scene, it revolves around specific club events and the rap groups that draw the crowd.

Much of the time is spent milling around, talking, drinking, and dancing. The live show often produces a welcome rise in the excitement level of the clubbers. Some events feature several live acts, often followed by a freestyle session. The rap show will usually begin between 1:00 and 1:30 A.M. Formats vary depending on the club and the event. "B-Boy Night" at R-Hall (organized by Crazy-A) was held one Sunday a month and would start with a long breakdancing show, with many groups each doing a five-minute routine. Then a series of rap groups would come on, each doing two or three songs. At other shows, like FG Night, sometimes a series of groups would perform, while on other nights only one group would do a show followed by a more open-ended freestyle. Nevertheless, there were many similarities, and a characteristic live show would proceed as follows. Two rappers take the stage (or step up into the DJ booth), as the DJ prepares the music. For people enamored of live bands, the live show of a rap concert may strike one as a bit lifeless. The music is either pre-recorded on a digital audio tape (DAT) or taken from the breakbeats section of an album.[3] The flourish of a lead guitar, bass, or drum solo is replaced in the hip-hop show by the manic scratching of a record by a DJ who deftly slides a record back and forth across the slip mat laid on the turntable and works the mixer to produce the rhythmic flurries of sampled sound.

The rappers begin with a song introducing themselves as a group. Every group seems to have its own introductory song of self-promotion:

rainutsutaa ga rainut shi ni yatte kita	Rhymester has come to rhyme
doko ni kita? Shibuya!	where are we? Shibuya!
hai faa za dopesuto da	we are By Phar the Dopest
oretachi kyo cho gesuto da	we are tonight's super guests
makka na me o shita fuktuô	The red-eyed owl [You the Rock]
ore tojo	I've arrived on stage

These songs tend to be brief, only a couple of minutes long. Between the first and second song, the rappers ask the audience how they feel. A common catchphrase was "How do you feel/My crazy brothers."[4] The group will introduce by name the rappers and DJ, and also make sure everyone remembers the name of the group. The rappers will comment about how noisy the crowd is. Crowds are more often criticized for not being worked up enough rather than praised for their excitement.

The second song tends to be the one the group is most famous for. On stage, each rapper holds a cordless microphone right up to his mouth, and a rapper might steady the mic by holding his index finger under his nose. The other arm is gesticulating, palm out in a waving motion at the audience. A bobbing motion in the head and shoulders can be more or less pronounced.

Between the second and third song, the group will usually demand some call-and-response from the audience, almost always as follows:

---

[3]The term "breakbeats" refers to the section of a song where only the drums, or drums and bass, play. It is the break between the singing and the melodies of the other instruments, hence "breakbeats." This section can be looped by a DJ using two turntables and a mixer with cross-fader, and produces a backing track suitable for rapping.

[4]In Japanese, *chôoshi wa dô dai/ikarera kyôdai*. The masculinity of Japanese rap is here indexed by the calling out to "brothers" and also by the use of the masculine slang *dai* instead of *da*.

Call	*Response*	*Call*	*Response*
ie yo ho	*ho*	Say, ho	ho
ie yo ho ho	*ho ho*	Say, ho ho	ho ho
ie yo ho ho ho	*ho ho ho*	Say ho ho ho	ho ho ho
sawage!	[screams]	Make noise!	[screams]

The third and usually final song tends to be a new song, often introduced in English as "brand new shit," a revolting image for English-speakers perhaps, but apparently heard by the audience as a cooler way of saying "new song" than the Japanese *shinkyoku*. If the song is about to be released as a record or CD, this information is also announced before the song's performance. If there are other rap groups in the audience, this is also the time for "shout outs" (praise for fellow hip-hoppers) as in "Shakkazombie in da house" or "Props to King Giddra" and once even, "Ian Condry in da house." After the third song, there is seldom talk besides a brief goodbye in English: "Peace" or "We out." Encores are rare, but freestyle sessions, discussed below, are ubiquitous. After the show, rappers retreat backstage or to the bar area, but never linger around the stage after performing. The year 1996 was also a time of a "freestyle boom," when most shows were closed with an open-ended passing of the microphone. Anyone could step on stage and try his or her hand at rapping for a few minutes. This has been an important way for younger performers to get the attention of more established acts. There is a back-and-forth aspect of performance in the clubs that shows how styles are developed, honed, and reworked in a context where the audience is knowledgeable, discriminating, and at times participates in the show itself.

It is important to understand that over the years, this kind of feedback loop has helped determine the shape of current Japanese rap styles. One of my main sites was a weekly Thursday night event that featured another collection of rap groups called Kitchens. Hip-hop collectives such as Kitchens, Little Bird Nation, Funky Grammar Unit, and Rock Steady Crew Japan are called "families" (*famirii*, in Japanese). The different groups often met at clubs or parties, at times getting acquainted after particularly noteworthy freestyle sessions. Over time some would become friends, as well as artistic collaborators, who performed together live or in the studio for each others' albums. Such families define the social organization of the "scene." What is interesting is how they also characterize different aesthetic takes on what Japanese hip-hop should be. Kitchens, for example, aim to combine a pop music sensibility with their love for rap music, and, like many such "party rap" groups, they appeal to a largely female audience. The Funky Grammar Unit aims for a more underground sound that is nonetheless accessible, and they tend to have a more even mix of men and women in the audience. Other families like Urbarian Gym (UBG) are less concerned with being accessible to audiences than with conveying a confrontational, hard-core stance. The lion's share of their audiences are young males, though as UBG's leader, Zeebra, breaks into the pop spotlight, their audiences are becoming more diverse.

The lull that precedes and follows the onstage performance is a key time for networking to build these families. In all, the live show is at most an hour long, at times closer to twenty minutes, and yet there is nowhere for the clubbers to go until the trains start running again around 5 A.M. It is not unusual for music magazine writers to do interviews during club events, and record company representatives often come to shows as well, not only as talent scouts but also to discuss upcoming projects. I found that 3:00 to 4 A.M. was the most productive time for fieldwork because by then the clubbers had mostly exhausted their supply of stories and gossip to tell friends, and were then open to finding out what this strange foreigner jotting things in his notebook was doing in their midst.

Japanese cultural practices do not disappear just because everyone is wearing their hip-hop outfits and listening to the latest rap tunes. To give one example, at the first Kitchens event after the New Year, I was surprised to see all the clubbers who knew each other going around and saying the traditional New Year's greeting in very formal Japanese: "Congratulations on the dawn of the New Year. I humbly request your benevolence this year as well." There was no irony, no joking atmosphere in these statements. This is a good example of the way that globalization may appear to overshadow Japanese culture, but one needs to spend time in clubs with the people to see how surface appearances can be deceiving.

In many ways, then, it is not surprising that rappers, DJs, breakdancers, record company people, and magazine editors all agree you cannot understand the music unless you go to the clubs. There is an intensity of experience in hearing the music at loud volume, surrounded by a crush of dancing people, while drinking alcohol and staying out all night, that gives the music an immediacy and power it lacks when heard, say, on headphones in the quiet of one's room. Indeed, it is difficult to convey in words the feeling of communal excitement during a particularly good show, when one gets wrapped up in a surge of energy that is palpable yet intangible. It is this emotional experience that in many ways counteracts any fears that it is all "merely imitation," which is the most common criticism of the music.

At the same time, going to a club involves a strange mix of the extraordinary and the routine. On one hand, you visit a place with bizarre interior design, listen to music at exceedingly high volume, stay out all night and, often, get drunk. It is a sharp contrast to an ordinary day of school or work. We must also recognize, however, that while a club may strive to be a fantastic microcosm, it is still embedded in Japan's political-economic structures, characteristic social relations, and the contemporary range of cultural forms. It is not by chance that clubs tend to attract people of specific class, age, sexuality, and to some extent locale. Moreover, if you go regularly to clubs, after a while it becomes just another routine. It is largely predictable what kind of pleasures can be expected, and also the generally unpleasant consequences for work or school after a night without sleep.[5] Clubbing of-

---

[5]Youthful Japanese clubbers use the mixed English-Japanese construction "all *suru*" (do all) to mean "stay out all night in a club." For example, the following exchange occurred between two members of the female group Now. Here, the sense of routine outweighs the excitement. A: *konban mo ooru suru ka na?* (Are we staying out all night again?) B: *Tabun.* (Probably) A: *Yabai.* (That sucks.)

fers freedom and constraints. This tension is the key to understanding how clubs socialize the club-goers by structuring pleasure in characteristic ways.

I have only suggested some of the ways that clubs offer insight into the ways that global hip-hop becomes transformed into a local form of Japanese hip-hop, but we can see how an idea of "genba globalism" can help us understand the process of localization. Globalism is refracted and transformed in important ways through the actual site of urban hip-hop clubs. Japanese rappers perform for local audiences in the Japanese language and use Japanese subjects to build their base of fans. In contrast to club events with techno or house music, hip-hop events emphasize lyrics in the shows and the freestyle sessions. There is a wide range of topics addressed in Japanese hip-hop, but they all speak in some way to the local audience. Dassen 3 uses joking lyrics ridiculing school and television. Scha Dara Parr is also playful, emphasizing things like their love of video games and the kind of verbal repartee characteristic of close buddies. When Zeebra acts out his hard-core stance, he tells of drug use in California, expensive dates with girlfriends, and abstract lyrics about hip-hop as a revolutionary war. Rhymester's lyrics are often set in a club or just after a show, for example, describing an imagined, fleeting love affair with a girl on a passing train. Some songs refer to cultural motifs going back centuries, such as a song performed by Rima and Umedy about a double-suicide pact between lovers, remade as a contemporary R&B and hip-hop jam.

Understanding Globalization in Local Terms

Rap music in Japan offers an interesting case study of the way popular culture is becoming increasingly global in scope, while at the same time becoming domesticated to fit with local ideas and desires. At the dawn of the twenty-first century, entertainment industries are reaching wider markets and larger audiences. The film *Titanic*, for example, grossed over $1.5 billion, the largest amount ever for a film, and two-thirds of this income came from overseas. In music, there are global pop stars too, like Britney Spears and Celine Dion. In rap music, the Fugees could be considered global stars. Their 1996 album "The Score" sold over 17 million copies worldwide. More recently, Lauryn Hill's 1998 solo album revealed that the transnational market for hip-hop is still growing, and most major rap stars do promotional tours in Japan. An important feature of pop culture commodities is that they tend to be expensive to produce initially, but then relatively cheap to reproduce and distribute. Compact disks are one of the most striking examples. Although studio time is expensive (between $25,000 for a practically homemade album to upwards of $250,000 for state-of-the-art productions), the CDs themselves cost about eighty cents to produce, including the packaging. Obviously, the more one can sell, the higher the return, and this helps explain the eagerness of entertainment businesses to develop new markets around the world.

Less clear are the kinds of effects such globalized pop culture forms might have. The fluidity of culture in the contemporary world raises new questions about how we are linked together, what we share and what divides us. The spread of popular culture seems in some ways linked with a spread in values, but we must be cautious in our assessment of how and to what extent this transfer takes place. It is safe to say that the conventional understanding of globalization is that it is producing a homogenization of cultural forms. From this perspective, we are witnessing the McDonaldization and the Coca-Cola colonization of the periphery by powerful economic centers of the world system. The term "cultural imperialism" captures this idea, that political and economic power is being used "to exalt and spread the values and habits of a foreign culture at the expense of the native culture."[6] In some ways, anthropology as a discipline emerged at a time when there was a similar concern that the forces of modernity (especially missionaries and colonial officials) were wiping out "traditional cultures," and thus one role for ethnographers was to salvage, at least in the form of written documents, the cultures of so-called "primitive peoples." Many people view globalization, and particularly the spread of American pop culture, as a similar kind of invasion, but the idea that watching a Disney movie automatically instills certain values must be examined and not simply assumed. In some ways the goals of anthropology—combatting simplistic and potentially dangerous forms of ethnocentrism—remain as important today as when the discipline was born.

The example of Japanese hip-hop gives us a chance to examine some recent theorizing on globalization. The sociologist Malcolm Waters offers a useful overview of globalization, which he defines as follows:

> A social process in which the constraints of geography on social and cultural arrangements recede, and in which people become increasingly aware that they are receding.[7]

A key aspect of this definition is not only that the world is increasingly becoming one place, but that people are becoming increasingly aware of that. This awareness may lead to a heightened sense of risk, such as global warming or the "love bug" virus, or to a rosy view of increased opportunities, for example, to get the most recent hip-hop news in real time or to download the latest music instantly via the Internet.

It is important to recognize, however, that globalization involves much more than Hollywood movies and pop music. Waters does a good job of analyzing three aspects of globalization, namely, economic, political, and cultural. He contends that globalization processes go back five hundred years, and that

[6]John Tomlinson, *Cultural Imperialism: A Critical Introduction* (London: Printer Publishers, 1991), p. 3.

[7]Malcolm Waters, *Globalization* (London: Routledge, 1995, p. 3).

the relative importance of economic, political, and cultural exchanges has varied over that time.[8] From the sixteenth to nineteenth centuries, economics was key. In particular, the growth of the capitalist world system was the driving force in linking diverse regions. During the nineteenth and twentieth centuries, politics moved to the fore. Nation-states produced a system of international relations that characterized global linkages with multinational corporations and integrated national traditions. Now, at the dawn of the twenty-first century, cultural forms are leading global changes in both politics and economics. Waters argues that a "global idealization" is producing politics based on worldwide values (e.g., human rights, the environment, anti-sweatshop movement) and economic exchanges centered on lifestyle consumerism. The key point is that while economics and then politics were the driving forces in globalization of previous centuries, it is cultural flows that are increasingly important today. If he is right, and I would argue he is, this points to the importance of studying the kinds of ideals that are spread around the globe.

What ideals are spread by hip-hop in Japan? Clubbing certainly promotes an attitude that stresses leisure, fashion, and consumer knowledge of music over other kinds of status in work and school. Although it is important to recognize that the effects of lyrics are somewhat complicated, it is worth considering, to some extent, the messages carried by the music. Although rappers deal with a wide variety of subjects, one theme appears again and again, namely, that youth need to speak out for themselves. As rapper MC Shiro of Rhymester puts it, "If I were to say what *hip-hop* is, it would be a 'culture of the first person singular.' In hip-hop, . . . rappers are always yelling, 'I'm this.'" Such a message may seem rather innocuous compared to some of the hard-edged lyrics one is likely to hear in the United States, but it is also a reflection of the kind of lives these Japanese youth are leading. In Japan, the education system tends to emphasize rote memorization and to track students according to exams. Sharply age-graded hierarchies are the norm, and may be especially irksome in a situation where the youth are likely to live with their parents until they get married. Moreover, the dominant ideology that harmony of the group should come before individual expression ("the nail that sticks up gets hammered down") makes for a social context in which the hip-hop idea that one should be speaking for oneself is, in some limited sense, revolutionary. At the very least, it shows how global pop culture forms are leading not to some simple homogenization, but rather adding to a complex mix that in many ways can only be studied ethnographically through extended research in local sites.

Another important theorist of globalization is Arjun Appadurai, who proposes that we consider contemporary cultural flows in terms of movement in five categories: people or ethnicity, ideology, finance, technology, and media. He adds the suffix "-scape" to each to highlight that the deterritorialization of cultural forms is accompanied by new landscapes of cultural exchange, thus we

[8]Waters, pp. 157–164.

have "ethnoscapes, ideoscapes, financescapes, technoscapes, and mediascapes" (others have added "sacriscapes" to describe the spread of religion, and one might add "leisurescapes" for the spread of popular culture). The key point about these landscapes is that they are "non-isomorphic," that is, they don't map evenly onto each other. Appadurai notes, for example, that the "Japanese are notoriously hospitable to ideas and are stereotyped as inclined to export (all) and import (some) goods, but they are notoriously closed to immigration"[9] (1996:37). Migration and electronic mass media are the main driving forces to Appadurai's theorization. One of the problems with Appadurai's theory, however, is that the notion of "-scapes" draws us away from considering how flows of technology, media, finance, and people are connected. An alternative is to consider key sites, *genba* if you will, of various sorts depending on one's interests as a way to see how new, hybrid forms of culture are produced. "Genba globalism" aims to show how artists, fans, producers, and media people are actively consuming and creating these new forms.

One thing that anthropologists offer to the advancement of human knowledge is a clear sense of the ways people interact in specific places. At one time, anthropologists would choose a village or island to map in elaborate detail. Now in a media-filled world, we face different analytical challenges, but the techniques of fieldwork—learning the language, participating in daily life, observing rituals, and so on—can still be used. One of Appadurai's conclusions is that exchanges along these different "-scapes" are leading not only to a deterritorialization of cultural forms, but also to an increased importance of the "work of the imagination".[10] In other words, as identities can be picked up from a variety of media sources, the construction of "who we are" arises increasingly from how we imagine ourselves, rather than from where we live. Life in urban areas seems to make this aspect of identity—as imagination and as performance—all the more salient. What I hope I have drawn attention to is the way the hip-hop nightclubs give us a chance to bring some of this work of the imagination down to the level of daily life.

Conclusion: Global Pop and Cultural Change

In the end, the globalization of popular culture needs to be understood as two related yet opposing trends of greater massification and deeper compartmentalization. On one hand, the recording industry is reaching larger and larger markets, both within Japan and around the world, as mega-hits continue to set sales records. On the other hand, there is an equally profound if less visible process by which niche scenes are becoming deeper and more widely connected

---

[9]Arjun Appadurai, *Modernity at large: Cultural dimensions of globalization* (Minneapolis: University of Minnesota Press, 1996), p. 37.

[10]Appadurai, p. 3.

than before, and in the process, new forms of heterogeneity are born. Although I have only been able to touch on a few of its aspects here, Japanese rap music is a revealing case study of the social location, cultural role, and capitalist logic of such micro-mass cultures. It is important to recognize, however, that these micro-mass cultures also have the potential to move into the mainstream.

The distinction between "scene" and "market" highlights what is at stake when we try to analyze the cultural and capitalist transformations associated with globalization. Information-based and service industries are growing rapidly, promising to reorganize the bounds of culture and commodities, yet we need close readings of how such emerging economies influence everyday lives. Although B-Boys and B-Girls go to great lengths to distinguish the "cultural" from the "commercial" in their favored genre, it is rather the linkage of the two in the circuits of popular culture that offers the deepest insight. In the end, the winds of global capitalism that carried the seeds of rap music to Japan can only be grasped historically with a close attention to social spaces, media forms, and the rhythms of everyday life.

Walking to a hip-hop club in Tokyo, one is confronted with a tremendous range of consumer options, and it is this heightened sense of "you are what you buy" that has in many ways become the defining feature of identity in advanced capitalist nations, at least among those people with the money to consume their preferred lifestyle. At the same time, it is important to be sensitive to the ways that, outward appearances notwithstanding, the consumers of things like hip-hop are embedded in a quite different range of social relations and cultural meanings. It makes a difference that B-Boys and B-Girls, listening to American hip-hop records, still feel it is important to go around to their friends and associates with the traditional New Year's greeting of deference and obligation. This is an example of the ways social relations within the Japanese rap scene continue to carry the weight of uniquely Japanese practices and understandings.

It is likely, too, that "global pop" will become more heterogeneous as the entertainment industries in other countries develop. There are reasons to think that, in music at least, the domination of American popular music as the leading "global" style seems likely to be a temporary situation. In the immediate postwar period in Japan, Western music initially dominated sales. But sales of Japanese music steadily grew and in 1967 outpaced Western sales. Today, three-fourths of Japan's music market is Japanese music to one-fourth Western. Moreover, although American music currently constitutes about half of global sales, this is down from 80 percent a decade ago. It is quite possible that as local record companies mature in other countries, they will, as in Japan, come to dominate local sales. Certainly, multinational record companies are moving in this direction of developing local talent and relying less on Western pop stars. Moreover, although Japan is a ravenous importer of American popular culture, it has some notable exports as well. Some are more familiar than others, but they include the Mighty Morphin' Power Rangers, karaoke, "Japanimation," *manga* (Japanese comic books), mechanical pets, Nintendo or the Sony Play-Station video games, and of course, Pokémon.

Just as it would seem strange to Americans if someone claimed Pokémon is making U.S. kids "more Japanese," it is dangerous to assume that mass culture goods by themselves threaten to overwhelm other cultures. The anthropologist Daniel Miller has been a proponent for taking a closer look at the ways such goods are woven into everyday lives. He argues that mass commodities are better analyzed in terms of an "unprecedented diversity created by the differential consumption of what had once been thought to be global and homogenizing institutions."[11] Miller's emphasis on the active and creative aspects of consumption is characteristic of a broad trend within the social sciences to view global commodities in terms of their local appropriations, and to represent local consumers with a greater degree of agency than found in other works that emphasize "cultural imperialism." It is this perspective that seems to me the best characterization of what is going on in Japan.

It is easy to see how the "sameness" aspect of globalization is promoted. Music magazines, TV video shows, and record stores promote similar artists whether in Japan or the United States. A new album by Nas is met with a flurry of publicity in the Japanese and English-language hip-hop magazines available in Tokyo. This relates in part to the structure of record companies and their marketing practices. In this sense, the widening and increasingly globalized market for popular culture does appear to be leading to greater homogenization. But it is primarily a process of homogenizing what is available, regardless of where you are. I would argue that the global marketing blitz of megahit productions like the film *Titanic* and the music of Celine Dion and Lauryn Hill reflect a homogenization of *what* is available, but not *how* it is interpreted. Although it is more difficult to see, in part because it is hidden beneath similar clothes, hairstyles, and consumption habits, different interpretations are generated in different social contexts. By attending to "actual sites" of cultural production and consumption, we can more clearly gauge the ways local contexts alter the meanings of globalization. "Keeping it real" for hip-hoppers in Japan means paying attention to local realities.

[11]Daniel Miller, "Introduction: Anthropology, modernity and consumption," in Daniel Miller (ed.), *Worlds Apart: Modernity through the Prism of the Local* (London: Routledge, 1995), p. 3.

Connection Questions

1. How does Ian Condry define globalization?

2. What does the hip-hop scene in Tokyo reveal about the globalization of popular culture?

3. Give two examples of how globalization has affected some of the forms of expressive culture described in Miller.

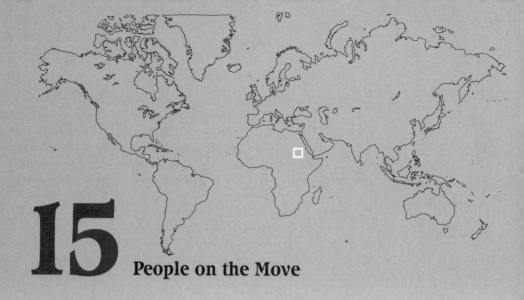

15

People on the Move

The Road to Refugee Resettlement

Dianna Shandy

In the early days of the discipline, anthropologists usually studied non-Western groups that they assumed were bounded and clearly definable. Such groups were named (often by outsiders) and were thought to have territories and a common language and culture. Although anthropologists recognized that many of the groups they studied had outside connections—that they freely borrowed culture, intermarried, and migrated—most still felt it was reasonable to talk about groups as if they were bounded units. However, the picture is changing, as this updated article by Dianna Shandy clearly shows. Today people are on the move. Some are migrants looking for economic opportunity; others are refugees. Here Shandy, using the case of the Nuer from southern Sudan, shows how refugees fleeing a perpetual civil war manage to gain relocation in the United States and how they have sought to adapt to the demands of life among Americans. A key to the process is the role played by the United Nations and social service agencies and the Nuer's own determination to better (in their terms) themselves.

Reprinted by permission of Dianna J.Shandy.

A Nuer youth, Thok Ding *(not his real name)* lies prone alongside two other boys on the dusty, clay ground on the outskirts of a village in southern Sudan. A man crouches over him with a razor blade. Beginning with the right side, the man makes six parallel cuts from each side of the youth's forehead to the center to create scars called *gaar*. This ritual scarification, which has been outlawed in Nuer areas since the 1980s, still marks entry into manhood for many Nuer young men.

A few years later in Minneapolis, Minnesota, Thok sits in pained concentration in front of a computer screen in a driver's license examination office. Still weak in English, he struggles to recall the multiple choice response sequence he memorized to pass the exam, in this stressful, but less painful, American rite of passage into adulthood.

When I began ethnographic work among Nuer refugees living in Minnesota, Iowa, and several other regions of the United States in 1997, I immediately was struck by the incongruity of their lives. The Nuer are a famous people in anthropology. They were the subject of three books by the well-known late British social anthropologist, Sir E. E. Evans-Pritchard, who described their pastoralist mode of subsistence, complex segmented kinship system, and religion. Evans-Pritchard conducted research among the Nuer in the 1930s. He described the Nuer as a tall, independent, confident people whose existence revolved around the needs of their cattle, especially the requirement to move the animals from high to low ground and back again each year. During the dry season from September to April, the cattle were herded to lower ground where there was still water and grass. During the rainy season, the lowlands became a swampy lagoon and the herds had to be moved to the highlands where rain had restored the range. This transhumant lifestyle and the need to guard cattle against raiders from nearby tribes had shaped Nuer society. (The Nuer were also the subject of a well-known ethnographic film, "The Nuer," made by Robert Gardner and released in 1970, which showed them to be much as Evans-Pritchard had described them.)

So when I first met Nuer people in Minnesota in the mid-1990s, these Northeast African pastoralists seemed out of place. Tall (most men are well over six feet in height) and still displaying the (for men) prominent forehead scars received at their initiations, the Nuer had come to live in one of the coldest parts of the United States. Why had they left their ancestral home? What did their status as refugees mean and how did they get it? How had they managed to come to the United States? Why had they been located, as it turns out, in more than 30 different U.S. states? How would a people raised as cattle herders adapt to U.S. urban settings? Would they remain in the United States on a temporary or permanent basis? How would they maintain a relationship with the families they left behind? And finally in a broader sense, what does all this tell us about the interconnectedness of a globalizing world and about anthropology's role in it?

Becoming a Refugee

Until recently, most Americans called the people who settled here *immigrants.* No distinctions were made based on the reasons people had chosen to come here or the circumstances they had left behind. In general, their arrival was encouraged and welcome because the country was spacious and their skills and labor were needed.

Today, things are different. There are immigrants and *refugees.* In the past, refugees were a kind of immigrant. They were people who came here to escape from intolerable conditions in their homelands, such as pogroms, the threat of military conscription, civil wars, and famine. The fact that they were escaping from something, however, did not affect whether or not they could enter the United States. Most people, especially those from Europe, were welcome.

Over the last 50 years, however, refugees have come to occupy a formal status, both in the eyes of the United Nations and U.S. immigration officials. They are not just *internally displaced persons (IDPs),* those who have left their homes but who are still in their own country. Officially, meaning how the United Nations and national governments define them, a refugee group is one that shares a "well-founded fear of persecution" based on any of five factors such as race, religion, nationality, membership in a particular social group, or political opinion, and who has left their home country. How the United Nations or national governments apply this definition when they seek to certify individuals as refugees varies. But the number of people that claim to fit this description and who seek asylum skyrocketed at the end of the Cold War in 1989 to an estimated 12 million in 2003.

Bureaucracies control who can be classified as a refugee. In 1950 the United Nations established a formal agency to help with the refugee "problem" headed by the United Nations High Commissioner for Refugees (UNHCR). The agency recognizes three options, or what it calls "durable solutions," to address the situation of refugees around the world: voluntary repatriation to the country of origin, integration into a country of asylum, or rarely, third country resettlement, meaning a move from one country of asylum to one that offers possibilities for a more permanent home. Initially housed in refugee camps, displaced people can apply for official refugee status with the hope of resettlement in another country, or that conditions will stabilize in their own country, allowing them to return home.

Many countries have agreed to take in a limited number of refugees as a way of settling them more permanently, and the United States is one of them. To do this, the United States sets a limit on the number of refugees it will accept each year and uses a bureaucratic process to screen prospective refugees it might be willing to take in. Over the past decade, the United States has resettled an average of 87,000 refugees here each year, with a sharp dip in numbers in the wake of September 11, 2001. The process is complicated by the fact that the criteria for admission can change, different government officials interpret the criteria dissimilarly, and resettlement policy can shift from one year to the next. It is also complicated by cross-cultural misunderstanding. The U.S. bureaucracy works differently from the way governments operate in the refugee's country of origin. Languages are a major barrier. Categories of meaning are not shared. The screening process is intended to determine "real" refugees, or those who cannot be protected by their home governments, and "economic" migrants who leave their home voluntarily to seek a better life. In practice the distinction is often difficult to establish.

The Nuer living in Minnesota and other regions of the United States have managed to come through this process successfully. They have made it to camps that process refugees, discovered how to enter the bureaucratic process designed to certify them as refugees, learned how to tell a sufficiently convincing refugee story to gain certification and found a way to get on the list to be resettled in the United States.

Thok Ding's life illustrates this process. Thok was born in southern Sudan and lived in a small village. As in most Nuer households, Thok lived with his mother, father, siblings, and his father's extended family. Thok had family members who lived in a nearby town and attended school, but there was no school in his village. His first memory is of going to the forest to take care of his calves when he was seven or eight. He would leave home in the early morning with other boys his age, taking food with him to eat while he was grazing the cattle and protecting the calves from wild animals. Girls, on the other hand, would stay closer to home and were charged with milking the cows.

When he was in his early teens, he, along with other boys who were the same age, underwent the ritual scarification *gaar* ceremony ushering him into manhood. After undergoing this painful ritual, Thok said that now that he was a man, he could be "free." "You can do whatever you like. You can have a woman. You can have a home by yourself. You can live away from your parents."

Shortly after his initiation, the civil war that wracked the southern Sudan caught up with him. Fueled by events that extend back much further in time, civil war has engulfed the Sudan since just before it gained independence from joint English–Egyptian colonial rule until the present, with just a brief interlude of peace from the early 1970s until 1983. This ongoing strife in the Sudan frequently is attributed to social distinctions based on geography (north–south), ethnicity (Arab–African), and religion (Muslim–Christian). But, as the recent Darfur crisis has illustrated, these are fluid categories. From a southern perspective, northern Muslim Arabs entered their land in the 1800s looking for ivory and slaves. Northerners were favored under colonial rule, which gave them more power and increased tension with people, such as the Nuer, living in the south. Today, it is the Khartoum government, located in the north, that is engaged in war with southerners who seek self-government.

Nuer society has suffered cataclysmic shifts in the decades since Evans-Pritchard conducted his fieldwork, a fact well documented by anthropologist Sharon Hutchinson in her book *Nuer Dilemmas* published in 1996. For example, instead of merely regulating Nuer seasonal cattle drives, the change of seasons in the southern Sudan also dictates the rhythm of the civil war. The dry season makes it possible to move heavy artillery across the clay plains; during the wet season the same plains are impassible. The war and the displacement of Nuer and other southern Sudanese it has caused are the major cause of migration.

In the late 1980s, government troops attacked Thok's village, killing many people including his father. Although many of the survivors elected to stay and to keep herding cattle, with his father dead Thok felt it was wisest to leave Sudan after this tragedy. He traveled on foot for three days with his mother and siblings and their cattle to an Ethiopian refugee camp called Itang.

One feature of camp life was the presence of a Christian mission school, which provided Thok with his first taste of formal education, something that would prove useful later as he sought refugee status. He advanced quickly in school, skipping several grades. Seventh grade stands out for him as the real beginning of his education, however, because he passed a national exam. As a result, he was transferred to Gambela, another Ethiopian camp, to attend school, leaving his mother and siblings behind. Food scarcity made life in Gambela very difficult. Thok recalls that students were given only a small amount of corn each month. They would grind the grain into flour, cook the mixture with water, and eat it plain without a stew.

His education at Gambela progressed nicely, but was ended when war broke out in Ethiopia. Threatened by the dangers it posed, Thok rejoined his mother and siblings. Together they returned to Sudan where the United Nations had established a temporary camp to care for the Sudanese refugees who were streaming back across the border from Ethiopia. Thok weighed his options and decided to return to Ethiopia on his own. He went to the capital of Ethiopia, Addis Ababa, where he encountered some friends from school who shared information on how to get to refugee camps in Kenya.

He traveled to Kenya by bus, negotiating his way past border and police checkpoints along the way. He was arrested once by Kenyan police and had to spend the night in jail before they turned him over to the U.N. authorities that ran the nearby refugee camp. Once in the camp, he filled out a form that documented his background, and requested that he be considered for resettlement in another country. Because Thok had no relatives who had been resettled in other countries, he applied for resettlement anywhere that would accept refugees from the Sudan. These included Australia, Canada, and Sweden as well as the United States, the country that finally admitted him.

Two years elapsed from the time Thok arrived in the camp until he was sent to the United States. Life in the Kenyan camp was much more difficult than the one he had stayed at in Ethiopia. There was nothing to do, no river, no place to keep cattle, and no garden plots. Thok did, however, meet some friends he had made earlier in school, and together they cooked food and found ways to pass the long days in the camp. He and his friends also listened to the stories other Nuer told of their encounters with the refugee officials who interviewed people requesting resettlement. In a tragic commentary on how devastation can seem "normal," they learned that the biggest mistake people made was to invent dramatic stories to make themselves eligible for resettlement. For example, one Nuer man said, "People feel they need a reason, so they tell the person interviewing them that they killed someone and if they return to Sudan they will be put in jail. But the story didn't work because the interviewer thought the refugee must be a violent man." The Nuer men who worked as interpreters in the camps believed there was a better approach. "We told the community, we need to tell them the reality. Don't say you killed someone, just say you were caught in the crossfire." They had learned that the refugee officials were looking for certain kinds of experiences to determine who fit the criteria for refugee resettlement.

In addition to recounting a plausible story that indicates why they would be persecuted if they returned home, refugees must also pass a medical screening, and they must also sign a promissory note to repay the cost of their airfare to the United States once they have settled and found work. Thok passed through this process successfully, and with a ticket provided for him by the International Organization for Migration, flew to the United States. He was met at the airport by a representative from Lutheran Social Services, one of many U.S. voluntary agencies responsible for resettling refugees.

Adapting to America

Some immigrants to the United States rely on family or friends to help them find a home, job, and place in the country. But many refugees depend on voluntary agencies or "volags" to help with settlement. These agencies are under contract to the U.S. government and receive a stipend for each refugee that they place. Volags help refugees with such necessities as finding a place to live, getting a job, learning to ride the bus, and buying food. They also help them complete paperwork documenting the existence of family members who were left behind, since there may be a chance to bring them over later. Volags emphasize how important it is for refugees to find a job and become self-sufficient. Volags provide refugees with a small initial cash stipend to help them get established. But the money doesn't last long and refugees are encouraged to start working as soon as possible, often within the first week or two after arrival. An agency helped place Thok in Minnesota, found him an apartment, and assisted with a job search.

There were about thirty refugees from Sudan and Somalia on Thok's flight from Nairobi, Kenya, to New York's JFK International Airport. When Thok boarded the plane, he knew no one. By the time he arrived in New York many hours later, he felt like the eight Sudanese men he had traveled with were his new best friends. In a wrenching sort of dispersal, the eight men were all directed by airline staff to different gates at the airport to await the next leg of their journey to far-flung destinations, like San Diego, California; Nashville, Tennessee; Dallas, Texas; and Minneapolis, Minnesota.

A representative from Lutheran Social Services and a volunteer from a local church greeted Thok when he arrived on his own in Minneapolis. His few possessions fit in a small bag that he carried with him on the plane. The man from Lutheran Social Services gave him shampoo and a toothbrush and took him to Burger King. Thok found the food very strange and difficult to eat. Thok stayed the first night in the volunteer's home—a widower in his mid-sixties who regularly helped Lutheran Social Services in this way. Thok spoke some English, but he relied mostly on gestures to communicate with his host. The next day the volunteer took Thok to Lutheran Social Services to complete paperwork.

When they finished with the paperwork, the case manager who had met Thok at the airport took him to what was to be his apartment. Thok found the place to be very dirty, particularly the carpeting that had not been cleaned after the last tenants departed. There was a strong smell of cigarette smoke, cockroaches in the kitchen, and a very leaky faucet in the bathroom. Despite these problems, Thok would have his own place that would be affordable when he got a job. Later, the man Thok had stayed with the previous night brought over some furniture that had been donated by church members.

Over the coming week, Thok met with his case manager to discuss getting a job. Where refugees work and the kinds of jobs that they can get depend somewhat on the level of education and training they received prior to arrival in the United States. Upon arrival, most Nuer have little formal education and can, unfortunately, only find jobs that most people born in the United States do not want, such as unskilled factory worker, security guard, parking lot attendant, fast food server, and nursing home assistant. Or, if they do have a degree when they arrive, like many immigrants, they are "underemployed," or work in jobs below their level of credentials. Many of the Nuer who have settled in the upper Midwest have found work in meat packing plants. Thok first got a job filling beverage trays for airplanes at the airport after he arrived in the United States. His back and arms ached from the lifting he was required to do, and he did not like his boss.

Several weeks later, Thok spotted another Nuer man while he was shopping at Target. Thok did not know him personally, but after they started talking he discovered that he knew the village where the man was from in the Sudan. It was good to see someone from "home," and Thok invited him back to his apartment to cook a meal and eat together. This man had moved to Minnesota from Iowa and was able to tell Thok the names and even the phone numbers of some Nuer who were living in Des Moines. Thok knew some of these people from the refugee camps in Ethiopia, and the next day he bought a phone card to get in touch. Thok could hardly believe his ears when he heard his friend John Wal answer the phone. After a conversation that lasted until the phone card expired, Thok decided to board a bus and leave Minnesota to move to Iowa. John had talked about the sizable Nuer community living in Des Moines and the well-paying jobs offered by a meat packing company. Thok called his case manager and left a message saying that he was going. He packed his personal items, left the furniture in the apartment, and boarded a Greyhound bus.

In Des Moines, Thok moved in with John and another Nuer man. Thok worked in a packing plant for a while, but found it very difficult. At first his job was to kill pigs as they entered the processing line. He found it so hard to sleep at night after doing this over and over again all day that he asked to be transferred to some other part of the line. He still found the work exceedingly hard.

One motivation to find a job quickly is to make it possible to bring over his family members to join him, but Thok has not managed to do this yet. In addition to his mother and siblings, Thok would also like to bring over a wife. There are roughly three Nuer men for every Nuer woman in the United States, and most of the women are already married or engaged to be married. Thok and other Nuer men struggle with what they perceive as "the unreasonable levels of freedom" afforded to women in U.S. society. One way to marry a wife with more "traditional" Nuer values, or so men think, is to let their family facilitate a marriage in the Sudan or in Ethiopia and try to bring the wife over as a spouse or a refugee.

Staying in Touch

Refugee groups are deliberately "scattered" geographically across the United States when they are resettled. Policy makers believe that dispersal increases individuals' ability to adapt successfully to their new environment and that it decreases any disruptive impact on the host community that receives the refugees. However, even though refugees are "placed" in particular locales in the United States, they seldom stay put. Hmong, originally from the highlands of South East Asia, and now residents of Saint Paul, Minnesota, are a case in point and, like the Nuer, are well known for moving frequently after arrival in the United States. Nuer, who moved regularly as part of their lives in southern Sudan, continue a kind of nomadism in the United States and move frequently—from apartment to apartment, from city to city, and from state to state. As a result of having been resettled in more than thirty different states in America, Nuer have many residency options to consider and have a tendency to move where they have relatives, friends, or jobs.

Staying in contact is very important to many Nuer refugees. They are adept at devising strategies for remaining in contact with other Nuer dispersed across the United States and those whom they left behind in Africa. The process of incorporation into the United States as a refugee is also about maintaining ties to Africa. One aspect of Nuer life that sets them apart from the experiences of previous waves of immigrants to the United States is the means by which they keep in contact with those who remain at home in the Sudan, in refugee camps in neighboring African states, and around the world.

Immigrants have always retained some ties with the homes they left. But, in a 21st century context the possibilities for frequent, affordable, and rapid contact are greatly expanded. Anthropologists refer to these crosscutting social ties that span the borders of nation-states as *transnationalism*. For instance,

Thok, who wants to marry, could phone his brother in Gambela, Ethiopia, to arrange the event. He can use Western Union to send money to his brother to buy cows to give to the prospective bride's father. In Nuer eyes, the groom does not even need to be present for the marriage to be legitimate, but this is not true in the eyes of immigration authorities. Even though the groom can do his part to sponsor the marriage from the United States, he still must travel to Ethiopia for the marriage to be recognized officially for immigration purposes. The bride can apply as a refugee herself but increases her chances of resettlement by also applying as a spouse joining her husband.

Sudan ranks third, after Palestine and Afghanistan, in a list of countries that has produced the most refugees. The number of displaced Sudanese exceeds three-quarters of a million people. Those in the diaspora maintain close ties with friends and family in the Sudan, in other African countries, and around the world. Therefore, a focus on the lives of Sudanese refugees in Africa is an important part of understanding Nuer refugees' lives in the United States. These transnational linkages influence Nuer peoples' decisions in the United States.

Conclusion

Refugees are a special category of immigrant to the United States. Often seen as victims of tragic circumstances, refugees are also amazingly adept at finding ways to survive these same circumstances. Refugees' lives depend on an international and national bureaucracy, and those who pass through the process represent a very small percentage of people who are displaced. Starting a life in a vastly different cultural environment than the one they were raised in presents a number of hardships. Refugees cope with these challenges by trying to maintain their original ethnic group identity. Transnational communication is one way to do this. So is moving to find people they know from their homelands.

Anthropologists, such as Evans-Pritchard, used to journey to faraway places to study distant "others." Nowadays it is often the objects of study that make the journey to the land of the anthropologists. Refugees such as the Nuer are among the latest newcomers to urban and suburban areas in the United States, and anthropologists can play a role in the adaptation process of Nuer in the United States. For example, some anthropologists work for voluntary agencies where what they learn about refugees through their ability to conduct ethnographic research helps to ease refugee adjustment to unfamiliar surroundings. Other anthropologists work at the federal and state levels to advise about the efficacy of the social programs designed to meet the needs of recently arrived populations and suggest changes if they are needed. Sometimes these roles take the form of advocacy.

But through it all, anthropologists still do fieldwork in much the same way. They learn the language of refugee populations, ask open-ended questions in interviews, conduct participant observation at such events as weddings, funerals, graduation ceremonies, and political meetings, and try to understand life from their informants' perspective.

Although he now knows an anthropologist, Thok Ding goes about his new life in the United States with the same independent determination that got him here in the first place. He will continue to move his residence if he thinks it will help him, increase his level of education, find better paying jobs, and eventually if all works out, marry a woman from the Sudan, bring his whole family to the United States and in the end, become a new American.

Connection Questions

1. What are the reasons for Thok Ding's migration to the United States?

2. How does Thok's story influence your views of U.S. immigration policies?

3. Provide some ideas about how anthropologists can contribute to migration policies and programs?

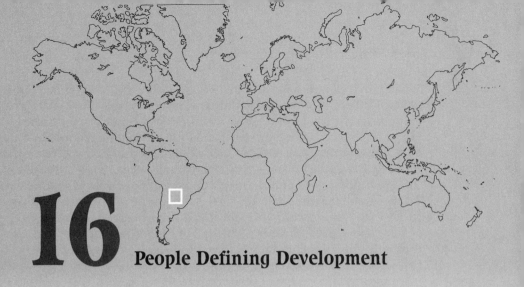

16

People Defining Development

Forest Development the Indian Way

Richard K. Reed

To most industrialized peoples, the practice of slash-and-burn agriculture seems wasteful. Horticulturalists use axes and machetes to fell forests, burn the debris, and then plant in the ashes. Within a few short years, the fields are abandoned and the farmer moves on. For people used to thinking of agriculture as intensively planted permanent fields, slash-and-burn agriculture seems destructive. In this article, Richard Reed challenges this simplistic notion. Describing the production practices of the Guaraní Indians living in the tropical forests of Paraguay, and detailing the destruction of their original way of life by the infiltration of colonos (non-Indian colonists), he shows that Indian slash-and-burn agriculture combined with commercial harvesting of natural products offers a more sustainable and economically sound means for all people to prosper in these fragile forests.

Reprinted by permission of Richard K. Reed.

When I arrived in Itanaramí that very first time, it felt like I had left the modern world behind. This small Guaraní Indian village was hidden deep in the Paraguayan forests, surrounded by hundreds of miles of wilderness. I took a jeep to the end of a rutted dirt road and followed winding footpaths for two days into the heart of one of South America's great natural areas. Trees shaded the trail I took over the low hills, and clear streams offered cool refreshment in the valleys. Entering the community, the path opened into a small clearing and Veraju's small thatch roof jutted up through the tangle of the family's overgrown garden. His family was busy in the house yard, preparing manioc from the garden and game from the hunt. The rest of the settlement was similarly embedded in the forest, each home set in a small clearing along the narrow footpath. Houses seemed isolated from the world, protected from modernity by the high trees and verdant foliage of this vast forest.

I soon discovered that the isolation was illusory. Their house lots were strewn with machetes from Costa Rica and clothes were sewn from Brazilian polyester cloth. Even the most isolated households bought salt and soap and fish hooks from traders.

Guaraní made their living by gardening and hunting, but they also obtained cash by gathering and selling goods from the forest, especially the leaves of the wild yerba-maté plant (*Ilex Paraguayensis*), which is brewed in a caffeinated infusion throughout southern South America. And the commercial work was not new. A little research showed that the Guaraní had sold the leaf to Brazilian, Argentine, and Bolivian merchants since at least 1590. They had developed a way to mine the forest for its wealth without destroying the resources on which they depend.

The Threatened Forests

But the Guaraní's environment was threatened even then. The world's great tropical regions had become prime targets for a new kind of economic development. Ranchers and farmers, from Brazil to Indonesia, flocked to the jungle frontiers armed with chainsaws and bulldozers. They built roads, clear-cut timber, and denuded the land of foliage, often burning the trees and brush as they went.

The scope of this human invasion staggers the mind. In recent times, development destroys hundreds of square miles of virgin tropical forest each day. In the Amazon alone, an area half the size of Louisiana is cleared every year. We are discovering that not only are the forests finite, but they are rapidly disappearing. At this rate, authorities predict that the forests will be gone by the year 2050!

The future of this development is as finite as the resources it depends on. The march of progress, which seems so powerful and necessary, will soon destroy the very resources it requires. We can either choose to abandon our current development strategies or we will be forced to change.

As a result, the modern world is searching for models of development that promote growth within the world's finite resources. This *sustainable development* differs from conventional strategies in several important respects. First, it recognizes that resources are finite and protects those resources even as we benefit from them. Second, sustainable development emphasizes the relationship between economic, ecological, and social systems, striving to protect the integrity of all three. Third, sustainable development promotes social stability by distributing the benefits and raising the standard of living of all people.

As the modern world searches for technological solutions to its increasingly obvious problems, I discovered that the Guaraní offered a proven model for sustainable tropical forest development. More than simply providing their subsistence, they had developed a *commercial* system that gave them access to the world marketplace without destroying the forests they depended on.

We may ask what accounts for this successful adaptation. What subsistence strategies permit them to live within the ecological limits of the forest? Can such people provide a model for successful tropical forest management? If so, perhaps indigenous peoples will be as important to our future as the oxygen-giving forests they live in. Let's look at the factors that allowed the Guaraní of eastern Paraguay to prosper in the forest and the lessons we may learn from them.

The Guaraní

Before the encroachment of outsiders, the Guaraní Indians were well adapted to their forest environment. Like most horticulturalists, they lived in small, widely scattered communities. Because their population densities were low, and because they practiced a mixture of slash-and-burn agriculture and foraging, they placed a light demand on forest resources. Small size also meant a more personal social organization and an emphasis on cooperation and sharing. Although of greater size and complexity than hunter-gatherer bands, Guaraní villages contained many of the cultural values found in these nomadic societies.

Since that first visit twenty years ago, I have continued to conduct ethnographic fieldwork in the small group of Guaraní villages that include Itanaramí. The residents of these communities are among the last of the Guaraní Indians still living in the forests of southern South America. They are the remnants of an ethnic group that 400 years ago dominated southern Brazil and Paraguay from the Atlantic Ocean to the Andes. The Guaraní have suffered as disease, slavers, and colonists have invaded their forests. Today, only 30,500 Guaraní remain in isolated settlements where the tropical forest survives—and even these are threatened.

The forests of Itanaramí have high canopies that shelter both animal and human populations. When I first arrived in the region, the expanse of trees was broken only by streams and rivers that drain westward to the broad, marshy valley of the Paraná River. Viewed from the ground, the density of the forest growth was matched only by the diversity of plant species.

Itanaramí itself is built along a small stream that gives the settlement its name. To my uninformed eye, it was difficult to recognize the existence of a village at all when I first arrived there. Homesteads—which consisted of a clearing, a thatched hut, and a field—were scattered in the forest, often out of sight of one another. A closer look revealed that pathways through the forest connected houses to each other and to a slightly larger homestead, that of the *tamoi* (literally grandfather), the group's religious leader. As in many small societies, households were tied together by kinship, which wove a tapestry of relations that organized social affairs and linked Itanaramí to other Guaraní communities.

I discovered that Guaraní culture emphasized sharing and cooperation. Sisters often shared work and childcare. Brothers usually hunted together. Food was distributed among members of the extended family, including cousins, aunts, and uncles. Families distributed abundance with compatriots who had less—and expected the same treatment in return. People emphasized the general welfare, not personal wealth.

The *tamoi,* although in no sense a leader with formal authority, commanded considerable respect in the community. He settled disputes, chastised errant juniors, and led the entire community in evening religious ceremonies where all drank *kanguijy* (fermented corn), danced, and chanted to the gods.

The people of Itanaramí not only lived in the forest, they saw themselves as of it. The forest was basic to indigenous cosmology. The people referred to themselves as *ka'aguygua,* or "people of the forest." Villagers often named their children after the numerous forest songbirds, symbolizing their close personal ties to the environment.

Sustainable Production

Guaraní had lived in their present locale for centuries and had dwelled throughout the tropical forests of lowland South America for thousands of years. During all this time, they had exploited flora, fauna, and soils of the forests without doing permanent harm. The secret of their success was their production strategy. The Indians mixed agriculture with gathering, hunting, and fishing in a way that permitted the environment to recover. They even collected forest products for sale to outsiders, again without causing environmental damage.

Guaraní farming was well suited to forest maintenance. Using a form of shifting agriculture called slash-and-burn farming, the Indians permitted the forest to recover from the damage of field clearing. The way Veraju, the tamoi of Itanaramí, and his wife, Kitu, farmed provides a typical example. When the family needed to prepare a new field, it was Veraju who did the heavy work. He cut the trees and undergrowth to make a half-acre clearing near his house. Then he, Kitu, and some of their five children burned the fallen trees and brush, creating an ash that provided a powerful fertilizer for the thin forest soils. When the field was prepared, Kitu used a digging stick fashioned from a sapling to poke small holes in the ground, and planted the staple Guaraní crops, beans and manioc root (from which tapioca is made). Interspersed with the basic staples, they added the slower-growing banana, sugar cane, and orange trees to round out their diet. When the crops matured, it was Kitu and her daughters who harvested them.

The secret to successful slash-and-burn agriculture is field "shifting" or rotation. Crops flourish the first year and are plentiful the next, but the sun and rain soon take their toll on the exposed soil. The thin loam layer, so typical of tropical forests, degenerates rapidly to sand and clay. Grasses, weeds, and insect pests, rare in the deep forest, eventually discover the vulnerable crops. By the third year, the poor soils are thick with weeds and grow only a sparse corn crop and few small manioc roots. Rather than replant a fourth time, Veraju and Kitu would clear a new field nearby where soils are naturally more fertile and the forest can be burned for additional ash fertilizer. Although fallow, their old field was not abandoned. They continued to return periodically for fruit and to root out the remaining manioc.

The surrounding forest quickly reclaims the old field; roots penetrate the opening from the forest edge and animals wander through it dropping seeds in their path. As the forest returns, the decaying matter once again strengthens the depleted soil. After several years the plot will be distinguished only as one of the citrus groves that are scattered throughout the unbroken forest. In this way, the forest produces a sustained yield without degrading the natural ecosystem.

The forest recovers sufficiently fast for the same plot to be cleared and replanted within ten or fifteen years. This "swidden" system results in the cyclic use of a large area of forest, with a part under cultivation and a much larger portion lying fallow in various stages of recomposition.

If farming formed the only subsistence base, the Guaraní would have had to clear much larger gardens. But they also turned to other forest resources—game, fish, and forest products—to meet their needs. Guaraní men often formed small groups to hunt large animals such as deer, tapir, and peccary with guns purchased from outsiders or with the more traditional bows and arrows they make themselves. A successful hunt provides enough meat to share liberally with friends. Men also trapped smaller mammals, such as armadillo and paca (a large rodent). They fashioned snares and deadfall traps from saplings, tree trunks, and cactus fiber twine. These were set near homesteads, along streams, and at the edges of gardens. Traps not only provided meat, but also killed animals that would otherwise eat the crops.

Fish also supplied protein for the Guaraní diet and reduced dependence on agricultural produce. Many rivers and streams flow near Itanaramí on flat bottomland. These watercourses meander in broad loops that may be cut off as the river or stream changes course during a flood. Meanders, called oxbows, make ideal fishing spots. In addition to hook and line, men captured the fish by using a poison extracted from the bark of the *timbo* vine. Floated over the surface of the water, the poison stuns the fish and allows them to be caught by hand.

The forest also supplied a variety of useful products for the Guaraní. They made houses from tree trunks and bamboo stalks; rhododendron vines secured thatched roofs. Villagers collected wild honey and fruit to add sweetness to their diets. If the manioc in the fields were insufficient, wild tubers provided a basic staple. Even several species of insect larva and ants were collected as tasty and nutritious supplements to the daily meal. Finally, the Indians knew about a wide variety of medicinal plants. They processed roots, leaves, flowers, and seeds to release powerful alkaloids, making teas and poultices for the sick and injured.

But the Guaraní were not isolated from commercial goods. Almost five hundred years ago, White traders entered the forests of the Guaraní and gave Indians access to world markets. The Guaraní continued to produce for most of their needs, but items such as machetes, hooks, soap, and salt were more easily bought than manufactured or collected. As they did with farming and hunting, Guaraní turned to the forest to meet such economic needs. They regularly collected two forest products, yerba-maté and leaves from wild orange trees, which have an oil used in flavorings and perfumes, to raise the necessary funds.

It is important to note the special Guaraní knowledge and values associated with subsistence activities. Because they lived in the forest for such a long time, and because they would have nowhere to turn if their own resources disappeared, they relied on a special and complex knowledge of how the forest works and how it can be used.

For example, Guaraní, such as Veraju, distinguished among a variety of "ecozones," each with a unique combination of soil, flora, and fauna. They recognized obvious differences between the high forests on the hills, the deep swamps of river basins, and the grassy savannahs of the high plains. But they made more subtle distinctions within these larger regions. For example, they called the low scrub along rivers *ca'ati.* Flooded each year during the rainy season, this region supported bamboo groves that harbored small animals for trapping and provided material for house construction. The forests immediately above the flood plain look like an extension of the ca'ati, but to the Guaraní they differed in important ways. This ecozone supported varieties of bamboo that were useless in house construction but that attracted larger animals, such as peccary, which they hunted. In all, the Guaraní distinguished among nine resource zones, each with distinctive soils, flora, fauna, and uses. These subtle distinctions among ecozones enabled the Guaraní to use the forest to its best benefit. By shifting their subsistence efforts from one zone to another, just as they shifted their fields from one spot to the next, the Guaraní assured that the forest environment, with its rich variety of life, would always be able to renew itself.

The Impact of Unsustainable Development

In the last few years, intensive commercial development has come to the region in which Itanaramí lies. Paraguay's deforestation rates are among the highest in the world, raising the specter of complete ecological destruction. White *colonos* (settlers), armed with chain saws and earthmovers, attack the trees. They vandalize the land without awareness of the carefully integrated ecozones. As the trees fall, the forest products, such as yerba maté, are destroyed. So are the mammals and fish, the bamboo and the rhododendron vines, the honey and the fruits, and the fallow fields. As these resources disappear, so does the economy of the once self-sufficient Guaraní. Without their traditional mode of subsistence, it has become impossible to maintain their kin-organized society, the influence of the tamoi, and the willingness to share. Indian communities are destroyed by poverty and disease, and the members who remain join the legions of poor laborers who form the lowest class of the national society. In short, the Guaraní lose their ability to survive as an independent ethnic group.

Recent intensive development began near Itanaramí with a road that colonists cut through the jungle to the village. Through this gash in the forest moved logging trucks, bulldozers, farm equipment, and buses. Accompanying the machinery of development were farmers, ranchers, and speculators, hoping to make a quick profit from the verdant land. They descended from their vehicles onto the muddy streets of a newly built frontier town. They cleared land for general stores and bars, which were soon filled with merchandise and warm beer. By day, the air in the town was fouled by truck noise and exhaust fumes; by night it was infused with the glare of electric lights and the noise of blaring tape players.

Soon the settlers began to fell the forest creating fields for cotton, soybeans, and pasture. Survey teams cleared boundaries and drew maps. Lumber gangs camped in the forests, clear-cutting vast tracts of trees. Valuable timber was hauled off to new lumber mills; everything else was piled and burned. Massive bulldozers created expanses of sunlight in the previously unbroken forest. Within months, grass, cotton, and soybeans sprouted in the exposed soils. Where once the land had been home for game, it now provided for cattle. Herds often clogged the roads, competing with trucks hauling cotton to market and busses loaded with new colonists. Settlers fenced in the fields and cut lanes through the remaining forest to mark off portions that would be private property (off-limits to Indians).

The road and fields reached Itanaramí in 1994. A cement bridge was built over the stream and chainsaws, logging trucks, and bulldozers assaulted the forests the Guaraní once used for gardens, farming, and hunting. The footpath that once carried Guaraní to the tamoi's house now carries their timber to market in Brazil. The families are left with barren house lots.

Moreover, by destroying the forest resources surrounding the Guaraní villages of the region, colonos set in motion a process that destroyed the native culture and society. Guaraní communities became islands surrounded by a sea of pastures and farm fields. Although the Indians held onto their gardens, they lost the forest resources needed to sustain their original mode of subsistence, which depended on hunting, fishing, and gathering in the forest as well as farming. These economic changes forced alterations in the Indian community.

First, without the forest to provide game, fish, and other products, the Guaraní became dependent on farming alone for their survival. Without wild foods, they had to plant more corn and beans. Without the forest production of yerba maté leaves to collect for sale, they were also forced to plant cash crops such as cotton and tobacco. These changes forced them to clear gardens that were over twice the size of their previous plots.

While the loss of the forest for hunting and gathering increased their dependence on agriculture, the fences and land titles of the new settlers reduced the land available to the Indians for cultivation. Families soon cleared the last of the remaining high forests that they controlled. Even the once forested stream banks were denuded.

After they had cleared their communities' high forest, Indian farmers were forced to replant fields without allowing sufficient fallow time for soils to rejuvenate. Crops suffered from lack of nutrients and yields declined despite additional effort devoted to clearing and weeding. Commercial crops, poorly suited to the forest soils, did even worse. As production suffered, the Indians cleared and farmed even larger areas. The resulting spiral of poor harvests and enlarged farms outstripped the soil's capacity to produce and the Guaraní's ability to care for the crops. Food in the Indian communities grew scarce. The diet was increasingly restricted to nonnutritious manioc as a dietary staple because it was the only plant that could survive in the exhausted soils.

The Guaraní felt the ecological decline in other ways. The loss of game and poor crop yields exacerbated health problems. Settlers brought new diseases such as colds and flu into the forest. The Guaraní have little inherited resistance to these illnesses and poor nutrition reduced their defenses even further. Disease not only sapped the adults' energy for farming and childcare, it increased death rates at all ages. Tuberculosis, which well-fed Guaraní had rarely contracted, became the major killer in the community.

The environmental destruction took a psychological toll as well. Guaraní began to fall into depression, get drunk on cheap cane liquor, and, all too often, commit suicide. A number of suicides were noted among the Guaraní in Brazil in the 1990s and subsequent research in Paraguay showed that indigenous peoples were killing themselves at almost fifty times the national average. The epidemic hit 15- to 24-year-olds the hardest. These young people saw little future for themselves, their families, and their people.

Deforestation also disrupted social institutions. Without their subsistence base, many Guaraní needed additional cash to buy food and goods. Indian men were forced to seek work as farmhands, planting pastures and picking cotton on land where they once hunted. Women stayed at home to tend children and till the deteriorating soils of the family farms.

The search for wage labor eventually forced whole Guaraní families to move. Many jobs were available on the new farms that had replaced the forest. Entire families left home for hovels they constructed on the land of their employers. From independent farmers and gatherers, they became tenants of *patrones* (landowners). Patrones prohibited the Guaraní farmhands from planting gardens of their own, so the displaced Indians were forced to buy all their food, usually from the patrones themselves. Worse, patrones set their own inflated prices on the food and goods sold to Indians. Dependence on the patrones displaced the mutual interdependence of traditional Guaraní social organization.

As individuals and families left the Guaraní villages in search of work on surrounding farms and ranches, tamoi leaders lost influence. It became impossible to gather disparate relatives and friends for religious ritual. The distances were too great for the elders' nieces and nephews to seek out counsel and medicines. Moreover, the diseases and problems suffered by the Guaraní were increasingly caused by people and powers outside the forest. The tamoi could neither control nor explain the changing world.

Finally, as the forest disappeared, so did its power to symbolize Guaraní entity. No longer did young Indians see themselves as "people of the forest." Increasingly, they called themselves *indios,* the pejorative slur used by their non-Indian neighbors.

Today, many of the Guaraní of eastern Paraguay remain in small but impoverished communities in the midst of a frontier society based on soybean farming and cattle ranching. The households that previously were isolated individual plots are now concentrated in one small area without forest for farming or privacy. The traditional tamoi continue to be the center of the social and religious life of the community, but no longer exert influence over village decisions, which are increasingly dominated by affairs external to the local community.

Development and Ecology

Some people might argue that the Guaraní need to learn from their new neighbors, that they need to change their traditional ways and adopt the economy and culture of the more modern, prosperous society. The problems the Guaraní suffer, they claim, are a result of their traditional economy and culture. Change might be painful for today's Indians, but will provide unequaled opportunity for their descendents.

Unfortunately, this argument ignores the fact that recent development is destroying the resources on which the new farming and ranching depend. The long-run implications of forest clearing are disastrous, not simply for the Guaraní and other Indians, but for settlers and developers as well. The tropical forest ecosystem is extremely fragile. When the vegetable cover is destroyed, the soil quickly disappears. Erosion clogs rivers with silt and the soils left behind are baked to a hardpan on which few plants can survive. Rainwater previously captured by foliage and soil is quickly lost to runoff, drying the winds that feed the regional rain systems. Although first harvests in frontier areas seem bountiful, long-term farming and ranching are unprofitable as the soils, deprived of moisture and the rejuvenating forces of the original forest, are reduced to a "red desert."

Returning to Itanaramí today, one notices that many of the fields first cleared by ranchers in 1996 have already been abandoned. And even worse, leaving the cleared land fallow does not restore it. Once destroyed, the forest plants cannot reclaim the huge expanses of hardpan left by unsustainable development.

Nor have developers been interested in husbanding the land. The colonos who clear the forests are concerned with short-term profit. Entrepreneurs and peasant farmers maximize immediate returns on their labor and investment, unaware of the environmental costs that subsidize their earnings. When the trees and soils of one area are exhausted, the farmers, ranchers, and loggers move farther into the virgin forest in search of new resources. The process creates a wave of development that leaves destruction in its wake. Unlike the Guaraní who have developed sustainable systems, developers do not stay and contend with the environmental destruction caused by their activities.

Indigenous Models for Sustainable Development

Rather than the Guaraní learning to adapt to our models of development, perhaps we need to take a lesson from indigenous peoples. If we hope to survive in the rain forest, we must learn from the people who have not only survived, but prospered commercially in this fragile environment. International agencies and national governments have begun to recognize that our development strategies are doomed to failure. Although deforestation continues unchecked in many regions of the Amazon Basin, forest conservation programs are using the experience of indigenous people to promote sustainable development in the forest.

Such is the case in Paraguay where a program is being implemented to preserve the remaining tropical forests. Groups like the Guaraní of Itanaramí, so recently threatened by encroaching development, are providing a model for newcomers to earn a profit from the natural resources, while protecting the existing environment. The natural forests of some of the Guaraní are the last remaining undisturbed subtropical forest in eastern Paraguay. With the help of Nature Conservancy, an area of 280 square miles has been set aside as a biosphere reserve. Although small, the program is attempting to protect a much larger buffer zone around the reserve by promoting rational land use by colonists. Aided by anthropologists who have made detailed studies of Indian commercial harvesting, planners are integrating the Indians' own models of agro-forestry into new production strategies for colonos. Guaraní techniques of commercial extraction have been of special interest, particularly the harvest of yerba maté, as it will economically outperform destructive farming in the long run. Teams of planners are teaching newcomers to tend and harvest their own tree crops. Far from being backward and inefficient, the mixed horticultural subsistence strategies of indigenous forest groups have turned out to be the most practical way to manage the fragile tropical forest environment.

Connection Questions

1. Explain the difference between sustainable development and unsustainable development.

2. Compare the situation of the Guaraní of Itanaramí with an example of development among indigenous peoples provided in the Miller chapter.

Index